HANDS-ON GUIDE SERIES®

Hands-On Guide to
Streaming Media

Focal Press Hands-On Guide Series

The Hands-On Guide series serves as the ultimate resource in streaming and digital media-based subjects for industry professionals. The books cover solutions for enterprise, media and entertainment, and educational institutions. A compendium of everything you need to know for streaming and digital media subjects, this series is known in the industry as a must-have tool of the trade.

Books in the series cover streaming media-based technologies, applications and solutions as well as how they are applied to specific industry verticals. Because these books are not part of a vendor-based press they offer objective insight into the technology weaknesses and strengths, as well as solutions to problems you face in the real-world.

Competitive books in this category have sometimes been criticized for being either technically overwhelming or too general an overview to actually impart information. The Hands-On Guide series combats these problems by ensuring both ease-of-use and specific focus on streaming and digital media-based topics broken into separate books.

Developed in collaboration with the series editor, Dan Rayburn, these books are written by authorities in their field, those who have actually been in the trenches and done the work first-hand.

All Hands-On Guide books share the following qualities:

- Easy-to-follow practical application information
- Step-by-step instructions that readers can use in real-world situations
- Unique author tips from "in-the-trenches" experience
- Compact at 250–300 pages in length

The Hands-On Guides series is the essential reference for Streaming and Digital Media professionals!

Series Editor: Dan Rayburn (www.danrayburn.com)

Executive Vice President for StreamingMedia.com, a diversified news media company with a mission to serve and educate the streaming media industry and corporations adopting Internet based audio and video technology. Recognized as the "voice for the streaming media industry" and as one of the Internet industry's foremost authorities, speakers, teachers, and writers on Streaming and Digital Media Technologies.

Titles in the series:

- *Hands-On Guide to Webcasting*
- *Hands-On Guide to Windows Media*
- *Hands-On Guide to Video Blogging and Podcasting*
- *Hands-On Guide to Streaming Media*

HANDS-ON GUIDE SERIES®

Hands-On Guide to

Streaming Media

An Introduction to Delivering

On-Demand Media

JOE FOLLANSBEE

ELSEVIER

AMSTERDAM • BOSTON • HEIDLEBERG • LONDON
NEW YORK • OXFORD PARIS • SAN DIEGO
SAN FRANCISCO • SINGAPORE • SYDNEY • TOKYO
Focal Press is an imprint of Elsevier

Focal Press

Acquisitions Editor: Angelina Ward
Project Manager: Paul Gottehrer
Assistant Editor: Rachel Epstein
Marketing Manager: Christine Degon Veroulis
Series Editor: Dan Rayburn
Cover and Interior Design Coordinator: Cate Barr
Cover and Interior Designer: Maycreate (www.maycreate.com)
Book Production: Borrego Publishing (www.borregopublishing.com)

Focal Press is an imprint of Elsevier
30 Corporate Drive, Suite 400, Burlington, MA 01803, USA
Linacre House, Jordan Hill, Oxford OX2 8DP, UK

 Recognizing the importance of preserving what has been written, Elsevier prints its books on acid-free paper whenever possible.

Library of Congress Cataloging-in-Publication Data

(Application submitted)

British Library Cataloguing-in-Publication Data
A catalogue record for this book is available from the British Library.

ISBN-13: 978-0-240-80863-5
ISBN-10: 0-240-80863-0

For information on all Focal Press publications
visit our website at www.books.elsevier.com.

06 07 08 09 10   10 9 8 7 6 5 4 3 2 1

Printed in the United States of America

This book is dedicated to my parents,

Jerry and Naomi Follansbee.

Table of Contents

Appendix A: Case Studies

Appendix B: Resources

Glossary 261

Index...277

Acknowledgments

The author would like to thank the numerous people who had a role in the journey that led to this book and its completion. Steve Mack first suggested I contact Focal Press about writing a book on streaming media, which resulted in the first edition of this volume, published under the title *Get Streaming! Quick Steps to Putting Your Audio and Video Online*. He served as technical editor for this edition. Angelina Ward got my proposal for a second edition approved, and Rachel Epstein was my indispensable contact at Elsevier and Focal Press. I'll never forget Joanne Tracy and Gina Marzilli's help at Focal Press in the first edition. Dan Rayburn, Shai Berger, and John Shay gave the first edition extra dimension and many of their contributions are incorporated in the second edition. Drazen Pantic, Tim Treanor, and Kevin Smith offered encouragement. Writing friends gained through the University of Washington Extension's writing program, including my teachers Nick O'Connell and Priscilla Long, cheered me on. And I would like to thank my former colleagues at RealNetworks. It was a baptism of fire.

About the Author

The first computer Joe Follansbee worked on was a DEC mainframe (he thinks), installed in the bowels of the Kingdome (now demolished) in Seattle in the early 1980s. The second computer was an Apple MacIntosh, which he used to write papers in 1986 while he was a student at The Evergreen State College in Olympia, Wash. The third computer he played with was actually a workstation at *The Daily Tidings* in Ashland, Ore., where he was a reporter. There was a succession of computers at radio news jobs, including a generic PC with an Intel 286 processor at Minnesota Public Radio. That's where he heard about streaming media. When he took a job at Progressive Networks (now RealNetworks) in 1996, he used a PC with an early Pentium processor. When he left the company in 2001, he built two Linux servers to host his own Web site and database. He wrote the first edition of this book in 2003 on a laptop in a basement office at his house. The book was published under the title *Get Streaming! Quick Steps to Putting Your Audio and Video Online*. He published *Hands-On Guide to Windows Media* in 2004. In addition to technology books, he writes articles for a variety of magazines, specializing in maritime history. He lives in Seattle with his wife Edith, and two daughters, Emily and Abbey.

About the Series Editor

Dan Rayburn is recognized as the "voice for the streaming media industry" and as one of the Internet industry's foremost authorities, speakers, and writers on streaming and digital media technologies for the past ten years. As a passionate leader and spokesperson in the field of streaming and digital media, Mr. Rayburn is noted for his expertise and insight pertaining to digital media business models, industry foresight, hardware and software products, delivery methods and cutting edge technology solutions globally.

He is executive vice president for Streamingmedia.com, a diversified news media company with a mission to serve and educate the streaming media industry and corporations adopting Internet-based audio and video technology. Its Web site (*www.streamingmedia.com*), print magazine, research reports, and tradeshows (Streaming Media East and West) are considered the premiere destinations both in person and online for professionals seeking industry news, articles, white papers, directories and tutorials.

Prior to StreamingMedia.com, he founded a streaming media services division for the Globix Corporation, a publicly traded NASDAQ company, which became one of the largest global streaming media service providers specializing in on-site event production for webcasts around the world. Prior to Globix, he co-founded one of the industry's first streaming media webcasting production companies, Live on Line, successfully acquired by Digital Island for $70 million.

An established writer, Mr. Rayburn's article on streaming media trends and technologies have been translated into four languages and are regularly published in major trade magazines and Web portals around the world. He is Series Editor for a new series of streaming media-related books for Focal Press entitled "Hands-On Guide" Series. He is co-author of the first business-focused book on the industry, *The Business of Streaming & Digital Media*. His second book, co-authored with Steve Mack, *Hands-On Guide to Webcasting*, was published in 2006.

Regularly consulted by the media for insight into business trends and technology, Mr. Rayburn has been featured in over one hundred print and on-line articles that have appeared in The New York Times, The Seattle Times, Crain's B2B Weekly, Broadcasting & Cable, Electronic Media, Mediapost.com, POST Magazine, ProAV Magazine, INS Asia, Internet.com, Radio Ink, EContent Magazine, Nikke Electronics and Wired.com among others. He has also appeared on many TV programs including those on CNN and CBS.

Mr. Rayburn also consults for corporations who are implementing digital media services and products in the broadcast, wireless, IPTV, security and cable industries. Over the past ten years he has helped develop, consult, and implement streaming media solutions for prestigious companies in the enterprise, entertainment and government sectors including A&E, ABC, Apple, Atlantic Records, American Express, BMG, BP, CBS, Cisco, Elektra, Excite.com, HBO, House Of Blues, ifilm, Indy 500, Intel, ITN, KPMG, Microsoft, MTV, NYTimes.com, Pepsi, Price Waterhouse Coopers, Qualcomm, RealNetworks, Sony Music, Twentieth Century Fox, United Nations, Viacom, VH1 and Warner Brothers among others.

For the past ten years, Mr. Rayburn has traveled internationally as a featured industry expert and has been sought out to keynote and speak on the current and future direction of streaming media technology, trends and business cases. A current technology advisor to many universities in the U.S., he has also taught Internet Broadcasting classes at New York University (NYU) and regularly lectures at numerous academic institutions. He is currently developing a series of distance learning classes with the Seattle Community Colleges, which will focus on teaching people the business and legal issues surrounding the implementation of streaming and digital media.

Mr. Rayburn holds board positions with various technology corporations in the U.S. and Europe and works with many non-profit organizations enabling them to utilize streaming media for their projects including The Museum of the Moving Image, The International Agency for Economic Development and the X PRIZE Foundation.

Dan Rayburn's contact infromation:
917-523-4562
www.danrayburn.com

Introduction

Hands-On Guide to Streaming Media Basics introduces you to the technology of "streaming," the process of sending audio and video over computer networks in real time. You will learn all you need to know to put music from your garage band, a recording of your child's first words, and video of your CEO's annual pep talk on the Internet or your internal corporate network. The book will teach you the basics of capturing sounds and moving images to a computer hard drive, converting them to files optimized for Internet transmission, and broadcasting them to whoever wants to listen or watch. Above all, the goal of this book is to get you excited about using this ground-breaking technology to broaden the impact of your communications.

Scope of the Book

Streaming media covers a broad range of options, software vendors, and networking technologies. This book will focus on the proprietary methods of four major manufacturers, which dominate 98% or more of the market. The leading vendors, followed by their major streaming brands, are:

- RealNetworks® (RealPlayer®/Helix™)
- Microsoft® (Windows Media® Services)
- Apple® Computer (QuickTime®)
- Adobe®/Macromedia® (Flash® 8 Professional)

The book will also detail some of the leading nonproprietary streaming technologies, notably the Motion Picture Experts Group (MPEG) set of standards, including MPEG Layer III (MP3) and MPEG-4.

The book won't discuss networking technologies in minute detail or application development, such as writing plug-ins to streaming media servers. The text also avoids specific computer hardware options, such as hardware audio or video encoders, although we will offer suggestions for building streaming media workstations.

Who Should Read This Book

You should read this book if you work with audio or video in any form, especially if you plan to deliver it over the Internet or a private computer network. Even if you work in a support role or as a decision-maker and don't get dirt under your fingernails, as they say, this book will help you understand an important new distribution channel for media properties. Some specific media professionals who will benefit include:

- Web designers
- Web programmers
- Videographers
- Audio engineers
- Media producers
- Post-production managers (audio and video)
- Educators
    - Communications and journalism
    - Distance learning
    - Computer science
- Business leaders who want to understand online media

Required Skill Level

The book makes some basic assumptions about your computer and Internet knowledge.

- Minimum one year of experience with a personal computer
- Familiarity with basic Internet tools, e.g., Web browsers and FTP programs
- Familiarity with basic computer terminology, e.g., CPU, RAM, and hard drive

By the end of this book, you'll have the basic knowledge to create streaming media all by yourself. However, we suggest you work closely with friends and colleagues as a team, especially when it comes time to broadcast your material over the Internet. Your experience of streaming media will go more smoothly and be more satisfying if you work collaboratively.

How to Use This Book

This book is organized to make your initial foray into streaming media as easy and efficient as possible. The book is laid out to follow in broad form the main parts of streaming media production: capture, encode, distribute, and playback. The book opens with a "quick start" chapter to get you learning by doing. In Chapter 2, you'll learn about the basic parts of streaming, with following chapters fleshing out each of the basics in detail. The final two chapters discuss alternative systems and advanced topics, including live streaming. If you want to understand live streaming in detail, it is recommended that you purchase another book in this series, *The Hands-On Guide to Webcasting*, by Steve Mack and Dan Rayburn.

Critical software procedures are put into step-by-step format with illustrations and screenshots. Ideally, you'll be able to complete a task by following these procedures exactly. You should also look for three other items that will help you understand key concepts:

 Alert – These are key facts and warnings that you should keep in mind as you practice streaming media skills.

 Author's Tip – These are suggestions from the author that will help you be more successful quickly.

 Inside the Industry – These are industry tips, tidbits and advice to give you a sense of what's happening in the streaming media business.

Conclusion

Though this book is an introduction to the basics of streaming media, it will give you a deep understanding of a rapidly growing and exciting industry. Always remember that streaming technology changes rapidly, so be ready to adapt. As you work with this book, take your time, let yourself make mistakes, and have some fun. If you're not having fun, there isn't much point in this streaming stuff, is there?

CHAPTER 1

Quick Start: Your First Streaming Media File

You've chosen this book to get up to speed quickly on streaming media and you're anxious to accomplish something right away. Perhaps you're on a deadline or just naturally impatient. This chapter gives you a taste of streaming, starting with the most basic procedure in streaming media: encoding.

As you'll learn later in the book, there are several streaming technologies to choose from. This chapter focuses on just one: Microsoft® Windows Media®. That's because most streaming technologies, including Windows Media, share several basic tools and procedures, such as encoding. And it's likely you already have Windows® Media Player®, the software that plays Windows Media files, on your computer.

In the following sections, you'll:

- Get a quick overview of streaming media
- Download and install a Windows Media® Encoder™
- Encode audio and video files into the Windows Media format

In order to get you going quickly, this chapter assumes that you have a source audio or video file in a "raw" format, such as **.wav** or **.avi**. If you're not sure about whether you have a raw audio and video file, don't worry. This chapter also helps you find files to encode.

A Quick Streaming Media Overview

The size of audio and video files blows every other type of file out of the water. A one-minute video file can be several megabytes (that's millions of bytes) in size, whereas a one-page letter might be only 20 or 30 kilobytes (that's thousands of bytes) in size. Trying to send enormous audio or video files across an average Internet connection, even a high-bandwidth connection such as cable or DSL (digital subscriber line), is like trying to pour Niagara Falls through a garden hose. You can do it, but it's going to take some time.

Streaming media engineers have solved this problem with a piece of software called an *encoder*. An encoder reduces the file size of the original file while maintaining as much of the aural and visual integrity of the original file as possible. Encoders can shrink the original file by as much as 80%. The resultant files can be transmitted much more efficiently and reliably. Plus, if you encode your files well, you should barely be able to tell any difference from the original file.

Installing a Windows Media Encoder

This section shows you how to download and install a Windows Media Encoder if you don't already have one. But before you do so, make sure you've got the right equipment.

Hardware Recommendations

Although encoding can be done on virtually any computer, it's best to have as much processing power, memory, and storage as possible when encoding streaming media files. For best results, Microsoft recommends the following:

- 500-MHz processor or higher, such as a Pentium III or AMD Athlon
- 128 MB of RAM
- Windows 2000 or XP
- 20 GB free hard drive space

ALERT Note that the hard disk recommendation is the absolute minimum. Even encoded files can be large, so build as much disk storage as you can.

The Installation Process

To install a Windows Media Encoder, follow these simple steps:

1. Point your browser to *http://www.microsoft.com/windows/windowsmedia/ 9series/encoder/default.aspx.*

2. Click the Windows Media Encoder 9 Series "Download Now" button, as shown in **Figure 1-1.**

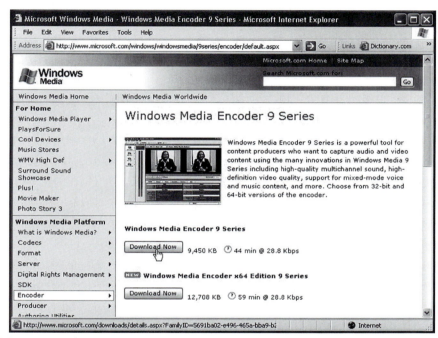

Figure 1-1
Click the Windows Media Encoder 9 Series "Download Now" button to begin installation.

ALERT You may see a link to the "x64" version of the Windows Media Encoder. This is an advanced version designed to take advantage of features in the next version of Microsoft's Windows operating system. Don't bother downloading this version of the encoder.

3. On the next page, click the "Download" button.

4. You may get a security warning. Click Run to continue.

5. If another security warning appears, click Run to continue.

6. On the encoder installer's Welcome screen, click Next.

7. Accept the agreement on the license agreement screen and click Next, as shown in **Figure 1-2**.

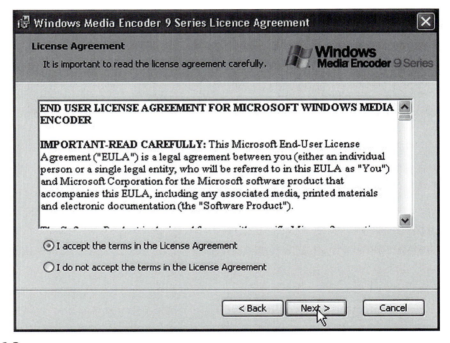

Figure 1-2
Accept the End User License Agreement for Windows Media Encoder.

8. On the "Installation Folder" screen, review the default installation folder, as shown in **Figure 1-3**, and click Next.

9. Click Install to begin the installation.

10. Click Finish when installation is complete.

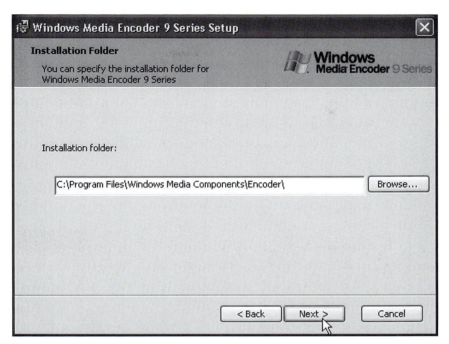

Figure 1-3
Review the folder where Windows Media Encoder will be installed.

To start the encoder, click Start → Programs → Windows Media → Windows Media Encoder. Note that a wizard dialog box appears by default. Click OK, then Cancel to see the main interface. (Normally, you'd use the wizard, but for the purposes of this tutorial, you'll close the wizard box to view the main interface.) The running program is shown in **Figure 1-4**. To see the main interface, click OK on the New Session dialog box.

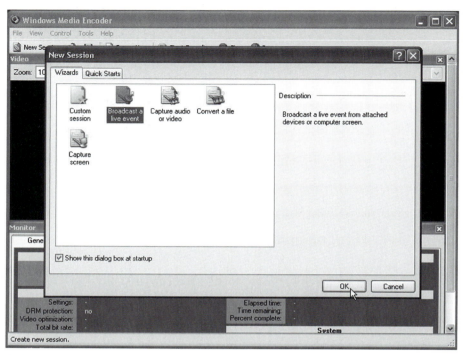

Figure 1-4
Windows Media Encoder at startup.

Encoding Audio and Video Files

Now that you've downloaded and installed an encoder, it's time to encode the raw or *source* file. The idea is to reduce the size of your raw audio or video file so it will "fit" into the maze of data pipes called the Internet. The following instructions assume you have audio and/or video content already existing on your computer. If you don't, you need to *capture* or *digitize* some content. Capturing and digitizing refer to the process of getting audio and video into your computer. For now, this chapter assumes you already have content that's ready to go.

Author's Tip

Capturing and digitizing are covered in more depth in Chapter 3, *Producing Audio and Video*.

When encoding content for streaming media delivery, it's always best to start with the highest quality source file possible. In the case of audio, that's commonly the WAV format. For video, it's commonly the AVI format (see "Audio and Video File Formats" sidebar). The problem is that these high-quality formats are too large to send across the Internet.

As mentioned earlier in this chapter, an encoder reduces the file size using advanced mathematical formulas while trying to maintain as much of the original fidelity as possible.

Essentially, the encoder throws away data that your brain doesn't need to understand the sound of Ricky Martin singing *Livin' La Vida Loca* or the image of the president giving the State of the Union address.

Author's Tip

Encoding is covered in more depth in Chapter 5, *Encoding Audio and Video*.

While you're going through these procedures, you'll see lots of potentially confusing options and terms. For the time being, ignore them and use the defaults as supplied by the vendors. They're usually good enough to get you started. We'll learn more about these options in a subsequent chapter.

Audio and Video File Formats

Before we start encoding, it's good to know something about file formats. The WAV format, pronounced, "wave," is the standard format for storing audio signals on the personal computer. It was invented jointly by Microsoft and IBM in the 1980s. The format can store all types of sound with virtually any quality, including stereo. You can play **.wav** files with dozens of applications, including all streaming media players. These audio files use the file extension **.wav**.

Video files come in several different formats, but we're going to stick with the most common, called AVI, which stands for *Audio Video Interleaved*. AVI files have the extension **.avi**. Like **.wav** files, **.avi** files can be played by streaming media players.

Author's Tip

Mac users: Most of the information about **.wav** files can be applied to Apple Computer's sound format, known as AIFF. The files have the extension **.aiff** or **.aif**. For video files, Apple uses the MOV file type, which uses the **.mov** or **.moov** file extension.

The main problem with **.wav** and **.avi** files is their size. They're just too big to stream reliably. AVI files in particular are among the largest files in the known universe. That's why we need to encode them before we can send them across the Internet.

Finding Files to Encode

To follow along with the encoding examples in the following section, you're going to need an audio and a video file. For the audio example, you'll need a **.wav** file. In fact you probably have dozens of them on your personal computer. You just don't know it. Microsoft loves to put **.wav** files on your computer for a variety of purposes. You know that "Ding!" sound you hear every time you goof? That's a **.wav** file. You'll use your operating system's search function to find a **.wav** file to play with.

ALERT The following procedure assumes you are using Windows XP as your operating system. Older Windows systems may require a slightly different procedure.

1. Click Start → Search → For Files or Folders.

2. Click the "All Files and Folders" link.

3. In the "All or part of the file name" box, type "***.wav**". The "*" is a wildcard character that tells the computer to find all the files with the **.wav** extension.

4. Select your local hard drive, usually C.

5. Click the "Search" button. Note the search results, as shown in **Figure 1-5**.

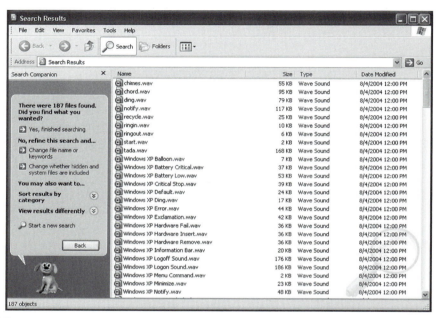

Figure 1-5
Search results for **.wav** files on a Windows XP computer.

6. The search will probably turn up dozens of files. Look for a file that lasts at least ten seconds when you play it, or has a large file size, say 100 kilobytes to 500 kilobytes. That will give you something substantial to work with, but won't take a lot of time to encode.

7. Copy the file to a temporary or working directory.

8. Give the file a new name to distinguish it from other projects. Many people put a project name, the date, and the producer's name in the file name.

To find a video file, you can try the operating system search trick we used above for finding a WAV file if you don't already have a video file to play with. Unfortunately, there aren't many **.avi** files on a typical hard drive. (One guess why: file size.) However, you can find public domain **.avi** files on the Internet for experimenting. The NASA archives at the NASA Web site provide a good source at *http://www.nasa.gov*.

Encoding an Audio File

Here are basic procedures for encoding an audio file with Windows Media Encoder.

1. Start the Windows Media Encoder by clicking Start → Programs → Windows Media → Windows Media Encoder.

2. Click Convert a File wizard in the wizards option box, as shown in **Figure 1-6**.

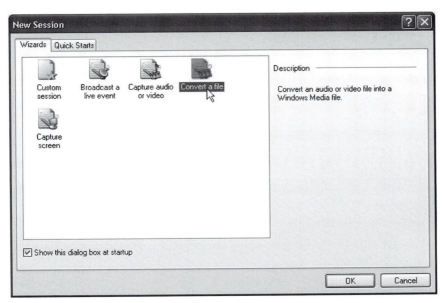

Figure 1-6
The Windows Media Encoder session wizard with Convert a File selected.

3. Use the Browse button to find your source audio file, select it, and click Open.

4. Note the directory location for the output file, as shown in **Figure 1-7**. Click Next.

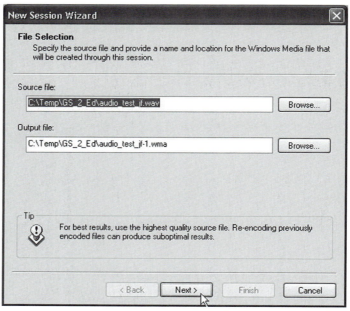

Figure 1-7
The location of the source audio file and the output file location in Windows Media Encoder.

5. In the Content Distribution dialog, click "Windows Media server (streaming)", as shown in **Figure 1-8**. Click Next.

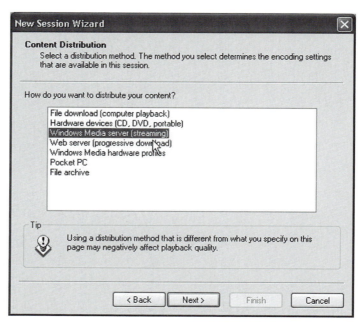

Figure 1-8
Select Windows Media Server in the Content Distribution dialog.

1. Quick Start: Your First Streaming Media File

6. In the Encoding Options window, look for the Bit Rate area. Scroll down and check the 19 kbps (kilobits per second) option in the Total Bit Rate column. Uncheck all other options, as shown in **Figure 1-9**. Click Next.

Figure 1-9
Check the 19 kbps option in the Total Bit Rate column.

7. In the Display Information dialog, fill in the form. (You can skip this, if you like.) Click Next.

8. In the Settings Review dialog, note the settings, including the location of your output file, as shown in **Figure 1-10**. Click Finish.

9. The encoding process commences, as shown in **Figure 1-11**. When the encoding is complete, click Close.

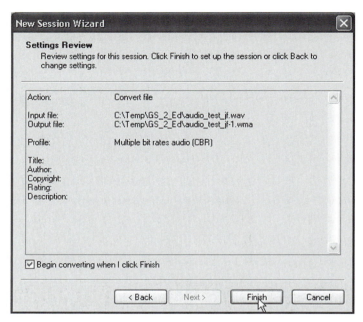

Figure 1-10
Note the settings for your encoded output file.

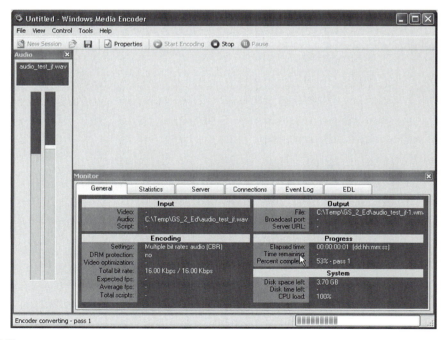

Figure 1-11
Windows Media Encoder encoding an audio file.

Look in your working directory for the newly encoded file with the extension **.wma**. Double-click the file to play it.

Encoding a Video File

This is the procedure for encoding a video file with Windows Media Encoder. Much of the procedure is the same as encoding an audio file, except that you're encoding a video file, of course.

1. Start the Windows Media Series Encoder.

2. Click "Convert a File" wizard in the wizards option box.

3. Use the Browse button to find your **.avi** file (the source video file), select it, and click Open.

4. Note the directory location for the output file. Click Next.

5. In the Content Distribution dialog, click Windows Media Server.

6. In the Encoding Options window, look for the Bit Rate area. Scroll down and uncheck the 282 kbps option and check the 43 kbps option in the Total Bit Rate column. Click Next.

7. In the Display Information dialog, fill in the form. (This is optional.) Click Next.

8. In the Settings Review dialog, click Finish, and the file begins to encode, as shown in **Figure 1-12**.

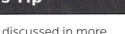

Author's Tip

"Bit rate" is discussed in more detail in Chapter 5.

9. When the encode is complete, click Close.

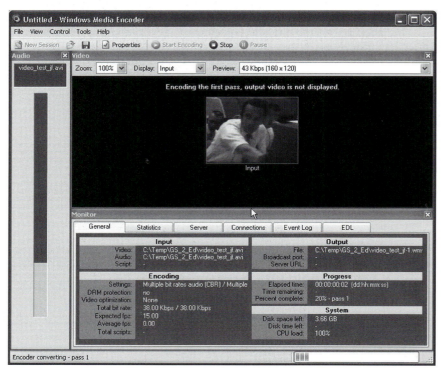

Figure 1-12
Windows Media Encoder encoding a video file.

You'll find a new file in your working directory with the **.wmv** extension. Double-click the file to play it.

Conclusion

You can get a taste of streaming media technology by trying out one of the basic streaming processes: encoding. This chapter focused on Windows Media encoding, although there are many other choices, which are discussed in following chapters. Chapter 2 introduces you to basic streaming media concepts and the other major streaming media platforms.

CHAPTER 2

The Building Blocks of Streaming Media

Before learning any new skill or technology, you have to understand the fundamentals. In streaming media, that means examining each of the technology's building blocks, including players, encoders, and servers. This chapter introduces you to the elements of sending audio and video over the Internet with streaming tools, though it focuses mostly on players. It's also important to understand how streaming media fits into the overall world of Internet technology.

In this chapter, you'll:

- Learn what streaming is and how it is used
- Learn about the current streaming media industry
- Learn how to upgrade existing streaming media players on your system, and install new streaming media players

Streaming Media Basics

Streaming is the continuous transfer of data from one computer to another in real time. Streaming media most often refers to the transfer of audio and video data, though it can be applied to almost any other kind of data, such as static images and text.

Most of this book discusses streaming in the context of audio and video. Outside this book, you'll see the word *stream* used for other types of data, such as stock quotes, which this book doesn't cover. Streaming is also frequently confused with *downloading*. Downloading also involves transferring a file from one computer to another, but with a critical difference: if it's a media file, such as a piece of music, you can't play it until the entire download is finished.

The Streaming Process

Most streaming media systems operate on the *client/server model*. A *client* requests data from a *server* on a computer network, and the server delivers the data to the client, which interprets the data. In simplest terms, the streaming media process consists of four steps: *capture*, *encode*, *distribute*, and *playback*, as shown in **Figure 2-1**. Here are the steps in more detail:

1. Images and/or sound are digitized and stored in a computer file.

2. The audio or video file is encoded into a format that can be streamed by an *encoder*.

3. The encoded file is placed on a *streaming media server*.

4. A client, referred to as a *media player* or just *player*, requests the encoded file and renders the data back into audio or video.

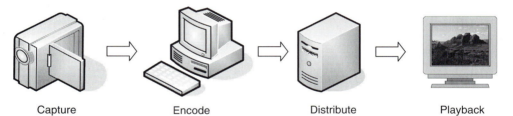

Capture   Encode   Distribute   Playback

Figure 2-1
The four steps of streaming: capture, encoding, distribution, and playback.

The book walks you through the installation process of players and encoders and shows you how to use the basic functions of each tool. You won't learn how to install and configure a streaming media server, however. That requires some administrative and networking expertise that's beyond the scope of this book. But you will get a good grounding in streaming server technology and terminology, so that you can talk about it intelligently to the powers that be.

Why Learning about Streaming Media Is Important

The Internet pervades everyone's life. It seems that everyone sends pictures of their children via e-mail, or shares them on a community site. People monitor the unfolding of world events on Web sites. And, increasingly, people listen to music and watch TV-style programming with streaming audio and video. Streaming media has helped the Internet evolve into a mass medium as important as print, radio, and television.

Arbitron/Edison Media Research, a marketing research firm, has tracked the growth of the Internet as a mass medium for audio and video since 1998, producing more than two dozen reports. In 2003, Arbitron declared that the Internet had entered the mainstream of American life. In 2005, the company said that 81% of Americans now have access to the Internet from home, work, or a public place, such as a library, up from 50% in 1999. Americans now spend more than an hour a day on average on the Internet.

Arbitron also tracks the growth of streaming media in particular. In its 2005 report, *Internet and Multimedia 2005: The On-Demand Media Consumer*, Arbitron estimated the monthly Internet video audience at about 35 million people. It said the weekly Internet video audience was nearly 20 million.

The growth of the streaming audience matches the growth of *broadband* Internet connections to the home. A high-quality audio or video experience depends on *cable* and *digital subscriber line* (*DSL*) bandwidth, and once people hook up, they start using streaming media. Arbitron says the number of Americans with broadband at home has more than tripled since 2001, from 13% to 48%, as shown in **Figure 2-2**. And once they have broadband, they almost double their time online, from 1 hour 16 minutes to 2 hours.

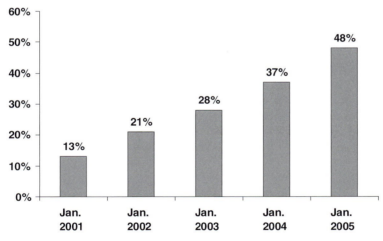

Figure 2-2
Streaming media growth has followed the growth of residential broadband connections. (Arbitron, 2005.)

Moreover, people have overcome their initial confusion about streaming technology. The Cable and Telecommunications Association for Marketing says in a 2002 report that 64% of Americans know how to listen to music on the Internet, including how to start and stop a stream, and 61% know how to listen to a live radio broadcast over the Net. And, according to Arbitron, people prefer short-form, "on-demand" style clips. In 2005, the company says, 11% of online Americans have watched a news clip in the past month, 9% have viewed movie trailers or previews, and 8% have seen a music video.

Why Use Streaming Media

In the days of the Internet boom, all you had to say was "It's cool!" for everyone to try a new technology. Those days are gone, thank goodness. Today, the response to many new technologies is "So what?" Decision-makers, especially those holding the purse strings, want to know whether a technology will move an organization toward its goals. Streaming media offers a number of benefits beyond the delight of seeing it work.

- **Cost-effective method of communication** – Organizations save money by reducing certain costs of media distribution. For example, you'd spend about $10 to duplicate and send out a VHS cassette of a training video to a branch office. If you work in a company with operations scattered over a wide geographic area, that cost could run into hundreds or thousands of dollars per video production. If you put that video on a streaming media server and invite employees to view it online, virtually all the duplication and distribution costs disappear.

- **Faster time to market** – Distribution of audio and video on physical media, such as CD, carries another cost: time. It takes days, weeks, or even months to distribute a video on VHS cassette, for example. However, once the audio or video is produced, you can place it on your streaming server within minutes or hours of its completion. Then you simply put a link to it on your Web site, announce it to your audience, and they come to you.

- **More delivery options** – Today's media environment is more fragmented than ever. People get information from newspapers, magazines, radio stations, television networks, Web sites, PDAs, even cell phones. Streaming media responds to the audience's desire for a variety of media channels. Adding streaming media as a communication channel increases your reach, giving you a better chance to reach your audience.

- **Tracking and profiling** – When you click on a streaming media link, information about that click is stored in the streaming media server's *log file*. Sophisticated streaming producers cull these log files for information on how their streaming content is used. By analyzing this information, you can discover what resonates with your audience and then hone your communication strategy further.

- **Global reach** – Radio and television signals are physically limited. Even large broadcast networks are limited by geography and international boundaries. Individual satellites cover only part of the globe. But any computer in any country on any continent can view your audio or video stream as long as they are connected to the Internet. Geographic and political boundaries become as porous as cheesecloth.

- **More efficient use of network infrastructure** – Offering downloads is still a popular way to distribute media files. And it may be right for you. However, downloading, especially in high-traffic situations, can clog your network and slow down all your other Internet-dependent business processes. Streaming media systems manage the use of your network bandwidth and other resources in a way that won't negatively affect other Internet-related activities.

Here are some common uses of streaming media. This list assumes you're working in an organization that divides its audience into people outside the organization and inside the organization.

- External audiences
- Online radio stations
- Market analyst calls
- Movie trailers
- Entertainment videos
- Infomercials
- Virtual tours of real estate
- Access to public meetings
- Internal audiences
- Private access to industry conferences
- Executive communications
- Employee training
- Product demonstrations

One of the fun things about technology is invention. See if you can come up with a new application of streaming that will sweep the globe!

Inside the Industry

 Most of the tools for viewing, creating, and in some cases delivering streaming media are available for free or very low cost. It's one of the great things about streaming.

However, you may see or hear the term "free software" thrown about in other contexts. What these folks really mean is "open source." In this case, "free" has nothing to do with cost. If you're curious about this, take a quick look at the section on open source software (OSS) in Chapter 10, *Alternative Systems*.

The Streaming Media Industry

Technology doesn't exist in a vacuum. It's important to understand streaming media in the context of the overall technical and business environment of the Internet. The chapter has already discussed the broader environment—i.e., the fact that the Internet is now deeply entrenched in everyday life and that streaming is catching on as a way to enjoy audio and video. Now let's review the technical and business environment of the streaming industry itself.

The Major Players

The streaming media industry is one of the most competitive in the Internet software business. The stakes are enormous. Everyone enjoys some form of audio and video, and streaming software manufacturers ultimately want to "own" the method by which you use it on the Internet. They fight for every percentage point of market share, and one of the ways they do it is by one-upmanship in technology.

RealNetworks

Progressive Networks (now called "RealNetworks") released the first commercially successfully streaming media technology in 1995. The software was called "RealAudio® 1.0." It included a server, an encoder, and a desktop clientplayer. RealNetworks' technology has gone through several iterations, though the player has always been called "RealPlayer." The server system, however, is today known as "Helix," though it's still sometimes called "RealServer."

Microsoft

In 1996, Microsoft released its answer to RealAudio, "Netshow," which was later renamed "Windows Media Services," which covers its player, encoder and server.

RealNetworks and Microsoft are regarded as the two major competitors in the streaming media marketplace, and until recently, the competition was bitter and acrimonious. In 2005, RealNetworks settled a long-standing antitrust lawsuit against Microsoft, and the two companies pledged to cooperate. Yeah, sure. You can bet your last computer byte that they will fight tooth and nail for the lucrative markets created by streaming media technology.

Apple Computer

Apple Computer entered the competition late with its QuickTime Streaming system in 1998. Despite the loyalty of Apple's user base among media professionals, QuickTime has never caught on as a streaming solution, although it remains important in the arena of digital media production. Sensing this, Apple has sought alliances with RealNetworks as a way to stave off the juggernaut of Microsoft. But the two "allies" get along only grudgingly.

Macromedia

The latest major entrant in the streaming media melee is Macromedia, one of the leading companies producing content creation tools for Web designers. Flash Professional 8, the latest version of its Flash animation technology, includes streaming media features. They aren't as sophisticated as the other three vendors. But Macromedia's deep penetration into the Web design and production industry suggests it could carve out a significant niche. In 2005, Macromedia was acquired by Adobe Systems.

Other Factors

Lurking in the wings are several smaller streaming media manufacturers, proponents of open streaming standards such as MPEG-4, media companies, and governments. Lawyers from every side are still hacking away at the Gordian knot of rights ownership in the digital age. The legal problems of Microsoft spice up the stew, although its problems in the antitrust realm seem to have abated for now. And don't forget the public relations people at each company. They put enough spin on their products to make planet Earth reverse its rotation. Streaming producers should keep an eye on all these factors, any one of which could affect your streaming plans over the long term.

Your Place in the Industry

Competition and debate may be good for innovation, wealth creation, and the American way, but it causes migraines for streaming media producers. Everyone wishes computer technology, including streaming media, functioned like other media technologies, such as radio and television. Just turn it on and it works. But as long as certain technology companies feel a need to dominate the streaming technological arena, and as long as no single company achieves domination, and as long as people disagree on the right approach to streaming, producers will have to take into account all the possible combinations and variations of each implementation when they offer streams to users. A radio producer doesn't have to worry about whether a listener's car radio can receive his station's signal. A streaming media producer, on the other hand, has to think about the user's computer, bandwidth, installed software, and a universe of other things. This book will help you make the right decisions.

Career Opportunities

Streaming media may excite you enough that you'll want to make it a career. The streaming media industry is still very new, but the streaming media specialist may soon emerge as a true career choice. Media production companies, Web hosting firms, and large corporations with internal communications departments will all need people with streaming expertise in the next three to five years. Jobs could appear in the form of regular full-time employment or as a contract work. You will most likely find yourself working in one of three departments, depending on the organization: media production, information technology, or corporate communications. Your best bet today is the IT department. But the pattern of job growth will likely follow the early days of the Internet. Web designers started popping up first in the IT department. Later, they transferred to other departments dealing with media and communications.

What is a Media Player?

Devices to play recorded media have been around since the invention of the phonograph by Thomas Edison in 1877. The phonograph is essentially a media player. It transforms sound encoded into the hills and valleys of a groove etched on a metal or wax drum (the media) into pressure waves humans hear as music or speech. The same goes for a cassette tape deck or a CD player. They just use different media. The term *media player* or *player* in the context of streaming media refers to a piece of software that transforms digital signals transmitted over a computer network into pressure waves and/or patterns of light and color. People interpret these waves and changes in light patterns as sound or video coming from speakers or displayed on a monitor. The technology may be more than a century apart in time, but the fundamental principle is the same, as shown in **Figure 2-3**.

Figure 2-3
Media players date back to the 19th century, starting with the phonograph, continuing with radio, television, and online media.

Find Your Media Player

You need to see if you have a media player installed. The streaming media market is dominated by four companies: RealNetworks, Microsoft, Apple Computer, and Macromedia. They make players under the brands "RealPlayer," "Windows Media," "QuickTime," and "Flash." If your computer is three years old or less, there's a very good chance you have at least one and possibly a number of these players already installed. If you're not sure, take a few minutes to browse your computer's hard drive for one of the brands listed above.

Update Your Media Player

You can assume you have at least one of the four major media players on your computer. The most likely suspects are RealPlayer, Windows Media, QuickTime and Flash. Depending on the age of your computer, the particular version of your player may be old. To avoid compatibility problems with older players, it's a good idea to upgrade your player to the latest version. The simplest way to do this is via the player's Update command. Start your player and look for the command in the Help menu, as shown in **Figures 2-4**, **2-5**, and **2-6**.

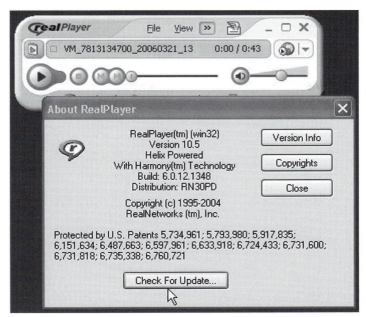

Figure 2-4
RealNetworks' RealPlayer update button under Help → About RealPlayer.

Figure 2-5
Microsoft Windows Media Player update under the Help menu. An easy way to reach this menu is Right Click over the "Now Playing" button and select Help → Check for Player Updates...

Figure 2-6
QuickTime Player's update feature under Help → Update Existing Software...

Author's Tip

When you run the Update command, you may have to navigate through dangerous shoals—namely a bunch of marketing messages. The software companies want you to buy players with more features or special services. These messages can be annoying. But if you patiently click the "No, thanks" buttons, your player will eventually start the update process. And you can rest assured that the free player will play any kind of file a "paid" player can.

What about Flash? The Flash player is actually a *plug-in* for your Web browser. It works within your browser behind the scenes to play media streams. Unlike the other vendors, there's no standalone Flash player. And there's a nearly 100% chance the Flash player is already installed on your system. To upgrade your Flash player, see the list of media player download pages in the following section, and use the Macromedia Flash Player link.

Installing a New Media Player

Even if you have a player already installed on your machine and have upgraded it to the latest version, you may want to hedge your bets by installing another media player. In fact, you can install all four major media players on one machine. Beware, however. The major software vendors are extremely competitive. You may get messages during the installation process that ask you to prefer one player over another, usually in terms of whether you want to associate a player with certain types of files. There may be other messages that suggest changes to certain settings. None of the changes will harm your computer. But read the messages carefully and make the decision you are most comfortable with.

Hardware and Software Requirements

Your computer may be relatively new and you have all the power you need to get good performance out of a new player. Here's a rule of thumb: If your computer is less than three years old, you're probably safe with what you have. But let's take a moment to look at some suggested hardware and software requirements before installing a new player from scratch, as shown in **Table 2-1**. If you're unsure about your installed hardware and software, see your information technology (IT) support person or call a computer retailer.

Table 2-1
Minimum and recommended hardware and software requirements for good performance by streaming media players.

Minimum Requirements	Recommended Requirements
233-MHz Pentium II processor	Pentium IV processor
64 MB of RAM	256 MB of RAM
56 kbps modem	Cable/DSL connection or better
16-bit sound card and speakers	16-bit sound card and speakers
65,000 color video display	65,000 color video display
Microsoft Windows 98	Microsoft Windows XP
Microsoft Internet Explorer 5.0 or later	Internet Explorer 5.0 or later

 ALERT Some businesses and other organizations restrict the types of software you can download and install on your system. Check with your IT department before downloading and installing any software discussed in this book.

Web Sites for Players

This book recommends free or low-cost software whenever possible. That means you should never have to pay a dime when you go to the following Web sites to download a new player. However, as we noted earlier, the software vendors may direct you to products or services that require a credit card number. (You may be asked for other information, such as your name and address. You'll have to give it to them to get your free download. But you won't need to give them a credit card number for a free download.) It's annoying, but, hey, they gotta make a living, too. Be persistent as you click around. You'll find the free download link eventually.

Here's a list of media player download pages:

- RealNetworks:
  http://www.real.com/freeplayer/?rppr=rnwk

- Microsoft:
  http://www.microsoft.com/windows/windowsmedia/player/download/download.aspx

- Apple Computer:
  http://www.apple.com/quicktime/player/

- Macromedia (Look for the "Macromedia Flash Player" link):
  http://www.macromedia.com/go/getflashplayer/

The Installation Process

The following procedures detail the steps for downloading and installing media players from RealNetworks, Microsoft, Apple Computer, and Macromedia.

ALERT If you're anxious about whether all this downloading and installing could break something on your computer, you should be. It's always a good idea to save any work you have, and perform a normal backup of your critical files before starting these procedures. If you don't have a backup procedure, this is a great time to create one!

RealPlayer

Progressive Networks, now called RealNetworks, introduced "RealAudio" and "RealVideo," which are among the most recognizable streaming media brands on the Internet.

1. Point your Web browser to *http://www.real.com/freeplayer/?rppr=rnwk*, as shown in **Figure 2-7**.

Figure 2-7
Select the appropriate link on the RealPlayer download page for your operating system.

2.   Click the download link appropriate for your operating system.

3.   *Study the new page carefully. This can be the most confusing part.* When you're ready, click the "Start RealPlayer Download" button.

4.   You may get a warning that asks, "Do you want to run this file?" as shown in **Figure 2-8**. Click Run.

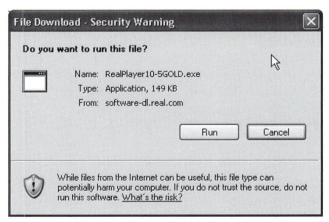

Figure 2-8
Click Run if shown this prompt.

5. You may get another warning that asks, "Do you want to run this software?" as shown in **Figure 2-9**. Click Run.

Figure 2-9
Click Run if shown this prompt.

6. If you get an error message, click the "Restart Download" button on the Real-Player installer confirmation page. (See step 3.)

7. The "Download Manager" will appear, and probably show you some advertising, as shown in **Figure 2-10**. Be patient as the RealPlayer installer downloads.

Figure 2-10
The RealPlayer Download Manager.

2. The Building Blocks of Streaming Media

8. When the download finishes, you'll see a "Preparing to Install" message, and then a screen showing the licensing agreement, as shown in **Figure 2-11**. Click Accept.

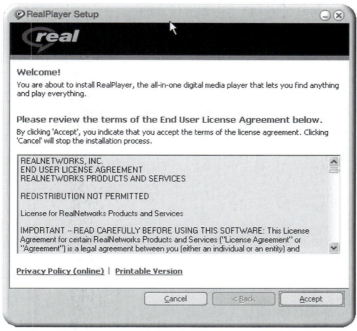

Figure 2-11
The RealPlayer licensing agreement screen.

9. In the "Select Program Location and Desktop Settings" Window, as shown in **Figure 2-12**, note the options, modify as needed, and click Next.

10. In the Universal Media Player screen, read the options, and click Finish, as shown in **Figure 2-13**.

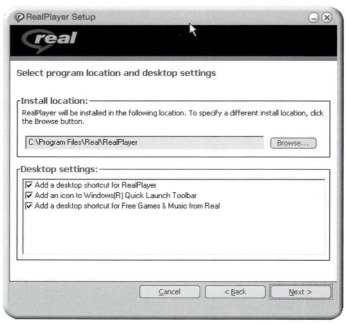

Figure 2-12
The RealPlayer Select Program Location and Desktop Settings screen.

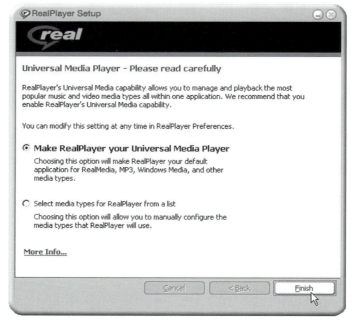

Figure 2-13
The Universal Media Player screen, which tells RealPlayer to play all known media file types or the media file types you select.

2. The Building Blocks of Streaming Media

11. The installer will ask you whether you want a "Premium" setup or "Basic" setup, as shown in **Figure 2-14**. Read these options carefully. Premium will cost money, charged monthly to your credit card, while Basic allows you to use RealPlayer free of charge. When you've made your choice, click Continue.

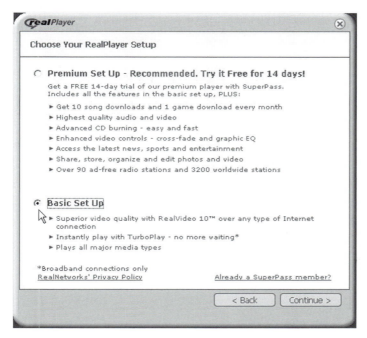

Figure 2-14
The "Choose Your RealPlayer Setup" screen. This screen is where you decide whether to pay for monthly extra services or use the basic, free services.

12. The installer now asks you for some information about yourself, as shown in **Figure 2-15**. Unfortunately, you have to answer these questions to go further. However, you can opt out of any promotional e-mails by unchecking the boxes. When done, click Create.

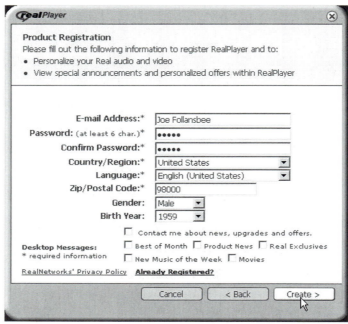

Figure 2-15
You will have to give some personal information to continue the installation.

13.   RealPlayer now starts a brief introductory presentation, and the Real Guide
        displays in the lower half of the player window, as shown in **Figure 2-16**.

Installation of RealPlayer is now complete.

Figure 2-16
The installed RealPlayer, displaying the Real Guide.

Windows Media Player 9 and 10

Windows Media Player probably has the largest installed base of all the media players. (Some companies, notably RealNetworks, will dispute this.) The procedure discussed in the following section is for Windows Media Player 10 on Windows XP. If you're installing a different version (see sidebar "Which Windows Media Player?") the process may differ slightly, but you should be able to follow along.

Inside the Industry

Which Windows Media Player?

Microsoft seems bent on deliberately confusing streaming media users when it comes to downloading and installing the company's players. The version of Windows Media Player you use will depend on your operating system. If you have Windows 98 SE, Windows Millennium Edition, or Windows 2000, you'll use Windows Media Player 9. If you have Windows XP, you'll use Windows Media Player 10, because version 9 is not available for Windows XP.

(continued on next page)

Downloading a Windows Media Player for Mac can be just as confusing. If you run OS 8.1 to 9.x, you'll need Windows Media Player 7.1. If you run OS X, you'll install Windows Media Player 9.

Essentially, all Windows Media players have similar functionalities, with newer versions having extra added features. Any Windows Media Player should be sufficient to follow along with exercises in this book. No matter which player you have to install, they are all available through the Microsoft Web site at:

http://www.microsoft.com/windows/windowsmedia/download/AllDownloads.aspx

1. Point your Web browser to (see **Figure 2-17**):

    http://www.microsoft.com/windows/windowsmedia/default.mspx

Figure 2-17
Click the Download Now button to begin the download.

2.	Click the "Windows Media Player 10" link.

3.	On the new page, click the "Download Now" button.

4.	You may get a warning that asks, "Do you want to run this file?" as shown in **Figure 2-18**. Click Run, and the file will begin downloading.

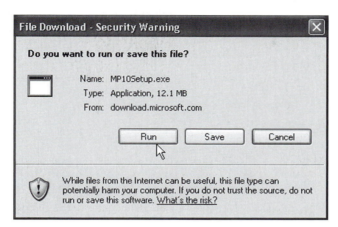

Figure 2-18
Click Run if shown this prompt.

5.	You may get another warning that asks, "Do you want to run this software?" as shown in **Figure 2-19**. Click Run.

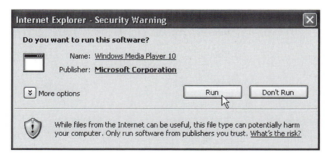

Figure 2-19
Click Run if shown this prompt.

6.	At the Supplemental End User License Agreement prompt, click Accept, as shown in **Figure 2-20**.

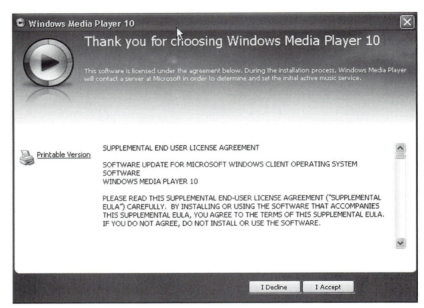

Figure 2-20
Accept the Supplemental EULA.

7. The player begins installation, as shown in **Figure 2-21**.

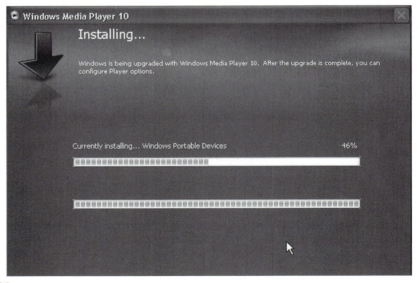

Figure 2-21
The player installation screen.

8. At the "Welcome to Windows Media Player 10" prompt, click Next, as shown in **Figure 2-22**.

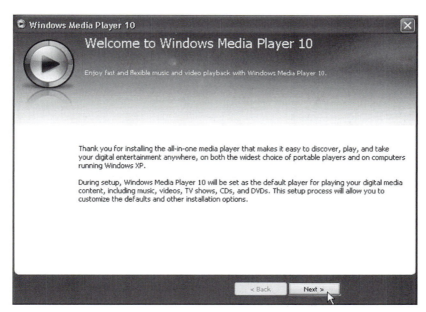

Figure 2-22
The player installation welcome prompt.

9. At the "Select Your Privacy Options," review your choices, including the choices selected by default, as shown in **Figure 2-23**, and click Next.

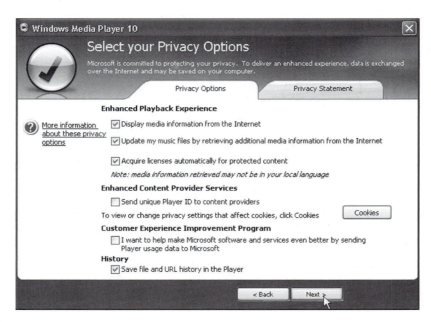

Figure 2-23
Select your privacy options.

10.   At the "Customize the Installation Options" prompt, review the File Types tab, as shown in **Figure 2-24**. The checked boxes mean that any time you want to view that file type, Windows Media Player will play that file by default. Review the Options tab, and click Finish.

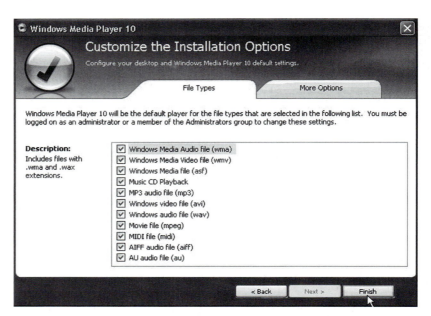

Figure 2-24
The File Types tab associates different media file types with Windows Media Player.

The Windows Media Player is now installed, as shown in **Figure 2-25**, which displays the Windows Media Guide. You can view the Guide by clicking the "Guide" tab near the top of the player interface.

Figure 2-25
The freshly installed Windows Media Player, with the "Guide" tab selected to show the Windows Media Guide.

QuickTime

The QuickTime file format (**.mov**) is one of the granddaddies of multimedia technology. QuickTime Player is bundled with Apple's iTunes® product.

1. Point your Web browser to:

    http://www.apple.com/quicktime/player/.

2. Click the "Free Download" button, as shown in **Figure 2-26**.

Figure 2-26
The Apple QuickTime download page.

3.   On the download page, click the "Free Download Now" button, as shown in **Figure 2-27**.

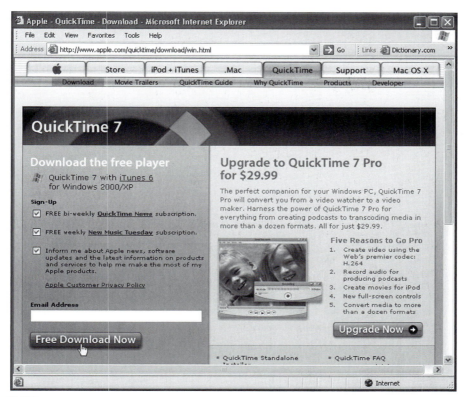

Figure 2-27
The Apple QuickTime download page.

4.   You may get a warning that asks, "Do you want to run this file?" as shown in
      Figure 2-28. Click Run, and the file will begin downloading.

Figure 2-28
Click Run if shown this prompt.

5. You may get another warning that asks, "Do you want to run this software?" as shown in **Figure 2-29**. Click Run.

Figure 2-29
Click Run if shown this prompt.

6. In the "Choose Setup Language" box, select the appropriate language, and click OK, as shown in **Figure 2-30**.

Figure 2-30
Select the appropriate language.

7. In the "Welcome to the iTunes 6 Installer" screen (note that it includes the latest version of QuickTime Player), click Next, as shown in **Figure 2-31**.

Figure 2-31
The iTunes and QuickTime Player installer welcome screen.

8.   At the "License Agreement" screen, accept the terms of the license agreement by selecting the appropriate button, and clicking Next, as shown in **Figure 2-32**.

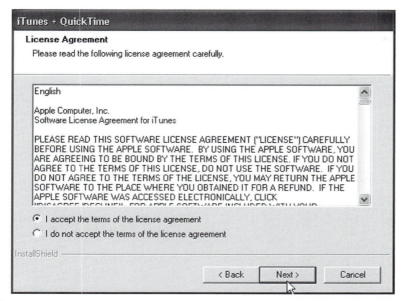

Figure 2-32
The software license agreement for iTunes and QuickTime.

9.   Read the "About iTunes" description, and click Next.

10. In the "Setup Type" screen, select which options you prefer, as shown in **Figure 2-33**.

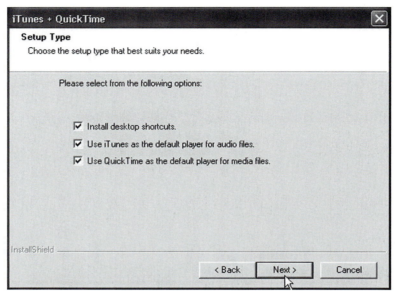

Figure 2-33
Choose which file types you want to play with QuickTime player.

11. Choose the destination location for the iTunes and QuickTime files (the default selection is fine), and click Next, as shown in **Figure 2-34**.

12. You may see one or more advertising screens from Apple. Click Next through these.

13. At the "Installation Successful" screen, click Finish, as shown in **Figure 2-35**.

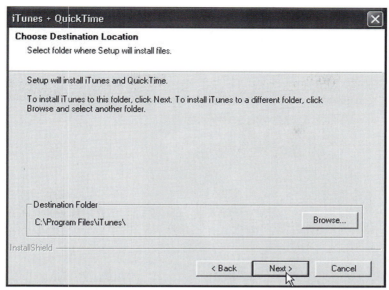

Figure 2-34
Choose the destination location for the QuickTime files.

Figure 2-35
The "Installation Successful" screen.

When installation is complete, launch the QuickTime Player by way of the Taskbar or the desktop link, and it will open to a screen similar to the Real Guide or the Windows Media Guide, as shown in **Figure 2-36**.

Figure 2-36
QuickTime Player installed and running.

Flash

Macromedia's Flash Player is the new kid on the streaming media block. But Macromedia is an old hand at tools for playing and creating online multimedia. One of the best things about Flash is the ease of installation. It's too bad all player installations aren't this easy.

1. Point your Web browser to:

    http://www.macromedia.com/downloads/.

2. Click the "Macromedia Flash Player" download link on the page, as shown in **Figure 2-37**.

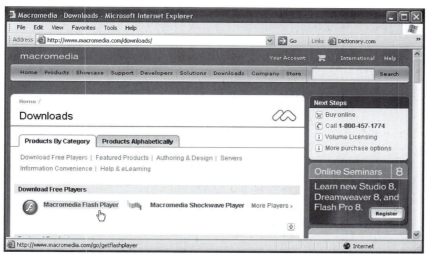

Figure 2-37
The Macromedia Flash Player download page.

3. In the "Macromedia Flash Player Download Center" page, check or uncheck optional software options, and click the "Install Now" button, as shown in **Figure 2-38**.

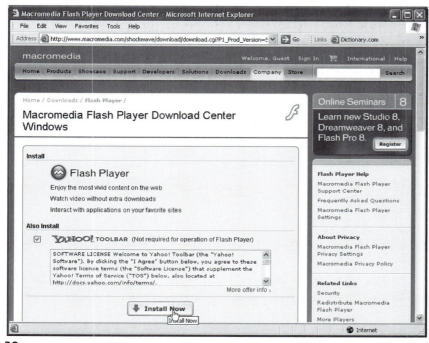

Figure 2-38
Check or uncheck optional software options before downloading the Flash Player.

4.   You may see a message in your browser saying that an "ActiveX" control may be required, as shown in **Figure 2-39**. Click the bar to continue.

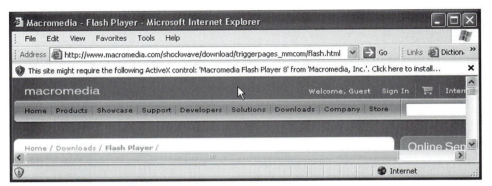

Figure 2-39
The browser may ask permission to install an ActiveX control.

5.   You may get a warning that asks, "Do you want to run this file?" as shown in **Figure 2-40**. Click Run, and the file will be installed.

Figure 2-40
Click Run if shown this prompt.

The Flash Player is successfully installed, as shown in **Figure 2-41**.

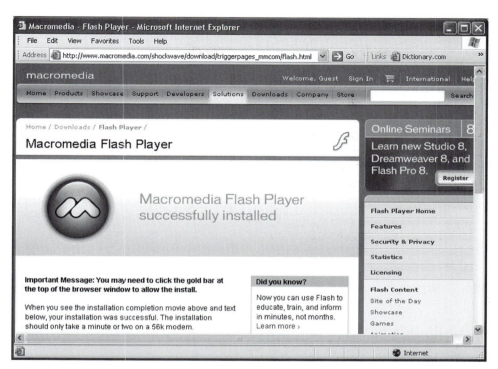

Figure 2-41
The message showing the Flash Player is successfully installed.

Note that the Flash Player is a browser plug-in, so there's no external media player to fiddle with. However, if you right click over the area in the Web page where the Flash Player is playing something, you may find some options to look at.

You have now successfully installed or updated all the major streaming media players.

Conclusion

Streaming media is the process of sending audio and video data over the Internet in real time. The streaming media industry is showing strong growth, and you can play a part as a streaming media producer. The streaming media process involves four basic steps: capture, encoding, distribution and playback. In this chapter, we learned how to manage our streaming media players, including updating already installed players and downloading and installing new media players. In Chapter 3, you'll learn about audio and video equipment suited for streaming media production.

CHAPTER 3

Audio and Video Production Tools

Now that you've learned some of the basic principles behind streaming media and updated your media player, it's time to get started with some of the tools you'll need to produce high-quality streams. Hopefully, you have a decent budget, but it's probably not bottomless, and the following sections take that into account.

In this chapter, you'll learn more about the equipment you'll need to buy or rent. You will:

- Review pre-production planning
- Learn about audio tool options
- Study video tool options
- Find out about hardware and software required to produce streaming media
- Learn about the importance of a good studio environment

Pre-Production Planning

Experts have written dozens of volumes about planning audio and video productions. It's really about "risk management"—that is, thinking ahead and reducing the potential for upsetting surprises. You're focused on the streaming media part, but it's worth reviewing a few of the pre-production basics for any audio/visual production.

The Script

The best productions start out with a dynamite *script*. Take the time to put down in words what you want the audience to hear and see. A script can be as simple as a one-page general description of the words and actions laid out in one or more scenes (the concept of "scene" applies to audio, too). Or it can be hundreds of pages of dialog and instructions. Your script is your first and most important planning document.

Budgets and Scheduling

Once you're happy with the script, work out a budget. Again, it can be as short and sweet as a single spreadsheet page. If you're renting equipment, include a line item for each piece. Labor is always the most expensive commodity; estimate the number of hours you'll need each crew member. Keep your scale in mind—you don't need to spend weeks working on a budget for a one-minute announcement by the CEO.

Location Scouting

Next, scout out the location or venue for your production. Visit the place physically, even if it's an unused office down the hall. Here are some questions to ask:

- Is there enough physical space for cameras, microphones, tripods, etc?
- Is there enough physical space for props, such as a desk and a chair?
- Are there enough grounded power outlets nearby?
- Is there access to the physical space during off hours for setup purposes?

Scheduling

When you've satisfied the location requirements, think about a detailed schedule. This is especially important for coordinating with people in leadership roles, such as corporate executives. Can the CEO show up for your recording session? Plan your production far enough ahead so you can accommodate their schedule. And keep in touch with their staff as recording or shooting approaches so you can revise your schedule if needed.

Connectivity

If you plan to broadcast your streams live, you will need a solid connection to the Internet at your shooting location. Ask the network manager how much bandwidth is available and where the network jacks are located. If all you have available is dial-up, find another venue. If you have a reliable DSL/cable connection or better, you're in business. Keep in mind, however, that your actual bandwidth varies with the specific type of DSL/cable connection.

Many broadband connections are *asynchronous*, meaning that they have different download and upload capacities. These lines are often advertised with these capacities listed, such as 1.5M/768. This means you can download at *up to* 1.5 megabits per second, and upload at *up to* 768 kilobits per second. However, these are theoretical maximums—it's always a good idea to test the connectivity well in advance. This is also a good time to determine whether you need an account of some kind to connect to the local network. Be sure to have all these details in place before shooting begins.

Even if you're not planning a live broadcast, you may need to quickly upload encoded files to a server back at the office. Or you may simply need to check last-minute e-mail. A method for connecting to your corporate network remotely could save you time and frustration.

Figure 3-1
Use only wired connections for streaming purposes. Wireless is not reliable enough.

Be Ready for Anything
When the poet Robert Burns wrote about the failure of "the best laid schemes o' mice an' men" in the eighteenth century, he must've had a premonition about working on the Internet. In short, be ready to tackle any contingency. Good planning will see you through.

Audio and Video Tools
Quality results require quality tools. This section talks about the audio and video recording equipment you'll need for high-quality production. The section also makes some specific equipment recommendations, although there are many more choices than those listed here.

This is probably as good a place as any to point out that video tape stores both video and audio signals. They are recorded on different areas ("tracks") on the tape. Audio tape, of course, records only audio signals. Video cameras record in a variety of formats, some of which are better for streaming media content than others. **Table 3-1** shows some of the most common formats and their appropriateness for streaming work.

Table 3-1
Video recording formats.

Format	Type	Quality
DigiBeta	Digital	Excellent
Betacam SP	Analog	Excellent
DV (DVCAM, MiniDV)	Digital	Very Good
Digital 8	Digital	Good
S-VHS/Hi-8	Analog	Avoid
VHS	Analog	Avoid

Start with Portable Equipment

You want to get started quickly, and that means selecting equipment that's easy to learn and to use. And you don't want to break your budget. To meet these goals, this chapter focuses on portable equipment, rather than equipment designed for studio use only. The good news is that most portable equipment can double as studio equipment in a pinch.

Digital vs. Analog Equipment

Audio and video recording devices fall into two main categories, *analog* and *digital*. Analog recording devices have been around for more than a century; electronic analog devices were invented in the 1920s. Analog tape recorders and cameras record light and sound as a continuously variable electrical signal, usually onto a magnetic tape wound in a plastic case, such as audio cassette or VHS. Analog devices store a virtually infinite range of sounds and color. On the other hand, even the best analog recorders are subject to the problem of *noise*, which is extraneous information often introduced by the equipment itself. Noise can sometimes be filtered out during later stages of production.

Digital equipment, on the other hand, stores sound and light as binary "bits," often called "1s" and "0s." The ordered combination of these values, when interpreted by a computer, results in what humans perceive as sound and light. Like analog devices, digital devices record onto magnetic tape, such as DAT for audio and DV or mini-DV for video. (See **Table 3-1** for a list of video formats.) Digital devices are less susceptible to the noise problem. However, some audiophiles insist analog devices record certain sounds better than digital, especially music. You may actually notice little quality difference in streams over 300 kbps. However, in the long-term, digital is probably a better investment.

Since streaming is a digital format, it makes sense to use digital equipment, especially since many digital formats allow you to transfer your audio and video files directly. However, if your budget is tight, or if you have existing A/V equipment, analog equipment will work just fine, though getting the signal from the recorder to the computer may require more work.

Portable Audio Recorders and Cameras

The following are some recommendations for portable audio recorders and video cameras. These are only recommendations; you should take some time to shop around for something that meets your specific needs and budget.

Analog

Marantz PMD 222

The Marantz PMD 222 analog tape recorder, as shown in **Figure 3-2**, is a standard portable cassette tape recorder for radio stations all over the world. It's inexpensive, rugged, and full-featured. It also has an all-important *XLR* microphone cable connector. (More about cables in following sections.)

Figure 3-2
Marantz PMD 222 portable analog tape recorder. (Image courtesy of Marantz America.)

Why Audio is Important to Videographers

Question to author: I'm a videographer, and I see a lot of audio-only material in this chapter and the book in general. Why do I need to know about audio-only recording equipment and techniques?

The author responds: Thank you for that question. Audio-only techniques are a great introduction to streaming media basics and an excellent step toward more complex video streaming methods.

Furthermore, high-quality audio is more important to successful streaming than to standard video production. Many video producers tend to focus on the "visuals" at the expense of audio quality. They love "whip" pans, fast dissolves, jump cuts, and other video techniques. At the same time, they forget basic sound-recording techniques, such as proper microphone setup. If you want to be a successful streaming producer, shift some of your production energy from visuals to "aurals."

Try this experiment in your office or at home. Turn on your television (or even start a video stream), and turn off the sound for two or three minutes. Watch the video. Then turn up the sound and leave the room for two or three minutes. Stay close enough so that you can hear the sound but can't see the pictures. Compare the "with sound" minutes to the "without sound" minutes. In which case did you receive the greatest quantity and quality of information? It was probably the "with sound" minutes. People generally use the Internet to gather useful information, and it's imperative that your streams be information-driven. And since most useful information in video is actually delivered by the audio, paying close attention to audio quality pays off. Poor audio quality will turn Internet users away.

Sony BVW-300

The Sony BVW-300 analog video camera with built-in recorder, as shown in **Figure 3-3**, is a broadcast standard that records in Beta SP *format*. (See **Table 3-1** for more on video formats.) The camera uses a charge-coupled device (CCD), a chip that transforms light into analog electrical signals.

Figure 3-3
The Sony BVW-300 analog video camera. (Image courtesy of Sony Corp.)

Digital

Tascam DAP1

The Tascam DAP1 digital audio recorder, as shown in **Figure 3-4**, is also used by broadcasters for field recording. It can record in stereo, as well as mono. And it uses digital readouts for elapsed time and other information.

Figure 3-4
Tascam DAP1 digital audio tape recorder. (Image courtesy of TEAC America.)

Canon GL-2

The Canon GL-2, as shown in **Figure 3-5**, is a solid entry-level, multi-use digital video camera. It's pricier than some others, but affordable. The camera records in mini-DV format.

Figure 3-5
The Canon GL-2 digital video camera. (Image courtesy of Canon USA.)

Support Equipment

Good audio and video production requires dozens of moving parts, so to speak. The following is a list of items every production team needs. To save money, you can rent some of these items or buy them used. Other items you'll use primarily in the studio.

Recording Tape

Magnetic recording tape varies in quality from manufacturer to manufacturer. Use a brand name and stick with it. It's also a good idea to use 60-minute blanks. The tape itself is thicker and more durable than tape in a 90-minute or two-hour blank.

Microphones

Next to the recorder, your microphone is the most important tool in your kit. Never rely on microphones built into the recorder, whether audio recorder or camera. Internal *mics* or camera-mounted mics can't record decent sound worth a dang. Here's three suggested handheld microphones.

- Electrovoice RE-50 (as shown in **Figure 3-6**)
- Shure SM-58
- Audix om7

And here's a couple of clip-on *lavalier* mics for video work.

- Audio Technica AT803B (as shown in **Figure 3-7**)
- Shure MX183

Figure 3-6
Electrovoice RE-50 handheld microphone. (Image courtesy of Telex Communications.)

Figure 3-7
Audio Technica AT803B lavalier (clip-on) microphone. (Image courtesy of Audio-Technica.)

Microphone Stand
The microphone stand, as shown in **Figure 3-8**, is an often-overlooked piece of equipment. Putting your handheld mic on a stand reduces the chance you might introduce noise when you move the mic around. It's also easier to point it toward a sound source, such as an actor's mouth.

Figure 3-8
A typical floor-type microphone stand. (Image courtesy of Millenium.)

Lighting Kit

It goes without saying that good video requires good lighting. An entry-level lighting kit starts with two lights and a carrying case. Lighting kits made by Lowel, as shown in **Figure 3-9**, are the standard.

Figure 3-9
The Lowel Rifa Pro 66 lighting kit, designed for interviews. (Image courtesy of Lowel Light.)

Headphones

Professional audio and video producers always monitor the audio via a good pair of head-phones. It's important to monitor what the microphone is picking up, so you can adjust placement and gain setting of the microphone accordingly. Be sure to buy headphones whose ear cups cover the entire ear, not just part of it. That keeps out room noise. Here are suggestions for headphones.

- AKG Acoustics K141M
- Sony MDR 7506 (as shown in **Figure 3-10**)

Figure 3-10
Sony MDR 7506 headset. (Image courtesy of Sony Corp.)

Cables/Connectors

Cables get the signal to and from devices. *Connectors* need to be strong enough to cope with the constant banging, jiggling and pulling they experience. Male connectors are used for outputs; female connectors are used for input. Cables should be balanced and shielded to avoid the introduction of noise from nearby electronic devices. Use XLR connectors whenever possible. These are the strongest available. Main types of connectors are shown in **Figure 3-11**.

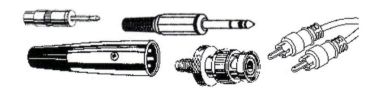

Figure 3-11
The main types of cable connectors, moving clockwise: mini, quarter-inch, RCA, BNC, and XLR. These are the male versions. (Images courtesy of Bux Communications, 1 Stop Electronics, and Stark Electronics.)

Audio Mixing Desks

You use a *mixing desk* to blend multiple audio signals together. For example, you can mix voice, music and natural or ambient sound onto a single track.

These can be used for an audio-only production or for creating a highly produced audio track in a video. (By the way, you can mix audio in software. But it's not as much fun.) Two good mixing desks are:

- Behringer MXB 1002
- Mackie 1202 VLZ-Pro (as shown in **Figure 3-12**)

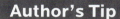

Author's Tip

Don't step on cables! There are smaller cables inside the sheathing, and stepping on them could rub off insulation, causing a short, or just plain break one in two.

Figure 3-12
The Mackie 1202 VLZ-Pro mixing desk. (Source: Mackie/Loud Technologies.)

Video Tape Recorders

You'll use a *VTR* (Video Tape Recorder) primarily for video tape playback, rather than re-cording. Like portable tape recorders and cameras, VTRs come in analog and digital ver-sions. Make sure you get one compatible with your other choices. And make sure your VTR has a FireWire/iLink connector. (More on FireWire later.) A couple of good VTR choices are:

- Sony DVR-20 (analog)
- Sony DSR-11 (digital, shown in **Figure 3-13**)

Figure 3-13
The Sony DSR-11 digital tape recorder. (Image courtesy of Sony Corp.)

<table>
<tr><td>

Author's Tip

If your camera has a FireWire connector, you can take the video/audio feed directly out of the camera and send it to your computer workstation. However, if someone else shoots the video and hands you an analog tape, you'll need a VTR. On the other hand, if someone hands you a DV tape, you can use your camera as the VTR.

</td><td>

Compressors and Proc Amps

Compressors help you manage the volume levels in your audio. Most professional-sounding audio is compressed. Here are a couple of options:

- Presonus Blue Max (as shown in **Figure 3-14**)
- FMR RNC1773

A *proc amp*, (short for "processing amplifier") cleans up video signals coming out of a camera. Options include:

- SignVideo PA-100 (single channel)
- SignVideo PA-200 (dual channel, as shown in **Figure 3-15**)

</td></tr>
</table>

Figure 3-14
The PreSonus Blue Max audio compressor. (Image courtesy of PreSonus.)

Figure 3-15
The Sign Video PA-200 dual channel proc amp. (Image courtesy of Sign Video.)

Equipment Bag or Rack

Invest in a set of sturdy portable equipment cases with wheels if you have lots of equipment and need to set it up quickly, as shown in **Figure 3-16**. Cases also make hauling equipment on airplanes much easier.

Figure 3-16
A sturdy equipment case will protect your investment.

Odds and Ends

Here are a few small but important items to add to your shopping list:

- Gaffer's tape
- Connector adapters (RCA to XLR, mini to 1/4" inch, etc.)
- Extra cabling
- Extra batteries and extension cords
- Small toolkit (Phillips and flathead screwdrivers, sharp knife, scissors, pliers)
- Pencil and paper
- A credit card to buy the things you forgot

Author's Tip

In a pinch, you can substitute cheap duct tape for gaffer's tape, but you'll be sorry. After your production you'll be left with sticky goo everywhere. Do yourself a favor and buy the good stuff.

Author's Tip

If you go out on location, find out where the nearest electronics store is, such as a Radio Shack. This will save you time if you discover you've forgotten a connector or you need batteries.

Places to Buy Equipment

You can buy most, if not all, of the equipment you need online. Here are a few suggestions.

- Broadcast Supply Worldwide (audio) – *http://www.bswusa.com/*
- The Broadcast Store (video) – *http://www.bcs.tv/*
- Online auction sites (Some people swear by these for mining good deals.)

Become Intimate With Your Equipment

Spend an hour getting familiar with all your new equipment. Read the manuals. Plug and unplug cables. Push buttons. Twist dials. Put in and take out tapes. As long as you're reasonably gentle, it's pretty hard to damage your new equipment.

Hardware and Software Requirements

Now that you've purchased or rented your audio and/or video equipment, it's time to talk about building an editing *workstation*. You can spend tens of thousands of dollars on nonlinear editing hardware and software packages. You can also spend a lot less by building your own from off-the-shelf parts and packaged software. You have to pay particular attention to some of the parts, notably the hard drive. But if you don't mind tinkering with computers, you can build a darn good workstation at no more than half the cost of a package deal.

The main points of difference between the hardware of a standard desktop computer you buy at a retail store and an editing workstation are:

- Processing power
- Memory (RAM)
- Storage (hard disk)

Rule of thumb for all these: More is better. So buy or assemble the most powerful equipment you can afford. See **Table 3-2** for some requirements and recommendations.

Author's Tip

Nonlinear editing (*NLE*) refers to the ability to move elements of video and audio around via an editing software package. It's very similar to cutting and pasting words, sentences or paragraphs in a word processor. Before computers, most editing happened in a linear fashion—that is, physical film clips or tape clips were assembled one after the other.

Table 3-2
Minimum and recommended requirements for an editing workstation.

Minimum Requirements	Recommended Requirements
1-GHz Pentium IV	2.5+ GHz Pentium IV processor
512 MB of RAM	1.24 GB of RAM
40 GB disk storage	500 GB disk storage
16-bit sound card and speakers	16-bit sound card and speakers
16-bit color video display	24-bit color video display
Microsoft Windows 2000 Pro	Windows XP Pro

Minimum hardware for Apple users is the PowerMac G5.

The hard drive recommendations in **Table 3-2** are actually pretty dinky. They'll get you started, but you're better off getting the biggest hard drive you can afford. And try to get a *SCSI* (pronounced "scuzzy") hard drive, not the standard IDE hard drive. SCSI drives are more expensive, but they perform better under the demanding conditions of audio and video editing. You may also want to invest in *Redundant Array of Independent Disk* (*RAID*) technology, which offers higher performance and more reliable storage for large amounts of data.

Author's Tip

Your editing workstation can double as a streaming media encoding workstation, though you may want to separate the two functions on two different computers.

Inside the Industry

One of the best hardware developments in recent years is *FireWire*, which was developed by Apple Computer as an ultrafast method of getting large amounts of data from one device to another. Also called *iLink* or *IEEE 1394* after the standards body that adopted it, FireWire is ideal for moving video and audio data from a digital recording device such as a DV camera to an editing and encoding workstation. You can move 400 MB of data per second over a FireWire cable up to 4.5 meters long. What does this mean to you? Make sure any video equipment you buy has FireWire capability.

Audio and Video Cards

Analog signals from analog audio recorders and cameras have to be digitized before a computer can manipulate them. Specialized hardware in the form of a *capture card* does this work. You'll need to install one or more of these cards before you can work with your audio or video:

- Audio Cards
    - Minimum: Factory-installed sound card
    - Recommended: Creative Labs Sound Blaster Audigy 4 Pro
- Video Cards
    - Minimum: ViewCast™ Osprey 210 (audio and video combined)
    - Recommended: ViewCast Osprey 500 DV (as shown in **Figure 3-17**)

Figure 3-17
ViewCast™ Osprey 500 DV video capture card. (Image courtesy of ViewCast.)

Most off-the-shelf personal computers include sound capabilities. As long as your computer has a *line in* input, that's enough to get you going. But if you really want to get the best quality, upgrade to a professional-level audio card.

Editing Software

Editing software lets you manipulate your audio and video files in ways unimaginable a generation ago. You can cut and paste portions of audio or video from the same file or different files. You can have an almost unlimited number of tracks. You can filter out certain kinds of audio-destroying noise or add video effects, such as fades. You'll find yourself spending hours just playing with these software packages. Here are a few choices:

- Audio Editing
  - Adobe Audition (formerly CoolEdit)
  - Sony Sound Forge
- Video Editing
  - Adobe Premiere
  - Sony Vegas Video

A Studio Environment

It's true you can produce audio and video on your desktop computer in your office, but a quiet, well-organized work environment devoted to audio and video editing is best. Think about converting an unused office into an editing booth. Put sound *baffles* on the walls and weather stripping around the door. Organize your equipment so that everything is in reach and cables and other equipment are properly stored. Make sure you have a good chair. You'll probably spend a lot of time in this room, so you might as well be comfortable!

Conclusion

Good results start with good tools. If you're serious about producing high-quality streaming media, invest in brand-name audio and video recorders, accessories, and supplies. You'll also need high-quality computer hardware and software to get the best results. And a studio environment is always the best option. In the next chapter, you'll discover the differences between analog recording and digital recording and some techniques for recording audio and video that will lead to good streaming media results.

Author's Tip

Many computers today come equipped with *Universal Serial Bus* (USB) and/or FireWire inputs. Many high-quality audio interfaces are available that plug directly into these inputs. These interfaces are usually very high quality, portable, and a great option for producing streaming media.

Author's Tip

Microsoft offers a simple capturing utility called Windows Media 9 Capture. You can download it from the Microsoft Web site.

CHAPTER 4

Production and Post-Production Techniques

The previous chapter helped you get started building an end-to-end streaming media system, starting with some of the basic equipment you need. This chapter explains the next step, getting your source audio and video from a recording device to a workstation in preparation for encoding and streaming.

In this chapter, you will:

- Discover the fundamentals of audio recording and video composition for streams
- Learn some audio and video theory related to streaming
- Pick up some ideas for a dream streaming workstation
- Optimize your audio in preparation for encoding
- Optimize your video in preparation for encoding

Fundamentals of Audio and Video Production

Streaming is a new method for delivering audio and video online. That doesn't mean you need to learn brand-new techniques for recording sound or composing a video shot. However, some things that work for television don't work well for streaming media. In this section, you'll review some of the fundamentals of audio and video production and learn some tips for adapting video techniques you may already know to a streaming environment.

Author's Tip

Why Not Just Record to the Hard Disk?

This chapter suggests that you should record your audio or video onto tape using specialized equipment, then transfer the data to your computer. But why not just record it directly onto a computer disk and save a bunch of steps? This makes sense. Several companies make specialized equipment for just this purpose, though most of it is designed for studio, not field, use. And it's very expensive. For now, avoid the temptation to record directly to your desktop personal computer or laptop. For one thing, recording on tape means you have an instant backup once you transfer all or part of your recording to your computer hard drive. The point is, whether you retain your tape or have it on Flash memory, which newer portable decks use, you'll have a second copy.

More importantly, your desktop was built for word processing and Web browsing, not the intensive production of time-based audio and visual information. Your disk drive and certain other components weren't designed for the large file sizes and huge data transfer rates required for intensive audio and video production. It's true that you can perform all of the activities and procedures described in this book on a desktop computer. But if you plan to create a large number of long-form productions—i.e., longer than five minutes each—consider buying one of the professional audio or video workstations.

Audio

Sound is an incredibly rich and rewarding medium. A whole chapter could be written about the right ways to record the human voice and the thousands of animate and inanimate objects that make sounds. However, you want to get on the right path immediately. So this section focuses on voice, because it's the simplest type of audio for beginners, and your first audio productions are likely to be voice only. You can build on these skills if you move on to more complex types of recording, such as music.

Simple Steps for Professional Results

Some simple steps for recording voice will get you through most situations. You'll need some time to practice and get used to working with the equipment, but you'll get the hang of it soon enough.

First, write down what you want to say—i.e., write a script. It can be anything from hand-written notes to a professionally edited script. Write it double-spaced and in all capital letters so it'll be easy to read.

Next, find a quiet place for recording. A studio is best, but any place where interruptions are few will work. Set up your equipment so that it's all within arm's reach, and make sure you can read the volume meter, for reasons explained further on.

Next, check all your connections. A loose one may sound solid, but a slight jiggle could cause a momentary loss of signal. Put on your headset and plug it into your recorder. You'll hear everything coming through the microphone and going on the tape. Gather up extra cable and put it where you won't kick it or trip on it.

Put your microphone near your mouth, ideally on a microphone stand. Experiment with the distance between your mouth and the microphone for best sound. The distance is usually three to six inches. Then place the mic at a slight angle to your lips. When speakers say the letters "p" or "t," they tend to make extra noises with their lips and teeth. Putting the mic at an angle mitigates this problem.

Volume Level

The most important concept in audio recording is volume level. A *volume level* is a measure of the power of the signal reaching the recording heads of the recording device. (The *head* is an electromagnet that rearranges metal oxides on the physical tape.) Too little level and the background noise caused by electronics and other factors could overwhelm the sound you really want to hear, your voice. Too much level could result in irritating distortion. Ever hear someone scream into a microphone? That grating sound you hear is *distortion*.

Monitor your levels by watching the volume meter on your tape deck. See **Figure 4-1** for an illustration of volume meters (sometimes called a VU, for "volume unit," meter) you're likely to encounter.

Author's Tip

Finding a quiet place to record will be harder than you think. Once you close the door, plug in your headset and listen to what the microphone picks up. If you're in an office, you might hear the whir of your computer's cooling fan, the whoosh of the air conditioning, or the buzz of fluorescent lights. If you have trouble finding a quiet room, try this trick. Get a light blanket or a large beach towel. Put it over your head and your microphone, as if you were in a tent. Then listen. Hopefully, the ambient sounds of your makeshift studio will be gone, or at least muted. This will lead to better sounding recordings, though you may look a bit silly to your friends and co-workers.

 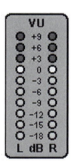

Figure 4-1
Two types of simple volume meter. The left VU meter is found primarily on analog equipment. The right one, often called an LED (light emitting diode) peak meter, is usually found on digital equipment.

Depending on your equipment, you need to treat the readings differently. On analog equipment, keep the needle out of the red zone as much as possible. A little bit is ok. If the needle barely nudges, your level is too low. On digital equipment, lights will be green, yellow and red. Say a few words. If the red lights blink a lot, your volume level is too high. If just a couple of green lights blink, the volume level is too low. If you see lots of green lights, with a smattering of yellow lights, your level is just right. On both digital and analog equipment, use the input gain or trim adjustment to modify your volume level up or down. Experiment and you'll find the right place. It might even be wise to turn your level down just a bit before you read your script. Some people increase their voice volume slightly when they actually start recording. By the way, ignore all the numbers and minus signs. Those are for experienced pros to figure out.

ALERT Don't confuse the volume level adjustment with the volume output into your headset. If you hear the volume in your headset go up or down, but the VU meter reading doesn't change, check whether you're turning the right dial.

Author's Tip

You can also try reading while you're standing. This lets you move at least one of your hands around, as if you were having a conversation.

Start Your Recording

If everything looks right, and you feel comfortable, push the record button (or the "play" and "record" buttons together), take a nice breath, and start reading your script. You're likely to rush through it the first time. This is a common problem for the inexperienced. Next time, cut your reading speed by half. It'll feel odd at first. But when you play it back, it'll sound normal and easy to understand.

Read your script several times and stop recording. Rewind and listen to all the takes. If you don't like any of them, read a few more times. When you're satisfied with a take, note its location on the tape, and remove the tape from the deck. Put it in a safe place and neatly store your equipment for later use.

ALERT The most expensive equipment in the world is no match for the human ear attached to a thinking brain. Use metering as a sanity check against your ears. But don't let metering overrule your own good judgment.

Video

The techniques of film and video have evolved over more than a century. When streaming video came along in the late 1990s, many producers assumed they could use the same editing techniques, shot compositions, special effects, camera movements and other common elements of visual language. Many people were disappointed when these creative options didn't automatically translate to the streaming medium.

However, this doesn't mean you can't have a sophisticated, well-produced streaming video. Just remember that streaming video is not the same as throwing a tape into a VCR or sending a video signal over the air. Think of streaming video and other types of video as different canvases with different palettes. Once you understand your streaming palette, you can create compelling stories.

Audio and Other Rules

Before getting into the video-only material, you might review the audio section above. All the suggestions and techniques for audio-only recording apply to audio recording for video with a few variations. In addition to writing a script, for example, you should consider story-boarding your script. A *storyboard* is a series of drawings that help you plan each video shot. A storyboard is akin to a visual outline of your video. It's an invaluable planning and time-saving tool.

When setting up your video shots, you may find that the microphones are a problem. You can use a microphone on a mic stand, but they are large and distracting. In the case of video, a lavalier mic is a better choice. These almost-invisible devices clip on to a blouse or tie and produce a high-quality audio signal. Don't forget to check your audio levels! A great picture with bad sound is worse than a great picture with no sound.

Lighting Is Critical

Light is everything in video recording. Cameras aren't as sensitive to light as you might think. The real reason shots look good, other than good framing, is the extra light thoughtfully cast on the scene. This helps the camera capture all the details, the correct colors, and the correct contrast between light and shadow. You definitely need extra light indoors. And you may need it outdoors as well.

Lighting a scene for video is an art in itself. Most techniques start with the classic *three-point lighting* system. Three lights bathe the subject in enough light for good color, contrast and definition. As shown in **Figure 4-2**, here are the elements for the three-point system:

- *Key light* – The key light is the main light source placed above the camera. It highlights the contours of the subject and throws deep shadows.

- *Fill light* – The fill light is softer than a key light, and "fills" some of the shadows. The fill light lowers the contrast between areas lit by the key light and shadows caused by the key light.

- *Back light* – The back light throws light behind the subject, and gives the subject a three-dimensional look by bringing the subject out of the background.

Key

Fill

Back

Figure 4-2
A simple three-point lighting setup.

If you shoot outdoors on a day with heavy overcast, you may need to add artificial light. On a clear day, the sun provides plenty of light, but the shadows may be harsh. A simple solution is a *bounce board*, a large flat panel painted white that reflects sunlight to fill in shadows.

Composition for Streaming

The video audience has grown used to productions using techniques that enrich the visual experience. Moving graphics, whip pans, fast dissolves, and soft focus have become part of our visual language. Unfortunately, most of this phraseology doesn't work with the current level of streaming technology. Why? Each time something moves in the frame, the information becomes more complex. To be displayed, the information has to be encoded into the file and the data rate of most streams isn't high enough to incorporate this properly. Therefore, you have to pare down your visual language. This doesn't mean you're limited to putting the camera on the tripod and locking it down. But it does mean you need to scale back some of your creative options and expectations.

ALERT Good video production requires an understanding of your audience. When you produce for a streaming audience, you need to ask two additional questions: How are they connected to the Internet and what is their connection speed? **Table 4-1** presents your options. If you think your audience will watch the video primarily at dial-up speeds, you are severely limited in your visual language. The amount of data that can be transferred in real time is tiny and simple visual changes from one shot to the next add enormous amounts of complexity. Fortunately, users are slowly migrating toward DSL/cable connections at home, and most medium-sized businesses and large corporations have faster speeds. This gives you more flexibility in your language choices. You'll learn more about audience analysis later.

Table 4-1
Typical bandwidths and creative flexibility.

Bandwidth	Flexibility
56 kbps Dial-up	Limited
DSL/Cable Modem	Moderate
T-1	Good
LAN	Excellent

Some Dos and Don'ts

The following are a few suggestions on techniques that translate well to streaming and those that don't. Good writing and storyboarding will help you get the most out of the techniques that work.

- Do
  - Close-ups
  - One and two-shots
  - Simple patterns in clothing
  - Simple, static backgrounds
  - Simple editing, including cutaways
  - Slow camera movements
  - Large font text and graphic elements with minimal detail
- Don't
  - Group shots
  - High-motion, such as fast pans, wipes or cinema verite
  - Quick cuts, such as too many shots in a brief period of time
  - Available light, unless full sunlight
  - Small text fonts or small graphic images
  - Moving graphics
  - Fast dissolves
  - Backgrounds with motion, such as rolling surf or flapping flags

Inside the Industry

 Many corporate video producers are shooting speeches or demonstrations that feature Microsoft PowerPoint presentations. These are great opportunities for adding visual variety to a stream without adding tons of digital information. Here's a simple technique:

1. Record the speech and get the PowerPoint file.

2. Have a graphics person extract the slides as JPEG files, or try the "Export to web" command in PowerPoint.

3. Using your video editing tools, drop each JPEG image into appropriate spots in the video, keeping the audio track underneath.

Now you have a video with switches between the talking head and their slides. It ain't Hollywood, but it's more engaging than just the speechmaker.

A Final Word About Audio

Experienced video producers may squirm at the creative limitations presented by streaming video. You could wait 10 or 15 years for the technology to catch up to your visual storytelling skills. But businesses and consumers are demanding streaming video now. How to cope? Think about your audio. You can deliver very high-quality audio even at low bandwidths. So consider spending extra resources on a killer audio track. It might make a dull visual experience a richer multimedia experience.

A Bit of Audio and Video Theory Related to Streaming Media

This book spends very little time on the theory behind digital audio and video. But this is a good opportunity to give you a little bit of background before delving into the details of the computer hardware and software.

How Digital Audio Works

Sound is complex analog vibrations in a medium, usually air, with variations in frequency and volume. These vibrations can have infinite variety, although the human ear is limited in the range of sound it can hear. Our ears convert these vibrations into analog electrical impulses. Our brain interprets and applies meaning to these impulses.

The first recording devices invented in the 19th century by Thomas Edison and others stored sound as variations in a continuous groove etched on a metal or wax cylinder or plate. To play the sound back, a motor powered by a spring or electricity turned the cylinder or plate at a constant speed. A diamond needle placed in the groove vibrated with the variations and transferred this mechanical energy to an amplifier. (Later devices used a magnet to rearrange and/or read the magnetic patterns of iron oxide crystals on Mylar tape.) The amplifier drove an electromagnet, which vibrated a rubber or paper cone. The cone's vibrations were transferred to the air, which humans hear as reproduced sound.

In the digital world, an electromechanical device (the microphone) picks up sound and converts it into analog electrical impulses, much like our ears. But when the sound goes into a digital tape recorder or a computer, usually via a sound card, the specially designed semi-conductor chips take *samples* of the sound. It's as if you were at a large buffet table. You see a huge bowl of strawberries. You can't eat them all. But you can sample them and get a good idea of what the rest probably taste like.

Audio sampling is no different. You can set your sound card to take just a few samples of the incoming signal, or you can tell it to take a lot. More samples mean more information and a better representation of the sound as a whole. The number of samples you take of a signal is called the *sampling rate*. The rate is expressed in *hertz*, a measurement of how often you take samples per second. Most samples fall in the range of 8 kilohertz (thousands of hertz, abbreviated kHz) to 44.1 *KHz*.

Each sample is a measurement of the incoming electronic waveform. This measurement can be stored using any number of bits, which is known as the *bit depth*. The *bit depth* determines the degree of accuracy of the sample, sometimes called the range of detail, resolution or depth. For example, you can measure length in yards, feet, or inches. Because inches are smaller, you need more digits to express the same value, but they are more accurate. Typical bit rates for digital audio include 8-bit, 16-bit, and 24-bit. (CD quality audio is 16-bit.)

Author's Tip

It's worth noting here that the greater the sample frequency and larger the bit depth, the larger the file. That affects your disk storage space. Look in the following section "Moving Your Audio and Video From Recording Device to Workstation" for a formula that can help you estimate file size.

How Digital Video Works

Light is waves of energy and magnetism that travel through space; the more precise term for light is "electromagnetic radiation." The waves travel at different wavelengths. Scientists measure a wavelength from the crest of one wave to the crest of the next, analogous to the waves caused by dropping a pebble into a pond, as shown in **Figure 4-3**. The wavelengths of light are measured in billionths of a meter. The range of electromagnetic wavelengths is enormous, but humans see only a small portion of it, known as "visible light."

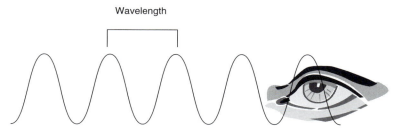

Wavelength

Figure 4-3
Light is measured in terms of its wavelength.

Like sound, light is also measured in frequency, and the human eye perceives different frequencies as color. Color frequencies range from 430 trillion hertz (red) to 750 trillion hertz (violet). Light travels through the iris of the eye through a flexible lens, which focuses it on the retina. Cells called rods and cones transform the light waves into electrical impulses that travel along the optic nerve to the brain. The 120 million rods in the average eye pick up dim light and motion. The six million or so cones specialize in color reception.

The first artificial light-gathering and storage device appeared in 1826, when a French inventor named Joseph Nicéphore Niépce made a picture of the roofs of some houses in his neighborhood. He gathered light using an old device called a *camera obscura* and stored the image on a pewter plate coated with a chemical akin to asphalt. Photography advanced to the point in 1895 when fellow Frenchman Louis Lumiere invented a camera that could take photographs quickly one after the other on long roll of cellophane film. Voila! Movies! (Lumiere's invention could also process and project the film.) Lumiere was a skeptic, though. He predicted the movie industry would never amount to anything.

With the invention of radio a few years later, inventors began to think of ways to send moving images electromagnetically. One technique that gained favor was developed in the 1920s by Philo T. Farnsworth. He found a way to scan the surface of a light-gathering device (called a *pickup*) and transform the signal into electrical impulses. Think of how you read a page in this book. You start at the top left, go across the page, and start again at the next line and repeat the process to the end of the page. A camera does this work at nearly the speed of light. A television reverses this process. You see an image because the scan happens so quickly. It's the same principle, known as *persistence of vision*, that makes the millions of images on film appear as one moving image. To store analog images, video engineers took a cue from audio engineers and created large versions of audio tape recorders to record visual and audio signals.

Farnsworth's analog methods dominated video technology until the 1980s and the advent of the digital camera. A digital video camera measures light in tiny pieces called *pixels*, assigns a value to each, and converts the value into "1s" and "0s." Like digital audio, digital video samples the video signal at a given rate and a given depth in bits.

However, digital cameras gather far more information than you can store efficiently. Therefore, electronics in the camera or elsewhere *compress* or remove some of the redundant information. To display the video information, the computer reverses the compression or *decompresses* the signal stored in the digital video signal or file and illuminates individual pixels on the monitor, somewhat like the drops that create an image in a Jackson Pollock painting.

Is Digital Really Better?
Many people still debate the relative advantages of digital recording over analog recording, despite the ascendance and dominance of digital. Here's a list to help you make up your own mind.

Advantages

- Copies are exact, without data loss when copies are made from copies.

- Easier to edit and manipulate.

- Cheaper to design and build digital recording and editing equipment.

Disadvantages

- Exact copies make piracy—i.e., theft—easier. (With analog, copies of copies look worse than the original.)

- Digital video files are large and awkward to work with.

- Some audiophiles believe digital recordings lack a certain warmth and smoothness.

Common Source File Formats

You'll come across a variety of file formats as you work with computer audio and video, as shown in **Table 4-2**. Source file formats, as far as this book is concerned, are formats used to store audio and video in a computer before they are transformed or encoded into streaming formats. (A *format* is simply a way to organize data on a storage medium.) To keep things simple, think of these formats as raw formats, just like the raw ingredients of a good pizza before they are cooked into a format specifically designed for Internet delivery.

Table 4-2
Common source data file.

Name	Type	Extension
AIFF	Audio	.aif, .aiff
AU	Audio	.au
MIDI	Audio	.mid, .midi
MOD	Audio	.mod
VOC	Audio	.voc
WAV	Audio	.wav
AVI	Video	.avi

Moving Your Audio and Video From Recording Device to Workstation

One of the most critical tasks you'll undertake as a streaming media producer is *capturing*. This is the process of moving data from your audio or video recording device to your computer workstation. It's important to do this well, because after you've captured the data, it's much harder to fix problems that may have been introduced by poor capturing technique.

Much of the capture procedure is driven by the particular hardware and software you use, although they share some elements. For example, you're likely to move data from your recording device to your hard disk via a cable and a capture card in your workstation. Read the instruction manual for both the audio and/or video capture hardware, particularly if you are unfamiliar with FireWire. (FireWire is cabling technology for transferring data to and from digital devices at speeds up to 400 megabytes per second.) Hardware manufacturers often bundle simple editing software packages with their cards. These give you a chance to experiment with the hardware, though the software is rarely up to professional production standards. If you have purchased editing software, be patient while you learn the software's intricacies. Fortunately, most editing software uses familiar concepts such as "play/pause/stop" and "record" for basic tasks.

You may want to optimize your workstation before capturing, especially if you've been doing some other intensive work. Here's a checklist:

- Defragment your hard drive
- Turn off network access and file sharing
- Close all other programs, especially those that access your hard drive
- Monitor your system resources to make sure the computer has enough power to keep up with the work it has to do

Prepare to Capture

Get yourself organized at your workstation with all your recording equipment. Hook everything up and make sure you can monitor output from your recorder via your computer. That way, you'll hear/see the same thing that's going on the hard drive.

Disk Space Needs

You'll be stunned how fast your hard disk fills up when you start capturing video, especially if you use *uncompressed* video. To avoid the dreaded "disk full" error, here's a quick formula for calculating how much disk space you need for a given clip. ("Color bit depth" refers to the amount of data that describes color, as in 8-, 16-, or 24-bit, and "fps" is "frames per second.")

```
width (in pixels) × height (in pixels) × (color bit depth) × (fps) × (duration in seconds) / 8,000,000
```

For example, here's a potential calculation for a two-minute clip, captured at 320 × 240, using 24 bits per pixel:

```
320 × 240 × 24 × 30 × 120 / 8,000,000 = 829.44 megabytes
```

Be aware that some Microsoft Windows and Apple Macintosh file systems limit individual file sizes to 2 gigabytes (2048 megabytes). That means if you have a long production, you have to either reduce certain parameters, such as color depth, or use editing software that can support file sizes greater than 2 GB. If you have a very long video, you may be able to glue individual pieces together after encoding with utilities provided by the encoding software vendor.

Time to Capture

Let's assume you have some tapes in front of you. Find the specific sections you want to capture. Don't capture the whole thing; that wastes time and disk space. Now choose your capture settings. This is critical! If you don't capture at the right settings, you could have trouble later when you encode. You may have to experiment some, but here's some basic audio capture settings.

- Bit depth: 16-bit
- Sample rate: 44.1 kilohertz
- Format: WAV (.wav)

You should also set audio levels in the editing software (see the previous section on volume levels).

And here's some basic video capture settings.

- Frame size: 320 × 240
- Frame rate: 30 fps (frames per second)
- Compression ratio: Lowest available (ideally uncompressed)

Video capturing offers a few other parameters to consider. Microsoft suggests that if you use a video monitor, adjust the *SMPTE* color bars (a standard color gauge in television and video production) and then adjust your computer monitor to match using a high-resolution computer bitmap of the SMPTE bars. Then adjust your video capture levels (*hue*, *saturation*, and *brightness*) so that the picture matches the video monitor. For a quick tutorial on adjusting your computer monitor, see the article "Using SMPTE Color Bars to Calibrate Monitor" at greatdv.com:

http://www.greatdv.com/video/smptebars.htm.

Microsoft also suggests you may want to capture using the YUY2 (4:2:2) pixel format for optimal use of its technology.

Now that you're ready to capture, click Record, and the hardware digitizes the analog signal from the recording device. The software applies the settings you specified and stores the data on your hard drive. In a few moments, you'll have your source audio or video file, all ready for encoding.

Author's Tip

If you use FireWire, you don't need to worry about setting frame sizes, frames per second, etc. The technology automatically transfers the digital video data at full-frame size and 30 fps using the built-in digital video compression.

Optimize Your Audio

Now that you've captured your audio and video, it's time to *optimize* it—that is, fix any problems and enhance it so that it sounds and looks best when streaming. In the case of audio, even the most experienced streaming pros find problems after it's been captured. For example, you may not have noticed the quiet buzz caused by an overhead fluorescent lamp. The whoosh of air conditioning may be particularly loud. Or the presenter has a few too many "aahs" and "umms." You can fix these problems using editing software. Furthermore, the software can manipulate the entire audio file to make the final encoded product sound even better.

It's best to perform these tasks in a certain order. Here's a quick checklist:

1. Editing
2. Equalization
3. Noise Reduction
4. Compression
5. Normalization

Editing

The art of public speaking has gone the way of the horse and buggy. You could argue that the advent of recorded speech meant the end of public speaking. That's because recordings can be manipulated to make a speaker sound better. This is an extreme view; witness the brilliant oratory skills of many clergymen and women.

Most people, of course, don't have these skills. Audio editing tools exist to compensate for the problems caused by long pauses, backtracking, coughs, cleared throats, and other distracting mistakes by public speakers. Experiment with your editing software to remove these errors, not just to make the speaker sound better, but to make the audio more "listenable." It's hard to listen to a presentation constantly interrupted by "aahs" and "umms." And don't forget that when you remove these things, you should listen to the change and fiddle with it if it sounds odd. Don't be afraid! Software editors are "nondestructive." You can always Undo.

Equalization

Sometimes you may find, despite your best efforts at recording and capturing, the file just doesn't sound "right." Trust these instincts and be fearless about manipulating the way the audio appears in your ears. You may discover, for example, that the speaker sounds "muddy." That's when there's a lot of lower frequency sound, but not a lot of higher frequency sound to give each word definition. One way to solve this problem is *equalization* or "*EQ*'ing."

Equalization is the process of turning up (boosting) or turning down (attenuating) small frequency ranges within audio. In the case of a muddy-sounding voice, you can try turning up the higher frequencies and turning down the low frequencies. Try attenuating frequencies below 100 Hz and boosting frequencies in the 1 to 4 kHz range. A typical software graphic equalizer is shown in **Figure 4-4**.

You may already have some equalization skills. Most home stereos and many car stereos have simple built-in graphic equalizers. These are the gizmos with "slide faders" that move up and down, changing parts of the audio. A popular EQ setting these days is a huge boost in bass response, which results in that "BOOM BOOM" sound favored by certain male juveniles. (Large bass speakers help.)

Your audio editing software should have a *graphic equalizer*, along with some presets. Again, don't hesitate to play with the settings and learn what works best. But work with moderation. You'll find that small adjustments go a long way.

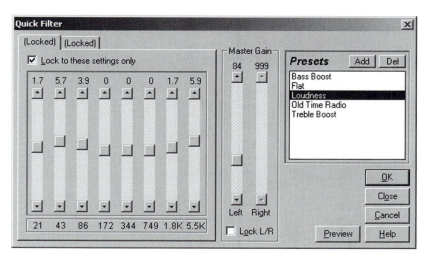

Figure 4-4
A typical software graphic equalizer (CoolEdit 2000).

The Difference Between Voice and Music

 It's important that you understand the basic difference between voice and music from an audio-engineering standpoint. Audio pros talk about the difference using the term *dynamic range*, which can be thought of as the span of volume from quiet to loud of all the sounds in a particular file. Music typically has a wide dynamic range. Think of Tchaikovsky's 1812 Overture. In the space of a few seconds, the music can go from the quiet of a few wind instruments to cannon fire. The music has a wide dynamic range.

Voice normally has a narrow dynamic range. The next time you have a lengthy conversation with your best friend, listen for the range of quiet places to loud places. Unless your friend likes to yell a lot, the dynamic range will be fairly narrow. Have you ever noticed how terrible music sounds over the telephone, while your best friend's voice can sound almost next door? That's in part because telephone lines are designed to handle the narrow dynamic range of the human voice, not the wide dynamic range of music.

It's also worth noting that music has a wide range of frequencies: The piccolo produces high-frequency notes, while the tuba produces low-frequency notes. Most normal human speech stays in a very narrow mid-frequency range. And telephones, by the way, are very good at reproducing mid-range frequencies, but not high or low frequencies.

Noise Reduction

In simplest terms, noise reduction identifies unwanted audio frequencies and, through complex calculations, attenuates them without affecting the rest of the audio. You pick a portion of the file with just the unwanted sound, highlight it, analyze it, and create a profile. Then you apply the profile to the entire file. Check your editing software manual for the specifics.

Use noise reduction carefully. It requires some advanced understanding of acoustics to get good results. If you're unsure, use equalization only.

Dynamic Range and Compression

One of the most important optimizations you perform on audio files is *compression*. Don't confuse this with encoding, which is sometimes called "compression." Encoding removes data from a file to make it smaller and streamable. Audio compression means turning down the loudest portions of the file, in effect narrowing the dynamic range. Compression lessens the chance your audio may sound distorted at the loudest points. Compressed audio also just sounds better.

Open up your audio editing software and the audio file you captured in Chapter 2. Find the function called "Compression" or sometimes "Dynamics Compression." To apply it, you'll probably need to highlight all or portions of the *waveform* (the squiggly line giving a visual representation of the audio). Most editing software packages offer compression presets, so you don't have to spend a lot of time figuring out the right settings. If you want to play with these settings (recommended!), try these:

- Threshold: –10 db

- Ratio: 4:1

- Attack and Release: 100 ms

- Output level: Add enough gain to restore the original signal level

 Alert   **Always use your ears to judge the results of your audio processing. If you don't like the results, change the settings or go with a preset. And always remember to listen to your results in headphones that block outside noise. At least listen to the results in high-quality speakers. Most music engineers carry personal speakers with them to each studio. They give them the cool name of** *monitors.*

Normalization

Streaming audio files sound best when they are loudest without distortion, sometimes called "clipping." *Normalizing* turns up the volume of an audio file to a point just before distortion occurs. Check your audio editing software for a Normalize function and normalize the file to about 95%, or –0.5 dB. Keeping normalization just under 100% or 0 dB gives the editing and encoding software a bit of wiggle room.

Optimize Your Video

Video capturing is an inexact science, and you may find unwanted artifacts or other problems with the video image once you have it on your hard drive. At the very least, the video probably doesn't start or end exactly where you want. You may see black bars along the edges. Or the video seems too dark or too bright. Now is the time to optimize the video. (Note that the audio optimizations above apply to audio tracks in video as well.)

Unfortunately, video files are not as plastic as audio files. This is why correct capturing technique is so important. Video has fewer "fixes" available to it than audio. But there are a few things you can do.

First, let's quickly review some good video capture settings from earlier in this chapter:

- Frame size: 320 × 240
- Frame rate: 30 fps
- Compression ratio: Lowest available

Once you get some experience, you might play with these settings a bit. You might try capturing at a larger frame size, say 640 × 480. (Remember to use a 4:3 ratio!) This is useful if you plan to stream at very high bit rates. And you should attempt to capture uncompressed video. This means you'll have all the video information you could possibly need.

However, a larger frame size can drastically increase your file size. Because the file size will be enormous, you will quickly eat up disk storage space. Furthermore, capturing at a large frame size requires a more powerful computer, or else you could lose video frames. Try it, but if you drop more than a few frames, go back to the smaller frame size.

As with audio, it's best to follow a certain order in your video optimizations to get the most out of them. The order isn't hard and fast, though.

1. Editing
2. Cropping
3. Video processing
4. Filtering
5. Resizing
6. Rendering

Editing

Editing moving images is an art form. It's not as simple as removing an "ahh" or an "umm." When you take out an "aah," the two pieces of audio on either side simply come together and the listener is none the wiser. But when you cut out a piece from a moving image, you wind up with something called a *jump cut*. The eye will notice that something was missing, even if the change is slight. The worst of these edits will break up the rhythm of the video, causing viewers to say unconsciously to themselves, "What was that?" Now you've lost the viewer's full attention.

A simple solution to the jump cut problem is a *cutaway*. When you're shooting your video, spend a few minutes recording some of the visual information around you. These could include shots of the audience, other participants in an event, or the general scene where the action takes place. These are called *covering shots*.

At your workstation, capture some of this video, using the same settings as your main video. When you come across a jump cut, take a piece of a covering shot, and "cover" the jump cut with the visual image, while maintaining the original audio, as shown in **Figure 4-5**. This takes some practice, but the transition will be much smoother and less likely to confuse the audience.

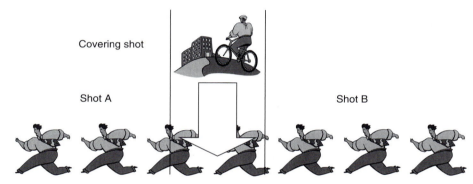

Covering shot

Shot A   Shot B

Figure 4-5
Use a covering shot to mask a jump cut.

Inside the Industry

 Television news editors use covering shots constantly. Next time you watch the evening news, look for a story about a speech or a press conference. You might see video of the speaker delivering an announcement or answering a question. Suddenly, the shot changes to a shot of all the cameras and their operators recording the event. Then the shot changes to the speaker again. Chances are the editor used a covering shot of the cameras to mask a jump cut. He or she may also have used the shot to give the scene a bit of variety in case the particular images or content was dull.

Use the video editing process to add simple *effects*. For example, it's a good idea to fade up from black at the beginning of a video and fade down to black at the end. This transition signals visually the beginning and end of a video. You can also add simple titles, called *slides*, to the beginning and credits at the end. (Don't forget to give yourself credit!) However, you should avoid the temptation to add a lot of effects that introduce too much information to the video file, such as wipes, whip pans, fast dissolves, etc. These generally don't translate well to streaming media, especially at low bit rates. To add visual effects, check your editing software manual for the exact procedures.

Cropping

If you have done any kind of photography beyond snapshots, you've probably cropped an image or two. Perhaps you needed to remove Aunt Argyle from the edge of a family portrait, because she's cut you out of her will. You probably used your photo manipulation software's *cropping* tool to symbolically, uh, punish her.

Streaming media producers use the cropping functions of video editing software to solve two less emotional problems, overscan and letterboxing.

Overscan

When you capture a video, you may notice black bars around the edges of the video images, as shown in **Figure 4-6**. These bars are normally covered by the plastic casing around a television's picture tube. Obviously, you don't need these bars, called *overscan*.

To solve this problem, use your editing software's cropping function. In many editing tools, video cropping works very much like the cropping tool in photograph manipulation software. Simply draw a rectangle inside the video image that leaves out the overscan area.

WARNING! Was the word "simply" used? Well, it ain't so simple. It is absolutely critical that the pixel dimensions of the cropped video (sans overscan) match the *aspect ratio* of the original video. If you're working with standard video, which has a 4:3 aspect ratio, this means for every four pixels you shave off the width, you need to take three pixels off the height. Otherwise, your video will suffer distortion later in the process.

Letterboxing

Movies shot in a wide-screen format such as Cinemascope are sometimes shown on TV in their original aspect ratio. This means black bars appear on the top and bottom of the image, as shown in **Figure 4-6**. This is called *letterboxing*.

In terms of streaming, these bars are just extra information you don't need to transmit over the Internet. Your viewers are better off without them. Use your video cropping tool to draw a square inside the actual image and lop off the unneeded bits. As with overscan, be sure your cropped image dimensions have a 4:3 ratio (or 16:9, if you're using high-definition video dimensions), or your image could become distorted later in the optimization process.

Figure 4-6
Overscan and letterboxing. Overscan is black border area around the image rectangles.

Video Processing

Television screens and computer screens use very different technologies to display images. Video generally looks darker on a computer screen than a TV screen. And the colors and contrast usually look different as well.

You'll remember the suggestion to buy a processing amplifier ("proc amp") in Chapter 3. These devices allow you to manipulate an incoming video signal. If you don't have a hardware proc amp, there's a good chance you can do similar manipulations using your video-editing software. And while hardware proc amps don't offer fine-grained control, software processing lets you change individual shots, even frames. The trick is to limit your urge to fix to the amount that gets the job done without introducing more problems.

The most likely change you'll make is brightness. As you play with it, you may notice the black areas of the video moving closer to gray. You'll just have to fiddle with the settings until you like what you see. Check your editing software manual for specifics.

Filtering

Most editing software packages and later versions of some encoders contain filters that take out certain artifacts introduced by the capturing process. The filters include *deinterlacing*, *inverse telecine*, and *noise reduction*.

Deinterlace

As mentioned previously, TV monitors display visual data differently from computer monitors. Video equipment records data in a way meant for display on televisions, which are *interlaced*. An interlaced video frame has two fields that overlap. If you imagine a TV screen as a set of vertical lines stacked on the other, one field contains the odd-numbered lines, the other holds the even-numbered lines. As shown in **Figure 4-7**, the lines of one field are shown first, and the second a moment later, although the human eye can't see the change.

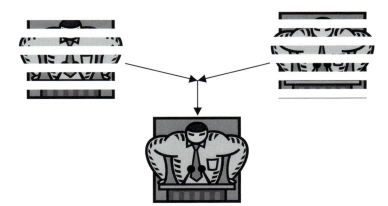

Figure 4-7
Televisions interlace two fields of lines to create a frame. To avoid artifacts created by this, use your editing software's deinterlacing feature.

When interlaced video is displayed on a computer screen, the two fields are combined to make a single frame of video. Artifacts are introduced under certain circumstances, especially when there's a lot of horizontal movement in the frame. Use your editing software's deinterlacing filter to remove these artifacts.

Inverse Telecine
Motion picture film is usually shot at 24 fps. Video is shot at 30 fps. (Actually, it's 29.97 fps.) When film is transferred to video, the process introduces duplicate frames to make up the extra six frames per second, as shown in **Figure 4-8**. This is redundant information you don't need for streaming. Use your editing software package's inverse telecine filter to remove these extra frames.

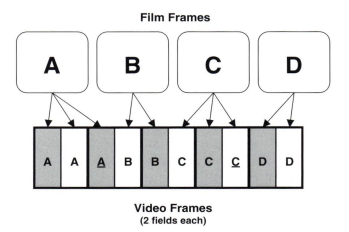

Figure 4-8
The telecine process, which creates extra fields (the underscored letter). These extra frames can be removed by the inverse telecine process.

Noise Reduction

Remember in Chapter 3 that you use the highest quality cameras and recording equipment you can. One reason is to reduce the chance for grainy pictures or general low quality. This "noise" can also appear as lines, snow, or any other unwanted electronic glitches. However, if you're trapped into using a cheap consumer video camera, you may be able to clean the image up a bit with your editing software's noise reduction. Be careful. Noise reduction may blur the image, introducing even more problems in an already problematic video image.

Rendering

The final step in the video optimization process is saving all the edits and optimizations into a file that will then be used to create your encoded streaming media file. This is called *rendering*. The most important rendering decision you'll make is image size. This should be the final size you want for the streamed image. You may want to render a master version of your edited video in the original size it was shot at, in order to have a high-quality master for later re-encoding.

You may decide to render two or more files, if you want one size for high-bandwidth users, and a smaller size for low-bandwidth users. A large image is closer to the TV experience most users expect. A smaller image size might mean a sharper image. The type of content you have—e.g., talking heads or fast action—may also influence your decision. As discussed in the section on cropping, make sure your image dimensions are in a ratio of 4:3 (or 16:9); the point is to maintain your original aspect ratio. Here are some standard streaming video image sizes:

- 640 × 480 (recommended only for very high-bandwidth streaming)
- 320 × 240
- 240 × 180
- 176 × 132 (FYI: This is the current standard size from streaming over mobile networks.)

If you're unsure how the video will look at different image sizes, take a small portion of your video and create a new file. Then render and encode the sample. That will save time and energy.

Now that you've optimized your video and chosen your image size, render your video. Depending on the length of the video and the power of your workstation, rendering could take thirty minutes or more. So take a break and get ready for encoding.

Author's Tip

Most video editing packages allow you to encode your video to a streaming media format directly from the timeline. This can save the time it takes to render your master video. However, it's always a good idea to render a master version for archival purposes.

Conclusion

Producing high-quality audio and video for streaming requires you to rethink your production techniques somewhat. Video producers, especially, may need to simplify some of their visual language. However, that doesn't mean your streaming productions have to be boring. They just have to be adapted to a different environment. The same goes for your post-production skills; you only need to tweak them in order to get maximum benefit for streaming. In the next chapter, you'll encode your material into streaming media files.

CHAPTER 5

Encoding Audio and Video

Now that you have produced and optimized your audio and/or video, it's time to encode. First, however, you need to decide what streaming media format to use. And before the chapter details the procedures, it will demystify one of the most important aspects of streaming: the *codec*. Like the famed Philosopher's Stone, which transformed base metals into gold, codecs and encoding transform large and unmanageable audio and video files into files that are smaller, yet still sound and look great.

In this chapter, you'll learn:

- How to choose the right streaming media format

- How to download and install streaming media encoders (not including Windows Media Encoder, which you installed in Chapter 1)

- How to choose the right codec

- How *multiple bit rate* encoding gives you more flexibility

- The basics and then some of audio and video encoding

Format Choice and Streaming Media Players

One of the decisions you'll make as a streaming media producer is which *platform*—that is, which one or more of the several streaming media technologies you'll favor for your project. You'll have to decide whether to use systems designed by RealNetworks, Microsoft, Apple Computer, Macromedia, an open standard such as MPEG, or some combination. Your decision will be driven in part by the installed base of players on the computers of your expected audience.

Media Players From Different Perspectives

A *media player* in the streaming context is software that receives audio and video data sent by a streaming server or a Web server. The data comes from an audio or video file specially modified (encoded) for continuous transmission over the Internet. During transmission, the media player is in constant contact with the server to ensure delivery of all the data. The media player converts the data into information that can be displayed on a screen or drive speakers to create sound.

Hmm. That's not totally accurate. Marketing experts might define a media player this way: A media player is an opportunity to capture the attention of an Internet user with a compelling audio and visual experience in order to impress the user with a particular brand and/or convert the user into a paying customer.

Actually, both descriptions are accurate. The point is that the major *proprietary* streaming media players double as media playback applications and opportunities to market goods and services. If you want to understand streaming media, you should understand that one doesn't usually exist without the other in some form. That's why media players offer so much more than play/pause/stop.

Software manufacturers sell their products primarily on the strength of the software's features. If you carefully examine all the features of the leading streaming media players, you'll find incredible similarity. They may look different, the commands and menus may have different names and layouts, and the underlying code may be different, but the number and types of features related to audio and video streaming are remarkably similar. This is especially true for the two heavyweights, RealNetworks and Microsoft. They are like two evenly matched boxers. Each punch and counterpunch keeps the score even. (Lately, they've made noises about being friendlier to each other, but look out for a sucker punch.) At this point, you should defer questions about which platform to use until you understand the audience you want to reach. That's discussed in the next section.

Inside the Industry

 You may ask, if the media players are so similar, how do the software companies make money with their media players? Basic business models are discussed in Chapter 11, *Advanced Topics*, but the short answer is "content." Ultimately, the user wants to hear or watch interesting things with his or her media player. The number and type of dooflickees and whatsits in the software are largely irrelevant in the long run. The streaming company that can deliver the most compelling content wins.

Evaluating Your Audience and Resources

Now comes one of your most difficult decisions. Which format(s) should I choose to serve my audience's needs? You'll struggle over this one. It might even keep you awake at night. The best way to cope is research, research, research. Understand and analyze your audience and the resources you have at hand as thoroughly as possible. That will lead to a good decision.

Professional media producers always start with the audience. Who is the man, woman or child you want to reach? What are their characteristics? Are you aiming at a mass audience or a niche audience? What makes your target audience different from the general audience? Once the audience is identified, the message is tailored to resonate as strongly as possible with the target.

Streaming media producers also start with audience. But they have to ask some very specific questions related primarily to the audience's capability to hear or view the content they produce. Put another way, television producers don't have to worry whether the family TV can show the video of the week. That's because television technology is just about the same everywhere. But the capabilities of office or home computers and their Internet connections differ wildly. Streaming producers have to take these variations into account.

Here are some variables to evaluate as you decide which streaming media platform(s) work best for your situation.

External vs. Internal

You can roughly divide the entire universe of streaming media users into people external to your organization or internal to your organization. For the external users, you have virtually no control over the types of hardware, software, or Internet connections they use. These users could include Joe Sixpack at his desktop computer surfing the Net for entertainment or information. External users can also be a very specific group of people, such as Joe Sixpack Who Drinks Triple Caffeine Sugar Juice. Whether it's a mass audience or a niche audience, you'll have to keep in mind a wide variety of computer configurations and Internet connection types.

You have much more control over an audience internal to your network, at least in theory. Most large organizations try to limit the configurations of desktop and laptop computers for ease of maintenance. Joe Sixpack's office computer is likely to be very similar to Jane Executive's desktop in the same company. And connectivity within an organization is likely to be similar across the network.

Internet vs. Intranet

The Internet has been described as a vast, undifferentiated cloud between the starting place of data and the destination. This means you have zero control over the network conditions at any given moment of your streaming media broadcast to an external audience, as shown in **Figure 5-1**. Some people have used the term *net weather* to describe the capricious nature of Internet conditions. One minute you may have summer sunshine, the next a winter blizzard. You simply have to accept this fact when streaming to large numbers of external users. You can take some comfort in the fact that streaming media systems are designed to cope with unpredictable conditions.

Figure 5-1
You have no control over your network delivery conditions once the data enters the Internet "cloud."

You have more control over conditions on an intranet, much as you have control over the heat and air conditioning in your house or apartment. Network administrators set the rules and parameters for network conditions on an *intranet*, which is a private network inside an organization. This is especially true for single buildings or corporate campuses.

Operating Systems and the Media Player
Consumers and corporations have only two choices for desktop/laptop *operating system* environments: Microsoft Windows and Apple Computer's operating systems. (Some say desktops and laptops running on the Linux operating system may gain traction in the next few years. But it's too soon to tell.) And Microsoft overwhelms Apple in terms of deployment in the marketplace.

Microsoft likes to tout this dominance as "creating a standard platform for personal computing." It ain't that simple. There have been six major versions of Windows: Windows 3.1, Windows 95, Windows 98, Windows ME, Windows 2000, and Windows XP. All are still in use somewhere, though newer versions tend to replace older versions over time. And Microsoft engineers are coding more versions of Windows. Apple also has several versions of its operating system still in use. And its latest product, OS X, is a radical departure from previous Apple operating systems.

These changes over the past ten years or so create enormous headaches for the streaming media producers, especially those who want to reach a large external audience. You don't have to worry so much about the operating system itself. But you do have to worry about the media players that work on that system.

Here's an example. Windows Media Player 6.4 was included with Windows 98. But streaming video quality in those days was poor compared to today's video quality. However, if you think you need to create video for those players, you may have to settle for inferior video quality, potentially alienating users with later versions of Windows and Windows Media Player. If you decide to cater to later versions of Windows/Windows Media Player, you may alienate users of Windows Media Player 6.4 by forcing them to upgrade, raising the hassle factor (see following section).

The problem is worse with RealPlayer, QuickTime Player and Flash. RealPlayer is bundled with Microsoft Windows by some computer manufacturers, and not others. RealNetworks has developed at least seven versions of its player since 1995. QuickTime Players are on virtually every recent Apple machine, but comparatively few Windows machines. Almost every Web browser has the Flash plug-in, but it has gone through at least eight versions since 1.0 in 1996.

Before you down another dose of your ulcer medication, consider your audience. Let's say you want to reach a niche audience of graphic artists and Web designers. Most of these professionals prefer the Apple platform. Perhaps you can safely choose QuickTime streams, because it's almost certain your audience has the QuickTime Player on its computers. Here's the lesson: Carefully analyze your audience for clues that can help you reduce the chance that your streams are incompatible with an individual audience member's operating system and media player.

The Hassle Factor

This chapter has mentioned the frustrating lack of knowledge and control you have about the operating systems and accompanying media players on the computers of an external audience. A related problem is lack of knowledge or control over specific pieces of software that may not have been shipped with a media player you're targeting. That can lead to player behavior that can confuse and alienate a user.

Say you've decided your audience has a certain version of a media player. You've encoded your file to match your knowledge of that player, based on your own testing. However, for one reason or another, a number of players out in the world don't have a key component installed by default. When the user tries to play your stream, he or she gets a message that suggests they download a component or upgrade the player completely. The message may intimidate the user, and he or she may stop the playback attempt. Or the user may be sophisticated enough to brush off the message, take the time to download and install the component or upgrade, and continue the session. Your analysis of your audience should give you some idea of how well an individual is likely to tolerate this hassle.

Again, producers targeting an internal audience have it easier. It's very likely your information technology department limits the time and method of component upgrades or new software installations. This means you don't have to worry as much about confusing messages related to media player capabilities.

Early Adopters vs. Late Adopters

Various technology observers divide people who adopt new technologies into four groups: Innovators, Early Adopters, the Early Majority, and Laggards. The rate of adoption rises with time, then falls as the population likely to risk the technology falls. Innovators try everything new just because it's new. Early Adopters see the competitive advantage of a new technology and try it out, even if it's not mature. The Early Majority follows the crowd. Laggards, whom you might call "Kickers & Screamers," would rather swallow molten lead than try any new technology. These categories can help you choose streaming formats that cater to your audience's attitude toward the online experience.

For example, you may determine that your audience is made up of gaming-crazy, extreme-sporting uber-geeks who think last week's product is so last week. Chances are they have the latest streaming media player running on the newest version of Windows or OS X. They probably have high-speed connectivity at home. You could take the risk of using the latest streaming codecs and high-bandwidth delivery. Using *codecs* from 1996 would definitely turn off this audience.

ALERT   Codecs are described and dealt with in more detail later in this chapter.

!

High Bandwidth vs. Low Bandwidth

The amount of bandwidth available to you and your audience may be the single most important factor determining your decision about platform and content. The more bandwidth on your side and the end user's side, the more likely you can satisfy your audience's expectation for a radio or television-like streaming experience. This is especially important if you want to reach an external Internet audience.

The trends are in your favor. Two-thirds of U.S. households are expected to have broadband connections by 2010, double the portion in 2005, according to Forrester Research. Streaming media usage and adoption tend to follow the broadband deployment trends.

Of course, the flip side is that about half of external users still access the Internet via a dial-up connection, according to Arbitron/Edison Media, and most of those people connect at 56 kilobits per second (kbps). The audio experience for this audience is acceptable, but the video experience can be frustrating. If you decide your target audience is primarily on dial-up, your audio options are decent. But your video options are extremely limited.

If you're focused on an audience within the boundaries of a corporate network, you have more options, as shown in **Table 5-1**. When you encode audio or video, you encode at a bit rate slightly lower than the maximum bit rate available in a given connection (more on bit rates later in this chapter). That's because networked computers need some *headroom* for transmitting certain kinds of network control information. You should also note that the bit rate can vary from moment to moment, but over time the rate will be about the number you choose.

Many small organizations with 10- or 100-megabit (and lately gigabit) Ethernet networks have more bandwidth than they can use, and you could take advantage of that extra capacity with streaming. You may face a different limitation: the number of people you can serve at one time. For example, if you have a 10-megabit local area network (LAN), and your boss will only accept high-quality video streams taking up 250 kbps each, you're limited to 40 simultaneous users (40 × 250 kbps = 10 megabits). Actually, the top number is really closer to 20; 40 simultaneous 250k streams would essentially freeze the entire network.

Table 5-1
Audience bandwidth targets.

Target Bandwidth	Maximum Bit Rate
28.8 kbps dial-up	20 kbps
56 kbps dial-up	34 kbps
Corporate LAN (intranet)	150 kbps
256 kbps cable/DSL	225 kbps
384 kbps cable/DSL	350 kbps
512 kbps cable/DSL	450 kbps

Organizational Relationships

Each and every organization depends on relationships with other organizations to thrive. An educational institution may depend on a particular set of major enterprise-funded foundations for annual support. A single individual donor may be the lifeblood of a community not-for-profit. The lion's share of a small business's revenue may come from a single customer. If your target audience includes people who form a key business relationship, it makes sense to check that group's streaming capabilities. If you choose Microsoft technology, and you later find out your key customer or client prefers RealNetworks' technology, you could be in deep trouble.

Organizational Capabilities

Your organization may have capabilities you don't know about. For example, you may already have Windows Media Services set up on your network. Or your account with your Internet service provider includes RealNetworks' Helix server. Talk to your Web developer. He/she may be familiar with QuickTime, but not RealNetworks or Microsoft streaming media systems. These existing capabilities will have a major influence on your choice of streaming format, even if your audience analysis goes contrary to your analysis of internal resources.

Making a Decision

You've done a careful analysis of your audience and your resources. But you're still having trouble deciding which streaming platform and format works best for you. A decision matrix that might help is shown in **Figure 5-2**. A decision matrix lists all the important criteria and weighs them according to their importance. Then you give each platform a rating. Multiply the rating by the weight for a score. Add up the scores, and see which platform wins.

Author's Tip

Audience Evaluation Scenarios

External Audience

You volunteer for a youth sports association in a community with a high percentage of technology workers. The sports association has received a generous technology grant from a locally based Fortune 1000 company that competes with Microsoft. The association's board has accepted your proposal to record its annual awards ceremony for archiving on the Internet. About half the town's residents have broadband connections at home. You decide that the most likely viewers are parents and friends of team members, and your informal telephone survey of parents shows they prefer RealPlayer. How do you use this knowledge to design your streaming?

- *Platform* – RealNetworks RealPlayer/Helix.
- *Media player version* – RealPlayer 8. (This is about three years old. Newer versions will be able to play streams designed for RealPlayer 8.)
- *Streams* – One audio stream for dial-up users. One 225k video stream for broadband users.

Internal Audience

You work for a health care company that depends on video training. About 1,000 employees work in several small buildings connected with a high-speed LAN. Most of the employees are comfortable with computers, but they are not technology workers per se. A few workers sometimes have trouble understanding things beyond simple printing or e-mail. Your chief financial officer spent 10 years at Microsoft before starting at your company last year, and he's approved spending for a desktop/laptop operating system upgrade to Windows XP. The upgrade project manager and the human resources director like your idea of providing video training online. How do you use this knowledge to design your streaming project?

- *Platform* – Microsoft Windows Media Services.
- *Media player version* – Windows Media Player 9 (bundled with Windows XP).
- *Streams* – One 225k video stream, limited to ten simultaneous connections. This would only consume approximately 2.5 Mbps, with little impact on the LAN.

ALERT Don't let the decision matrix make your decision for you. It's just a way to quantify intangibles. Ultimately, you have to make the final judgment based on your knowledge and experience.

		Streaming Media Platforms and Formats							
		RealNetworks		Microsoft		Apple		Macromedia	
Audience Criteria	Weight	Rating	Score	Rating	Score	Rating	Score	Rating	Score
External									
Internal									
Internet									
Intranet									
Operating Sys.									
Media Player									
Low Bandwidth									
High Bandwidth									
Innovator									
Early Adopter									
Early Majority									
Laggard									
Hassle Factor									
Relationships									
Resources									
	Totals								

Figure 5-2
A streaming media platforms and formats decision matrix.

Author's Tip

Product Reviews: Useful or Not?

One way to evaluate a streaming media platform is product reviews. Many consumer and industry magazines review each new release of streaming media software using internally developed benchmarks. They develop their own hardware configurations and they hire independent consultants. For example, *Network Computing* gave Apple Computer and RealNetworks grades of "B+" in a 2002 comparison. Microsoft got a "C−" (Macromedia wasn't reviewed). On the other hand, an independent study by the University of Ferrara in Italy rated Real-Networks, Microsoft, and Apple Computer one, two and three, respectively, in a quality test of mobile streaming systems (again, Macromedia wasn't reviewed).

Product reviews are like movie reviews. When a vendor gets a good review, a hyperventilating press release follows within ten seconds on a slow day. About the only thing missing is the full-page newspaper ads that scream "Brilliant!" or "Ground breaking!" or "Cool!" If a vendor gets a bad review, it may cry "Foul!" and try to discredit the tester's criteria or methodology. So then, reviews may not help much after all.

Installing Other Media Encoders

Much of this chapter details the encoding process. Unless you have done so already, you need to install encoders from all the major streaming media vendors. The following procedures detail the steps for downloading and installing encoders from RealNetworks, Apple Computer, and Macromedia (remember, you installed Windows Media Encoder in Chapter 1).

RealNetworks RealProducer Basic

You'll find links to free versions of RealNetworks' encoder, along with free versions of other RealNetworks products, throughout the RealNetworks Web site.

1. Point your browser to:

    http://www.realnetworks.com/products/producer/basic.html.

2. Scroll down the page and look for the link to "RealProducer Basic," as shown in **Figure 5-3**. Note that the download is free. Click the link.

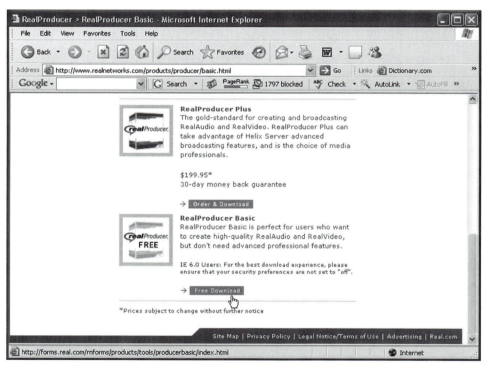

Figure 5-3
The link to RealProducer Basic on the RealNetworks Web site.

3. On the page that appears, read the licensing information and fill out the form. Click the "Download Now" button.

4. On the next page, click the appropriate download link. Don't be confused by messages suggesting the purchase of other products.

5. After you click the link, you'll likely see a security warning, as you did for player downloads in Chapter 2. Click Run to continue.

6. You may get another security warning. Click Run to continue.

7. As the installation starts, you'll be asked to accept the license agreement, as shown in **Figure 5-4**. Accept the agreement and click Next.

Author's Tip

Note the reference to "RealProducer Plus." This is the pay version of the RealNetworks' encoder, and it contains several features not available in the free encoder. If you prefer, you can purchase and download the Plus version, and the procedures for encoding in this chapter and later in the book will work fine.

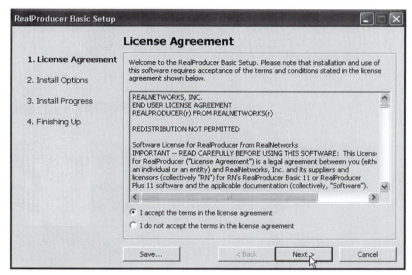

Figure 5-4
Read and accept the RealProducer Basic license agreement.

8. At the "Install Options" screen, review your options, and click Install, as shown in **Figure 5-5**.

9. At the "Finishing Up" screen, check your options, including whether you want to read the README file, and click Finish.

Author's Tip

Inexperienced computer users often ignore the README file. Don't make this mistake. README files can contain critical information about bugs, new features, and sometimes information about the people who made the software. Get into the habit of reading README files.

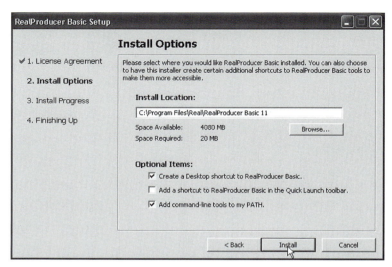

Figure 5-5
Review the installation options in the RealProducer.

RealProducer Basic is now installed, as shown in **Figure 5-6**.

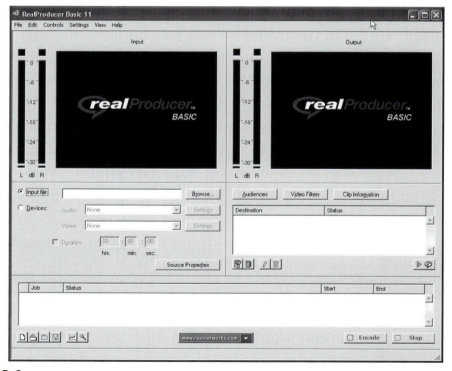

Figure 5-6
RealProducer Basic.

Apple Computer QuickTime Pro

Apple is the only company that has combined its encoder with its streaming media player. It's also the only company that requires you to purchase an encoder with no trial period. However, they make the process very simple:

1. Start QuickTime Player.

2. Click Edit → Preferences → Register.

3. Click "Buy QuickTime Pro," as shown in **Figure 5-7**.

Figure 5-7
QuickTime Player's Registration dialog under the Settings tab.

4. In the browser window that appears, follow the instructions to purchase Quick-Time Pro. This takes numerous steps, including a credit card purchase. via the Apple Computer Web site. Once the purchase is made, the key is e-mailed to you immediately.

5. Enter the registration key and the registered name into the boxes in the Register tab. Click OK.

6. To verify that you now own a working copy of QuickTime Pro, open the Edit menu. All commands, such as Copy and Paste, should now be available to you.

Macromedia Flash 8 Professional

Macromedia added streaming media capabilities to its Flash multimedia authoring system in 2002. Web designers immediately used it to embed streaming audio and video into Flash presentations. Originally called "Flash MX," it's now labeled "Flash 8." You'll need to download and install the Flash authoring system, which is rather expensive and complex if you're not a multimedia authoring specialist. However, you can test the waters with the trial version of Flash 8. You'll need the Professional version for the examples, because that includes the Flash 8 Video Encoder.

1. Point your browser to:

    http://www.macromedia.com/downloads/.

2. Find the Flash Professional 8 section, and click the "Try" link.

3. Fill in the form to get to the download page.

4. Once you reach the download page, select a language version, and click Download, as shown in **Figure 5-8**.

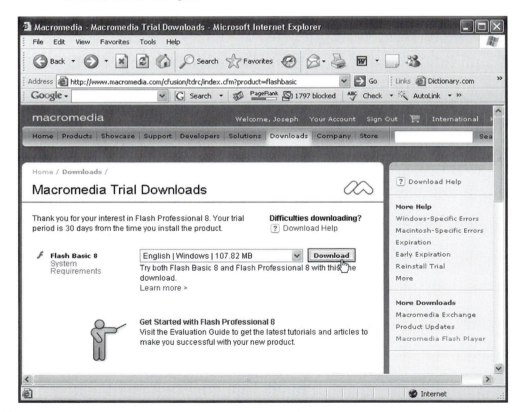

Figure 5-8
The download page for Macromedia Flash 8.

5. If you get a security warning, click Run to continue.

6. If you get a second security warning, click Run to continue.

ALERT Macromedia Flash 8 has fairly stiff system requirements, compared to the other streaming media encoding systems. No matter which system you use, however, it's a good idea to check system requirements for each before installing. Look for a link on the download page that displays these requirements.

7. At the installer welcome screen, click Next.

8. In the license agreement screen, accept the agreement and click Next, as shown in **Figure 5-9**.

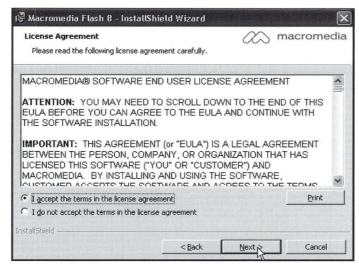

Figure 5-9
Accept the license agreement for Flash Professional 8.

9. In the "Destination Folder" screen, review the default installation folder and other options, as shown in **Figure 5-10**, and click Next.

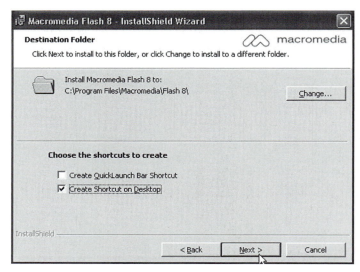

Figure 5-10
Review the folder where Flash Professional 8 will be installed.

10. In the next screen, check or uncheck the option to install the latest version of Flash Player. (You may have already done this via the procedure in the previous chapter in the subsection "Flash Player.") Click Next.

11. In the "Ready to Install" screen, click Next.

12. In the "Wizard Completed" screen, review the README file (optional), and click Finish.

13. To start Flash 8, click Start → Programs → Macromedia → Macromedia Flash 8 Video Encoder. A registration screen will appear, as shown in **Figure 5-11**.

14. Select the "I want to try Macromedia Flash" option, and click Continue.

15. In the "Select Flash 8 Trial Edition" screen, select Flash Professional 8 and click OK, as shown in **Figure 5-12**.

ALERT As long as you run the trial edition of Flash 8, a "nag" screen will display asking you to buy the program. You have to check the "try" option for every session. Or you could choose to buy the program, though it's the most expensive encoder by far, at several hundred dollars.

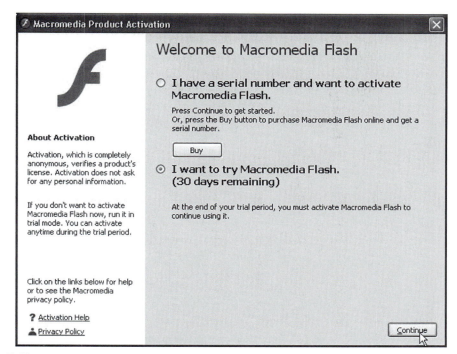

Figure 5-11
The activation screen for Macromedia Flash 8.

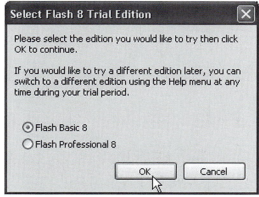

Figure 5-12
Select Flash Professional 8 in order to access the Flash 8 Video Encoder.

Choosing the Right Codec

One of the first questions asked by people who've learned a little bit about streaming media is "What codec should I use?" They often ask this question without thinking very much about the entire process, and not really understanding the place of codecs in the production stream. Codecs, which are complex mathematical formulae that remove unnecessary information, are also rather mysterious and slightly scary. Some people say it means enCOde/DECode. Others say it means COmpress/DECompress. Even the word "codec" has a certain Klingon-dialect feel to it.

These perceptions are probably the fault of the vendors, who compete strenuously on the quality of these critical components of their streaming systems. They spend large amounts of money researching or buying the rights to use these algorithms, which become massively hyped points of differentiation. In other words, the competition sometimes boils down to "Our codec is better than their codec." Codecs are also a way of tying a customer to a particular system. Once a producer settles on a vendor's proprietary codecs, it's hard to move to another vendor. The switching costs are just too big.

It's important to keep codecs in perspective. You're correct if you understand the central importance of codec choice. And you'll see how to make that choice in this section. But, hopefully, you've gathered from the rest of this book up to this point that codecs are only one piece of a bigger puzzle. Don't get hung up on them.

What Humans Perceive and What Codecs Do

Streaming media is just one of many ways producers can deliver sound and light to an audience. Professionals in every medium, from music to painting to filmmaking to codec engineering, start with research into the way humans perceive sound and light. Without this knowledge, codec design would be impossible.

Sound

Humans hear sound in the range of 20 Hz (low) to 20,000 Hz (high). Information on either side of this range is inaudible. Musical tones can take up a large portion of the audible spectrum. The range of a human voice tends to be narrower, with most of the information falling in the 500 Hz to 4,000 Hz range. Sound can be represented as a wave, as shown in **Figure 5-13**.

When audio is *digitized*, or captured to a hard drive, the sound card takes continuous measurements of the incoming electronic wave, and then stores these values sequentially. These values can then be played back to recreate the original waveform. The problem is, to represent the wave accurately requires a lot of data. A lot. Way too much to transmit across the Internet. That's where the codec comes in.

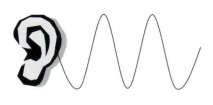

Figure 5-13
The human ear responds to pressure variations in the air, which can be captured electronically as a wave, and then digitized into a series of 1s and 0s.

Codecs work by removing information irrelevant to the perceptual experience of sound. These codecs are referred to as *lossy*, because information is "lost" in the encoding process. (Codecs that don't lose information are called *lossless*.) The codec's job is to try to maintain as much fidelity as possible, while reducing the file size as much as possible.

You'll see audio codecs roughly divided into music and voice, because of the different characteristics. Because of the narrow range of human speech, voice codecs can make certain assumptions about the audio and get good results at very low bit rates. Voice codecs were among the first truly successful codecs, because you could transmit very high-quality speech sounds over dial-up Internet connections. Music, however, is much more difficult to encode because of the wide frequency and dynamic range.

Light and Motion
Light and color are central to the human experience. And human eyes are especially tuned to motion, which is one reason why action movies can be so riveting. The amount of data the millions of rods and cones in retinas gather and send to the brain is almost beyond comprehension. In fact, the brain can't handle it all, and it has evolved internal filters to help decide which data to pay attention to and which to ignore.

Lossy video codecs attempt to do something similar. Because the Internet cannot handle the sheer number of bits in an uncompressed video file, codecs look for information that's redundant and gets rid of it. In conventional film or video, the information in each frame replaces the information in the previous frame. But much of this information is the same, frame to frame. Maybe it's the color of the sky or the lamp in the background. Instead of replacing all the information frame to frame, codecs replace only the parts that change. Every few seconds, a codec inserts a *key frame*, which becomes a reference point until another key frame appears. (The other frames are called *difference frames*, because they only contain information different from the previous frames.)

Video codecs can be tuned depending on the type of video content you're trying to encode, whether it is low action or high action. Key frames require a lot of bits to encode, whereas difference frames can be quite economical depending on how much motion there is in the frames. Therefore, the idea is to strike a balance between the number and the quality of the key frames.

Low action video, such as a speech or a "talking heads" program, has relatively small amounts of change. Therefore, the difference frames will be very small, so a codec can encode very high-quality key frames. Low action content can work well at dial-up speeds.

High action content, on the other hand, has less repeated information frame to frame. That means the difference frames will be fairly large, and therefore the quality of the key frames will have to be degraded a bit to keep the bit rate constant. High action content, such as music videos or movie trailers work best on high bit rate connections, at least cable/DSL.

Inside the Industry

Proprietary and "Standards-Based" Codecs

Codecs can also be divided into proprietary and *standards-based*. As discussed above, streaming media vendors compete to offer the best audio and video codecs. They guard the codec designs jealously, because these formulas are built as competitive advantages. They also tie ("ensnare" is perhaps a better word) a customer to the vendor's products.

Standards-based codecs, sometimes called *open codecs*, are based on publicly agreed on technical principles, which a company or individual may or may not own. Streams encoded with these codecs can play, theoretically, across multiple platforms. The best known of these standards in the context of streaming is MPEG-4. Of course, vendors have to decide to support open standards, which could mean loss of a competitive advantage. You'll hear more about MPEG-4 and open standards in Chapter 10, *Alternative Systems*.

Constant Bit Rate Encoding vs. Variable Bit Rate Encoding
In the language of encoding, the bit rate is the amount of data available to the media player for playback. Data can flow at a constant rate or a variable rate, depending on the scenario.

In streaming media, all audio and video files must be encoded at a *constant bit rate*, or *CBR*. This means that the data flows from the streaming server over the Internet to the player at a steady, predictable rate. CBR encoding provides a better experience over unreliable Internet connections. However, because CBR encoding demands that the data rate remain the same over time, a sudden change in the content may result in visual glitches. For example, if a boring news report suddenly switches to an exciting car commercial, the data rate may not be enough to encode the commercial (complex music, faster editing) as well as the low-action content, and the impact is diluted.

Variable bit rates actually reflect real life more closely. As suggested previously, a video image can instantly transform from slow and steady storytelling to quick and dynamic action. In *variable bit rate* encoding, or *VBR*, the codec can increase the data rate to account for these changes in speed and timing. However, because the Internet doesn't deal well with large bursts of data, it isn't really suitable for streaming media. VBR encoding is usually applied only to files that will be played back on devices, such as a compact disc player or a DVD player.

ALERT Variable bit rate encoding is getting used more and more often, especially for files that will be downloaded and placed on portable media devices, such as Apple Computer's iPod.

Making the Choice

Which codec should you use? You should first analyze your content. What types of information does it contain? Audio content is relatively easy to analyze. When you deconstruct video content, you'll analyze a video track and an audio track. And you'll apply the results of your audience analysis conducted in the previous section. The answers to the questions below should help you make a final choice.

- Is the audio primarily voice, music, or a mixture of voice and music? If it's a mixture, is the music just for variety or is it critical to the message?

- Is the video primarily one or two people speaking, such as a lecture or panel discussion, with only a few scene changes?

- Does the video contain numerous scene changes or lots of movement in the frame, such as music video or an action thriller movie?

- What streaming platform and Internet connection speed do you expect for your target audience?

Inside the Industry

 For a detailed discussion of audio and video codecs, read *A Practical Guide to Video and Audio Compression: From Sprockets and Rasters to Macro Blocks*, by Cliff Wootton, published by Focal Press.

Media Player Behavior and Multiple Bit Rate Encoding

There's one more set of principles to cover before you get to the actual encoding. Most media players behave in similar ways that every streaming media user experiences. Some of these behaviors can be very frustrating. Fortunately, you can mitigate some of the frustration with good encoding practices. This section explains some of the behaviors and a suggested solution.

When an end user at home or the next cubicle clicks a link to a streaming media file, the media player attempts to contact the streaming media server to get the stream. The player shows this by displaying a "Connecting..." or similar message. A logo may spin or flash as well. When the connection occurs, the player may then say "Buffering..." or "Loading..." This could go on for several seconds or longer, depending on the connection speed, the network conditions, and player settings.

Here's what's happening. The player is filling a reservoir of *random access memory* (*RAM*) with data from the stream. When the reservoir is filled, the audio or video starts to play. In the meantime, the player continues to receive data from the streaming server. It tries to keep the reservoir, also called the *buffer*, filled so that playback continues without interruption, creating a smooth user experience from the beginning of the clip to the end. All this is shown in **Figure 5-14**.

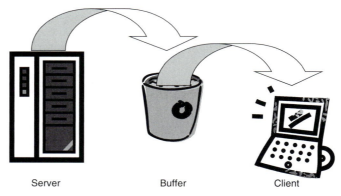

Server   Buffer   Client

Figure 5-14
A media player keeps a buffer of memory filled with streaming data to maintain a smooth user experience.

The unpredictability of the Internet can sabotage a player's valiant attempt at smooth playback. One minute, network conditions may be perfect. The next minute, something in the great cloud goes haywire and the media player stops receiving data from the streaming server. The media buffer empties, and playback stops while the player asks the server for more data to refill the buffer. The player tells the user what's going on by redisplaying a "Buffering..." or "Loading..." message. As with pre-roll, *rebuffering* can seem to take forever.

You can't control net weather, at least for users outside your own network. However, you can mitigate the problem with *multiple bit rate* encoding. This means combining several bit rates into a single encoded file. For example, if you combine encoding settings for a 56-kbps dial-up connection with settings for a 256-kbps cable/DSL connection, the server can send the appropriate stream to different audience members. What's more, if the Internet connection should suddenly constrict, the server can "shift down" to a lower bit rate stream (if it is available).Of course, a downshift could cause a loss in quality because 56-kbps streams carry much less data than a higher bit rate stream.

ALERT

For multiple bit rate encoding to work, the player's connection speed must be set correctly. For example, if it's set to receive streams for a dial-up connection only, it will never ask for the 256-kbps stream.

Encoding

Here's the part you've been waiting for: *encoding*. All your preparation of the audio or video file will now pay off with a high-quality encoded file that will reflect the high quality of your original work. And in some ways, the encoder is the simplest tool in the streaming media system. At bottom, it's just a front end for the codec, which does the work of taking large amounts of data and compacting it into a more manageable size, as shown in **Figure 5-15**.

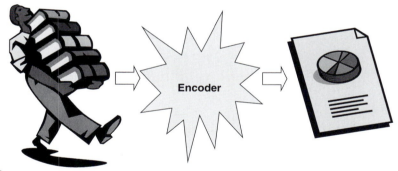

Figure 5-15
A streaming media encoder removes unneeded or repetitive data to make audio and video files smaller and more suited to streaming over the Internet.

The next sections take you step by step through the encoding process for each of the four major vendors: RealNetworks, Microsoft, Apple and Macromedia. If you lose track of your encoded files, you can recognize the format by its extension, as shown in **Table 5-2**.

Table 5-2
Common file extensions for streaming media files.

Vendor	File Extension
RealNetworks	.ra, .rm, .rv
Microsoft	.asf, .wma, .wmv
Apple Computer	.mov
Macromedia	.swf

If you haven't done so already, download and install the free RealNetworks RealProducer Basic and the Microsoft Windows Media Encoder. You will need to purchase an Apple Quick-Time Pro license to encode with the QuickTime Player. You can encode for Macromedia Flash 8 with the evaluation version of Flash 8 Professional.

The following sections assume you have a **.wav** file and/or an **.avi** file as your source file. If you don't, review Chapter 1 for instructions on finding a file to practice on.

ALERT **Tell the User About Title, Author and Copyright**

All of the major encoders let you add title, author, copyright and description information to the encoded file. This is an obvious feature but is often overlooked or ignored. The title, author and copyright information usually appears in the media player as it's playing, giving users crucial information. Keyword and description data may also help you identify and index files later, especially if you encode large amounts of material.

Encode Your Audio

Each encoder treats the audio encoding process slightly differently, often with wildly different interfaces. This section takes you through the basic steps.

RealNetworks RealProducer Basic Step-by-Step

1. Open RealProducer Basic.

    Make sure the "Input file" radio button is selected. (Review **Figure 5-6** for a screenshot of RealProducer.)

2. Click the Browse... button.

3. Find and highlight the file you wish to encode and click Open.

4. Click the Audience button.

5. In the Encoding Settings area, select the Audio Mode appropriate for your content from the drop-down menu, as shown in **Figure 5-16**.

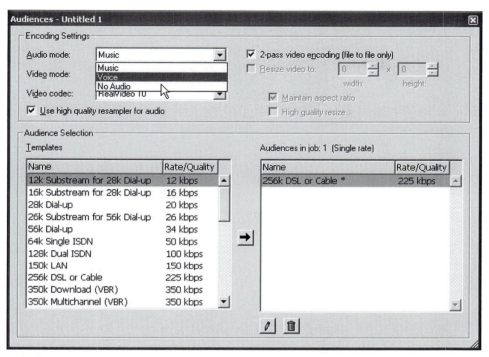

Figure 5-16
Select the Audio Mode.

6.   In the Video Mode drop-down menu, select No Video. This grays out the Video Codec drop-down menu.

7.   In the Audiences in Job box, note the audiences already listed. These are the different bit rates the stream will be encoded into.

8.   If you want to remove any audiences from the list, highlight the item with your mouse, and click the Trash icon below the box.

9.   If you want to add any audiences, highlight one of the items in the Templates box and click the arrow. This will add the audience to the audiences list.

Figure 5-17 shows a typical configuration for an audio stream targeted to dial-up and cable/DSL users.

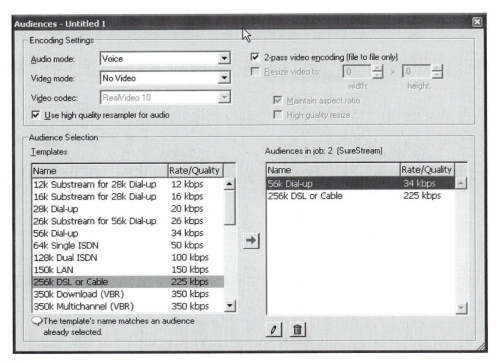

Figure 5-17
A typical audience configuration for audio streaming to dial-up and cable/DSL.

10.   Close the Audiences dialog box by clicking the "X" in the upper right corner.

11.   Click the Clip Information button and fill in Title, Author, Copyright, Keyword, and Description information. Also, choose a rating for your encoded file from the drop-down menu.

Inside the Industry

 The *Platform for Internet Content Selection* (*PICS*) specification enables labels (metadata) to be associated with Internet content. Originally designed to help parents control content accessed by their children, PICS also facilitates other code signing, privacy, and other types of content labeling.

12.   Close the Clip Information dialog box by click the "X" in the upper right corner.

13.   Note the file name in the Destinations box. This will be the name of your file once it's encoded. It will be placed in the same directory as your source file.

To change the name of the encoded file and its destination, click the Pencil icon or right-click the default file name and select Edit Destination.

If you are satisfied with your settings, click the Encode button. The file begins to encode, as shown in **Figure 5-18**.

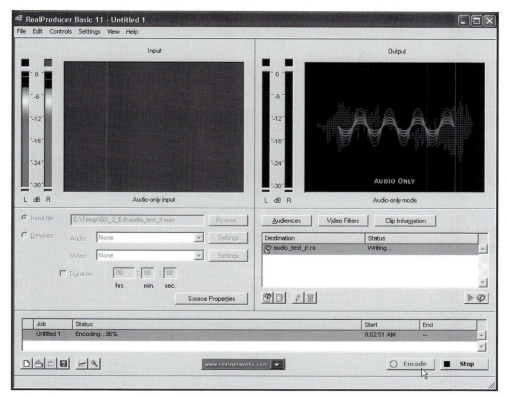

Figure 5-18
RealProducer Basic encoding a **.wav** file.

When encoding is complete, click the RealPlayer logo under the Destination box to play the file. Or open the file in your RealPlayer. It will have the **.ra** extension.

Author's Tip

To see further options for each audience in RealProducer, highlight one of your audience selections, and click the Pencil icon next to the Trash icon. The paid version of Real-Producer allows you to modify audio and video codecs and other parameters for these audience settings. You can also create custom templates. These features and others are not available in the free RealProducer.

Windows Media Encoder Step-by-Step

This section repeats some information from Chapter 1, while adding more detail. It also uses Custom Session features to give you a better idea of Windows Media Encoder's capabilities.

1. Start the Windows Media Encoder by clicking Start → Programs → Windows Media → Windows Media Encoder.

2. In the new session wizard, select "Custom Session," as shown in **Figure 5-19**. Click OK.

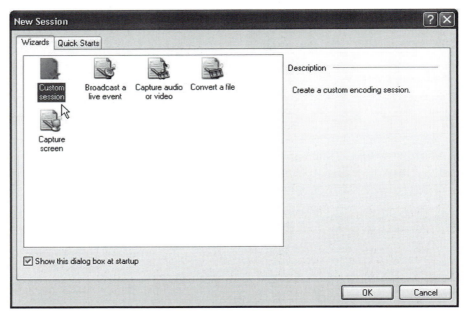

Figure 5-19
Select "Custom Session."

3. In the Sources tab, click the File radio button, and then click the Browse... button and locate the file you wish to encode, as shown in **Figure 5-20**.

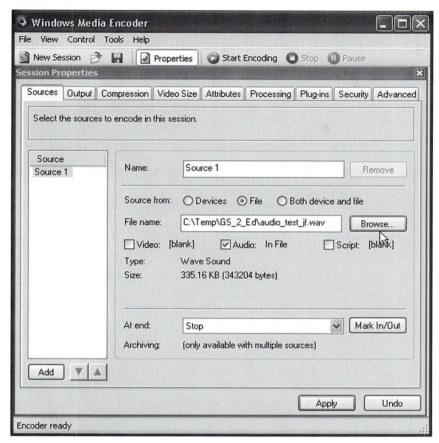

Figure 5-20
Click the File radio button and locate the file you wish to encode via the Browse... button.

4. In the Output tab, check the Archive to file check box. The text label changes to Encode to file, as shown in **Figure 5-21**.

5. Uncheck all other options, as shown in **Figure 5-21**.

6. In the Output tab, click Browse... to name the output file and place it in a directory where you will find it, as shown in **Figure 5-21**.

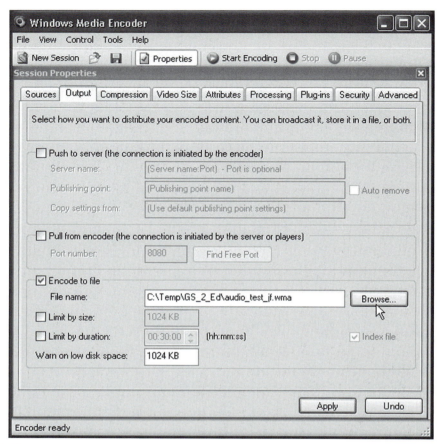

Figure 5-21
Check the Archive to file check box and locate a place for the output while giving it a name.

7.   In the Compression tab, select "Windows Media Server (streaming)" from the Destinations drop-down menu, as shown in **Figure 5-22**.

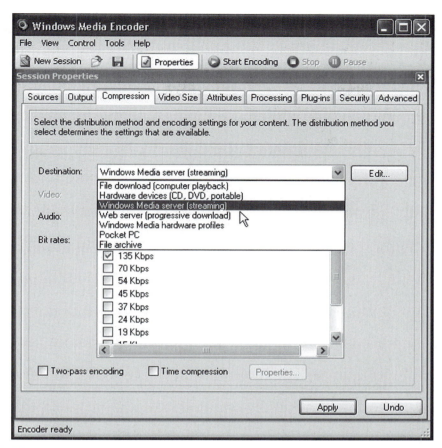

Figure 5-22
Select "Windows Media Server (streaming)" from the Destinations drop-down menu under the Compression tab.

8.   In the Compression tab, select "Multiple bit rates (CBR)" from the Audio drop-down menu, as shown in **Figure 5-23**.

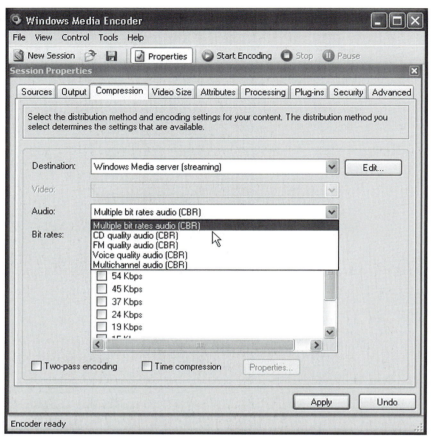

Figure 5-23
Select "Multiple bit rates (CBR)" from the Audio drop-down menu.

9. Select two audio bit rates in the Bit rates area, as shown in **Figure 5-24**. (135 kbps and 45 kbps are shown selected.)

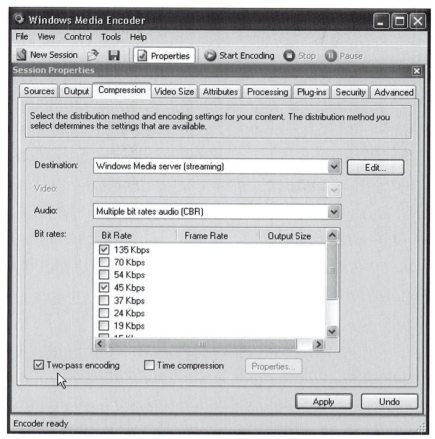

Figure 5-24
Select two audio bit rates and check the "Two-pass encoding" check box.

10. Check the "Two-pass encoding" check box, as shown in **Figure 5-24**.

11. In the Attributes tab, add Title, Author, Copyright, Rating and Description information.

12. Click the Apply button to apply all your settings.

13. Click Encode and the encoder will begin encoding your audio file, as shown in **Figure 5-25**. (You may need to select View → Audio Panel to monitor the encoding.)

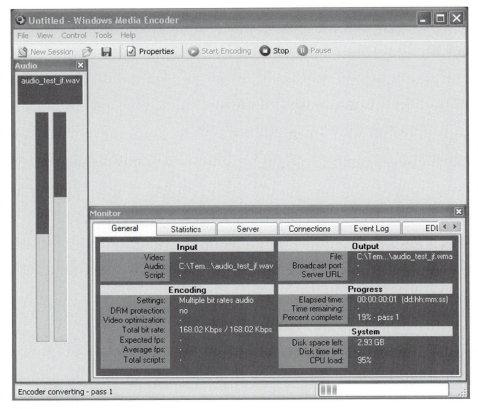

Figure 5-25
Windows Media Encoder encoding an audio file.

Author's Tip

Windows Media Encoder allows you to create custom audio compression profiles for later re-use. To create a profile, click the Edit button next to the Destination drop-down menu under the Compression tab in the Session window. Change the parameters as needed, and give the profile a descriptive name to help you identify it later. Click Export and give the new profile a file name.

Windows Media Encoder also has a number of ready-to-go profiles. To use one of these, click Import and select one of the profiles. You'll also use the Import function to retrieve your own custom profiles.

At the end of the encoding process, a file with the extension **.wma** will be saved in your working directory. Click Play Output File in the Encoding Results box to hear your work.

Apple Computer QuickTime Pro Step-by-Step

Apple Computer does not offer a free encoder. You will need to purchase a QuickTime Pro license from Apple to use the QuickTime encoding features.

1. Open QuickTime Player Pro.

2. Select File → Open File...

3. Locate the folder containing your **.wav** file.

In the "Files of type" drop-down, select Audio Files, as shown in **Figure 5-26**.

Figure 5-26
Select Audio Files from the "Files of type" drop-down.

4. Select the file you want to encode, and click Open. A new QuickTime Player Window appears with the file loaded. If you like, you can close the first window.

5. In the new player window, select File → Export As...

6. From the Export drop-down, select Movie to QuickTime Movie, as shown in **Figure 5-27**. (Even though your file is audio only, it is referred to as a "movie" by QuickTime.)

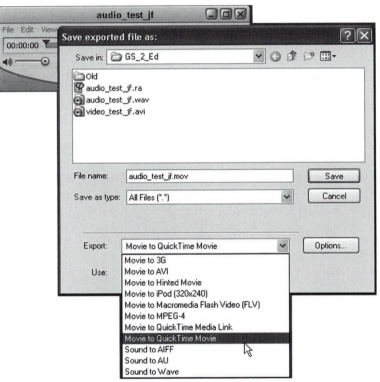

Figure 5-27
Select "Movie to QuickTime Movie" as your Export option.

7. In the Use drop-down menu, select your target audience, as shown in **Figure 5-28**. In this case, "Streaming - Medium" is selected.

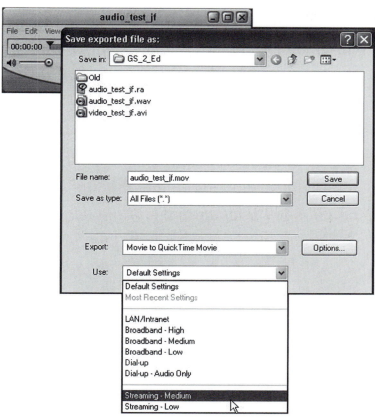

Figure 5-28
Select your target audience.

8. Click the Options button, which opens the Movie Settings dialog, as shown in **Figure 5-29**.

9. In the Movie Settings dialog, click the Settings button under the Sound check box.

10. Click the Advanced Settings check box. This opens all the options in the Settings dialog, as shown in **Figure 5-30**.

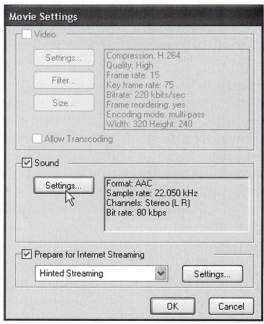

Figure 5-29
The Movie Settings dialog.

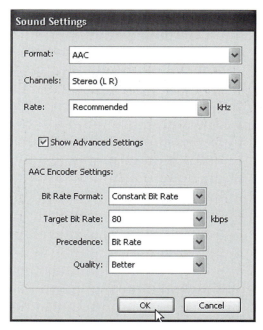

Figure 5-30
The Sound Settings dialog under the Movie Settings dialog. Note that the Show Advanced Settings check box is checked.

5. Encoding Audio and Video

11.   Open the format drop-down, and select a codec, as shown in **Figure 5-31**.

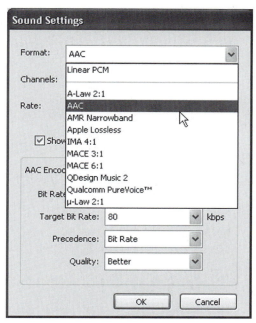

Figure 5-31
Select a codec from the Format drop-down.

ALERT The default audio codec in QuickTime Pro 7 is AAC, or *Advanced Audio*
Coding. The codec is automatically selected, probably because Apple
is pushing it as the best option for its iPod device. The company believes this codec should replace the highly popular MP3 codec, though
there's no sign MP3 is fading away.

12.   Click OK on the Sound Settings dialog.

13.   Check the Prepare for Internet Streaming
check box.

14.   Select "Hinted Streaming" from the drop-
down menu.

Author's Tip

Note that the Advanced settings
area changes as you modify the
codec. Each codec has its own
special features. Review the Quick-
Time Pro help file for details on
each codec.

QuickTime files encoded for streaming using the QuickTime Streaming Server (see Chapter 7, *Streaming Media Distribution*) need a special track called a *hint track* that tells the server how to package the streaming data for delivery.

15.   Click Settings.

16.   Check the Make Movie Self-Contained check box as shown in **Figure 5-32** and click OK.

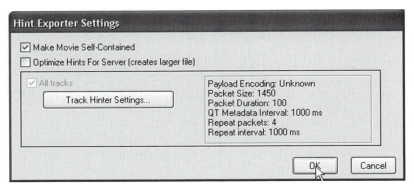

Figure 5-32
Hint Exporter settings.

17.   Check Optimize Hints for Server.

18.   Click OK in the Movie Settings dialog box.

19.   Click Save in the Save exported file as dialog box and encoding will begin.

To play the file in the QuickTime Player, select File → Open File... and look for the new file with the **.mov** extension.

Macromedia Flash 8 Audio Encoding Step-by-Step

This book assumes that you'll deliver your Flash via a dedicated streaming server. Many Flash presentations are delivered via HTTP, but that is not true streaming and is only suitable for certain restricted applications. For more on streaming via HTTP, please refer to Chapter 10, *Alternative Systems and Methods*.

1. Start Macromedia Flash 8 Video Encoder by clicking Start → Programs → Macromedia → Macromedia Flash 8 Video Encoder.

2. Select the "try" option in the nag screen and click Continue.

3. Add your source files to the encoder by dragging them into the application, or by clicking the "Add..." button (see **Figure 5-33**).

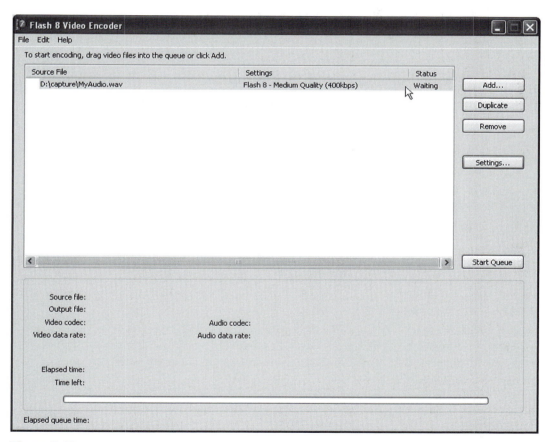

Figure 5-33
Drag files from any window into the Flash 8 Video Encoder.

4. Click the Settings... Button.

5. In the Flash Video Encoding Settings Window, click the Show Advanced Settings button. This reveals the advanced settings options (see **Figure 5-34**).

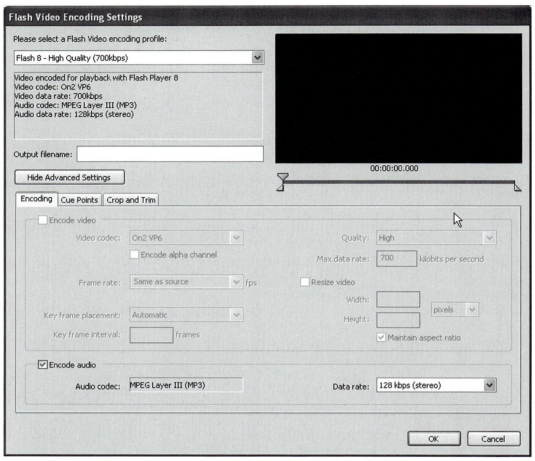

Figure 5-34
The Advanced Video Settings options.

6. You'll see that the video encoding options are grayed out. Select a bit rate from the Data rate drop-down menu, bearing your audience in mind.

7. Click the OK button to return to the main encoder interface.

8. Click the Start Queue button to encode your audio file.

9. You'll see a green progress bar along the bottom of the encoder window, along with elapsed-time and time-left readouts. When your file is done, it will be placed in the same directory as your original file, with a **.flv** file extension.

Unfortunately, you can't simply play back a **.flv** file, because there is no standalone Flash player. To test your file, you'll have to create an embedded Flash player. This is covered in Chapter 9, *Embedding Streams in Your Web Pages*.

Encode Your Video

Most of the steps for video encoding are the same as audio encoding above, except for the addition of video settings. Remember, streaming video is actually two streams, audio and video, that run synchronously. In video encoding you make choices for your video stream as well as your audio stream.

RealNetworks RealProducer Basic

1. Open RealProducer Basic.

2. Make sure the Input File radio button is selected.

3. Click the Browse... button.

4. Highlight the file you wish to encode and click Open.

5. Click the Audiences button.

6. In the dialog box, select the Audio Mode appropriate for your content from the drop-down menu.

7. Select the Video Mode appropriate for your content from the drop-down menu, as shown in **Figure 5-35**.

Author's Tip

RealProducer's Video Mode Choices
The RealNetworks RealProducer Basic offers the streaming media producer five Video Mode choices: Normal Motion Video, Sharpest Image, Smoothest Motion, Slide Show, and No Video. These affect the quality of the image, no matter the video codec.

- *Normal Motion Video* – For clips with the widest range of motion.

- *Sharpest Image* – Keeps the image sharper, but at a lower frame rate.

- *Smoothest Motion* – Keeps the motion smoother, but at the cost of image clarity.

- *Slide Show* – Creates the illusion of numerous still photos.

- *No Video* – Strips the audio track off a video file.

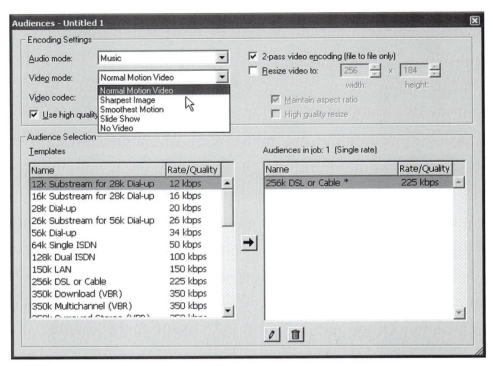

Figure 5-35
Select the Video Mode.

ALERT

Note that the Video Codec drop-down menu is defaulted to RealVideo 10. If you want more choices, you will need to buy the full version of RealProducer. *Warning*: Using RealVideo 10 means RealPlayer users with older RealPlayers may not be able to play your video. If they try to play video encoded with RealVideo 10 codecs, the media player may ask them to upgrade. Consult your audience analysis for guidance on whether your audience is tolerant of the hassle factor.

Author's Tip

2-pass encoding ("Two-pass" in Windows Media Encoder) means the encoder will analyze the file once for the optimal application of the codec. Then the encoder applies the codec on the second pass.

8. Check the 2-Pass Video Encoding check box.

9. In the Audiences in Job box, select the audience bandwidths you want to target. To remove audiences, highlight the item with your mouse, and click the Trash icon below the box. If you want to add any audiences, highlight one of the items in the Templates box and click the arrow.

10. Close the Audiences dialog box by clicking the "X" in the upper right corner.

11. Click the Clip Information button and fill in Title, Author, Copyright, Keyword, and Description information. Also, choose a rating for your encoded file from the drop-down menu.

12. Close the Clip Information dialog box by clicking the "X" in the upper right corner.

13. Note the file name in the Destinations box. This will be the name of your file once it's encoded. And it will be placed in the same directory as your source file.

14. To change the name of the encoded file and its destination, click the Pencil icon or right-click the default file name and select Edit Destination.

15. If you are satisfied with your settings, click the Encode button. The file will begin encoding, as shown in **Figure 5-36**.

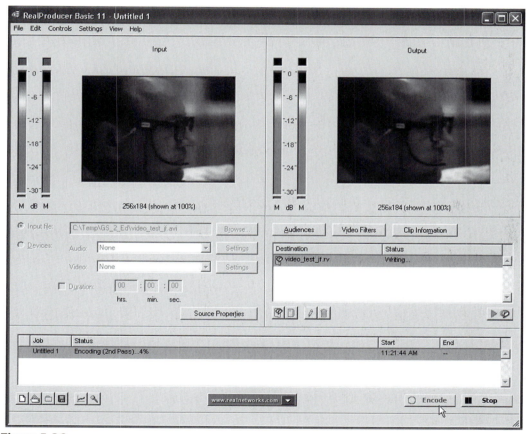

Figure 5-36
RealProducer Basic encoding an **.avi** file.

When encoding is complete, click the RealPlayer logo under the Destination box to play the file, which will have the **.rv** extension. Or open the file in your RealPlayer. The file will begin playing.

Using Image Manipulation Features in Encoders

Encoders offer options such as image resizing, cropping, de-interlacing and inverse telecine. For example, in Windows Media Encoder, under the Video Size tab in Session Properties, you can modify the image size, as shown in **Figure 5-37**.

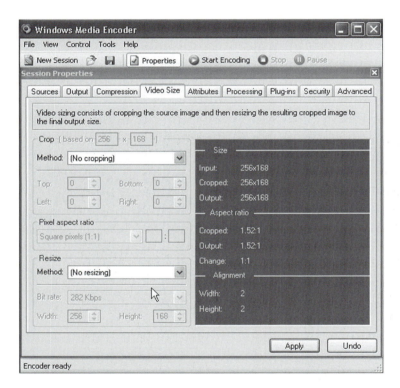

Figure 5-37
Cropping the video in Windows Media Encoder.

Windows Media Encoder Step-by-Step

1. Open Windows Media Encoder by clicking Start → Programs → Windows Media → Windows Media Encoder.

2. In the wizards dialog box, select Custom Session. Click OK.

3. In the Session Properties window, click the File radio button.

4. Click the Browse button and select the video file you wish to encode.

5. Click the Output tab. Check the Archive to file check box. The text label changes to "Encode to file." Uncheck all other options, and enter a file name for your encoded file.

6. Click the Compression tab.

7. Select "Windows Media Server (streaming)" from the Destination drop-down menu.

8. Select "Multiple bit rates (video)" from the Video drop-down menu, as shown in **Figure 5-38**.

9. Select "Multiple bit rates audio (CBR)" from the Audio drop-down menu. Choose the bit rates of your target audience from the "Bit rates" box.

10. Check the "Two-Pass encoding" check box.

11. Click the Attributes tab.

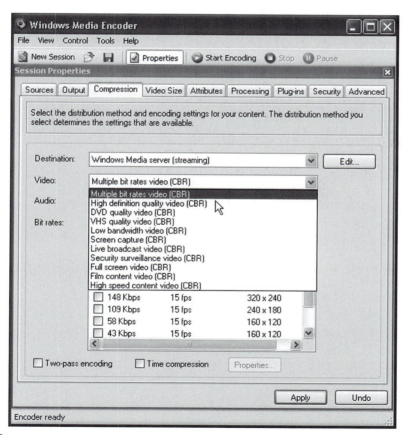

Figure 5-38
Select "Multiple bit rates video (CBR)" from the Video drop-down menu.

12. Select the Title, Author, Copyright, Rating and Description fields and click Edit to add the appropriate information.

13. If you are satisfied with your settings, click the Apply button.

14. Click the Start Encoding button to start the encoding.

When the Encoding Results dialog box appears, click the Play Output File button to review the encoded file. Click the Close button to end the encoding session. You'll find a file with the extension **.wmv** in your working directory.

Author's Tip

Advanced Windows Media Encoder Session Customization

Windows Media Encoder allows you to customize numerous encoding settings. Here's how to do this:

1. In the Compression tab, check the bit rate selections appropriate to your target audience.
2. Click the Edit button next to the Destination drop-down menu.
3. In the Custom Encoding Settings window, you'll see a General tab and at least one other tab corresponding to your bit rate selection(s).
4. Click a bit rate selection tab.

In the tab, you'll find a number of options, as shown in **Figure 5-39**. The most important ones are:

- *Audio Format* – You can adjust the amount of bandwidth used by the audio track in your video. If you select a lower audio bit rate, you can assign more bits to the video track.
- *Frame Rate* – You'll sometimes see "29.97" as the frame rate. This is commonly referred to as "30 frames per second." ("29.97" is the rate specified by a television engineering group for analog video transmission.) You can often change this to 15 frames per second without losing too much quality.
- *Video Bit Rate* – You can adjust the number of bits used to transmit video data up or down, depending on your target. Make only small adjustments here. If large adjustments are called for, Cancel the dialog. Then go back to the Compression tab and select another bit rate.
- *Video Smoothness* – Adjust this number up or down to regulate the sharpness of the image. However, sharper images may mean jerky motion.

(continued on following page)

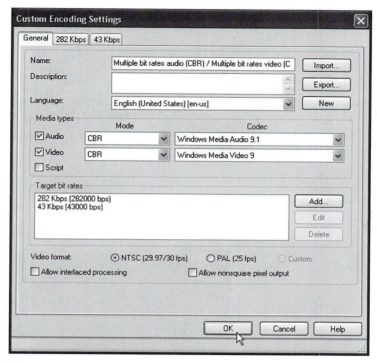

Figure 5-39
Windows Media Encoder Custom Encoding Settings window.

- *Key Frame Interval* – Modifying this number changes the number of seconds between each key frame. If you have a lot of motion, a lower number may be called for. However, don't wander too much from the defaults. Streaming media must be encoded at a constant bit rate. So if you lower the key frame interval, the encoder will be forced to encode them at a lower quality to keep the bit rate constant. In other words, you could cause more problems than you solve.

- *Total Bit Rate* – As you adjust the bit rate allocations, pay attention to the totals in the lower part of the window. This will help you track whether your final file will match the bandwidths of your target audience. Note also the Overhead total. This tells you that a portion of bandwidth is allocated to special kinds of data needed by the streaming server and media player to communicate efficiently and deliver the content reliably.

(continued on following page)

Ideally, you should take care of all these items in the source file before you encode. That gives you maximum control over the final output. And it limits the encoder to its true job: encoding files for streaming. But you may find these options useful if you have no time to fix the issues in the source file. You can also experiment and see if you get better results by resizing, for example, in your encoder rather than your video editing application.

Apple Computer QuickTime Pro Step-by-Step

1. Open QuickTime Player Pro.

2. Select → File → Open File…

3. Find the directory where your file is located.

4. Select your video file and click Open. A new QuickTime Player window opens, as shown in **Figure 5-40**.

Figure 5-40
An **.avi** file loaded into QuickTime Player Pro.

If you have more than one Quick-Time Player window open, you may want to close other QuickTime windows to avoid confusion.

5. Select File → Export. (If you do not see the Export menu item, you will need to purchase a Quick-Time Pro license and install it to encode with QuickTime Player.)

6. Choose "Movie to QuickTime Movie" from the Export drop-down menu.

7. In the Use drop-down menu, select your target audience.

8. Click the Options button to open the Movie Settings dialog box.

9. Check the "Video" check box, if it is not already checked, as shown in **Figure 5-41**.

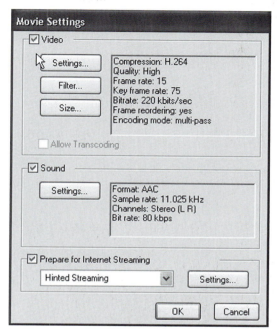

Figure 5-41
The Movie Settings dialog with the "Video" check box checked.

10. Click the Settings button under the Video check box.

In the Standard Video Compression Settings window, select a codec from the drop-down menu, as shown in **Figure 5-42**. Your other options in this window may change depending on the selected codec.

11. Alter your compression settings as needed and click OK.

12. In the Movie Settings window, click the Filter button under the Video check box.

13. In the Choose Video Filter window, you'll note several options. Depending on the codec, you may be able to modify various attributes of the video image. (For more information, see the Author's Tip, "Using Image Manipulation Features in the Encoders.") Click OK.

14. In the Movie Settings window, click the Settings button under the Sound check box.

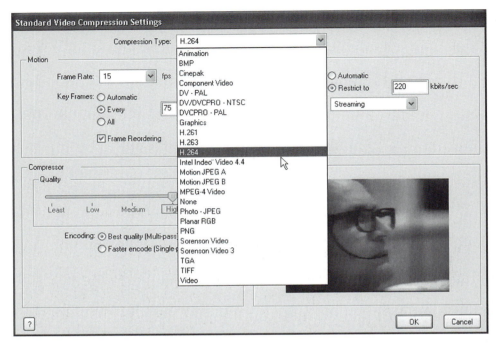

Figure 5-42
Select your video compression settings.

In the Sound Settings window, select a codec in the Compressor drop-down menu. Your options may change depending on the codec you choose. Click OK.

15. Check the Prepare for Internet Streaming check box.

16. Select "Hinted Streaming" from the drop-down menu.

17. Click Settings.

18. Check the Make Movie Self-Contained check box and click OK.

19. Check Optimize Hints for Server.

20. Click OK in the Movie Settings dialog box.

21. Click Save in the Save exported file as dialog box and encoding will begin.

To play the file in the QuickTime Player, select File → Open File... and look for the new file with the .mov extension.

Macromedia Flash 8 Professional Video Encoding Step-by-Step

1. Start Macromedia Flash 8 Video Encoder by clicking Start → Programs → Macromedia → Macromedia Flash 8 Video Encoder.

2. Select the "try" option in the nag screen and click Continue.

3. Add your source files to the encoder by dragging them into the application, or by clicking the "Add..." button (see **Figure 5-33**).

4. Click the Settings... Button.

5. In the Flash Video Encoding Settings Window, click the Show Advanced Settings button. This reveals the advanced settings options (see **Figure 5-43**).

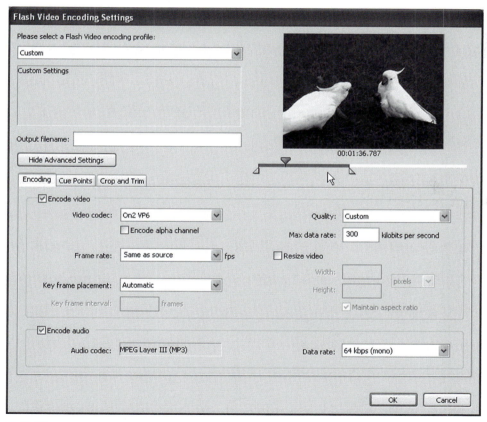

Figure 5-43
The Advanced Video Settings options.

6. You now have a number of options to set for your video quality. Use the upside down triangle below your video to *scrub* through your video. You can use the small triangles under the time line to set the beginning and end of your video clip.

7. The default settings for Flash 8 are for the On2 VP6 video coded. This provides the highest quality Flash video, but requires Flash player 8 for playback.

Inside the Industry

Macromedia uses two codecs in Flash 8 Professional: Sorensen Spark and On2 VP6. Sorensen Spark is a proprietary video codec licensed from Sorensen Media, and requires Flash Player 7. On2 Technologies' VP6 codec is a higher quality codec, but requires Flash Player 8.

As of March 2006, Macromedia claims the Flash 8 player is on over 50% of all desktops. They also claim they will be over 80% penetration by June 2006. (Source: NPD Online study, 12/2005.)

8. To create a video file for broadband streaming, choose the Flash 8 – Medium Quality (400 kbps) from the encoding profile drop-down at the top of the interface.

9. 400 kbps is a little aggressive for the total bit rate. To reduce this, choose Custom from the Quality drop-down menu, and then change the Max. data rate to 300.

10. The default audio data rate of 96 kbps is also a bit much for a 300-kbps file. Change this to 64 kbps (mono).

11. Click the OK button to return to the main encoder interface.

12. Click the Start Queue button to encode your video file.

13. You'll see a green progress bar along the bottom of the encoder window, along with elapsed-time and time-left readouts. When your file is done, it will be placed in the same directory as your original file, with a **.flv** file extension.

As mentioned in the preceding audio encoding section, you can't simply play back a **.flv** file, because there is no standalone Flash player. To test your file, you'll have to create an embedded Flash player. This is covered in Chapter 9, *Embedding Streams in Your Web Pages*.

Conclusion

Choosing the right streaming media format takes careful consideration of your audience, including the streaming media players they prefer, their likely bandwidth, and their expectations about quality. Once you understand your audience, you can encode in any format and deploy your streams with a better chance of success. In the next chapter, you'll learn some techniques for working directly with streaming media files.

Author's Tip

Flash 8's "Cue Points" and "Crop and Trim" Features

Flash 8 features two other encoding options at this point, "Cue Points" and "Crop and Trim." Cue Points allow Flash designers to embed triggers to other actions in the presentation. For example, when the video reaches a certain point, the background color of the presentation could change.

Crop and Trim allows developers to change the size and shape of the video image in the encoder. However, most streaming professionals crop their video image to the correct size before encoding.

CHAPTER 6

Working with Streaming Media Files

Streaming media encoders are highly versatile tools. You may find as time passes that you need to modify your streaming media files, especially information such as title, author or copyright. And you may also need to embed certain actions in a file, such as a command to open a Web address in a browser window. To do this, expert producers manipulate encoded files with *utilities* included with the encoder packages, or take advantage of several command line options available with encoding software. Large encoding tasks can also be automated via these options. In this chapter, you will:

- Edit encoded streaming media files
- Embed events into the files
- Learn how to encode several source files at one time

A caveat: Once your source audio and video files are encoded into streaming media files, they are ready to be placed on a streaming media server and published. In general, you shouldn't try to modify the files at this point, since this can often introduce more problems than you solve, as explained in the next section. If you do so, proceed with caution.

Editing Streaming Media Files

Encoded streaming media files are highly specialized files designed for a single purpose: transmission and playback over the Internet in real time. As such, you shouldn't fiddle with them. If you notice a major error in the file, such as a poor edit in a video shot or poor audio, it's best to fix the source file and re-encode. If you used the wrong codec, you have no choice but to re-encode. However, some errors, such as misspellings in the title data embedded in the file, can be fixed without re-encoding. The following sections introduce you to the simple tools that modify encoded streaming files.

RealAudio and RealVideo

RealNetworks' RealProducer comes with a tool called "RealMedia Editor," which allows you to modify encoded RealAudio or RealVideo files. The following procedures demonstrate some simple editing tasks.

Change the Beginning and Ending of a File

1. Start RealProducer.

2. Select File → Edit RealMedia File.

3. In the RealMedia Editor (see **Figure 6-1**), locate and open the encoded audio or video file you wish to edit.

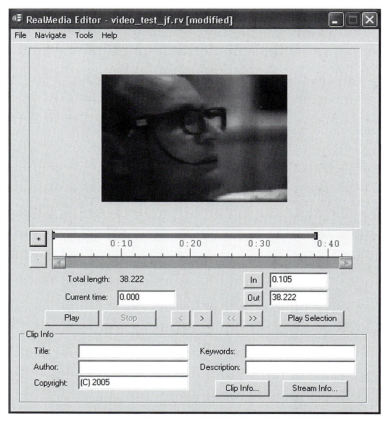

Figure 6-1
RealMedia editor with an encoded video file loaded into the program.

4. Locate the new beginning of the file by clicking the red vertical line with your mouse and dragging it to the new beginning time, as shown in **Figure 6-2**.

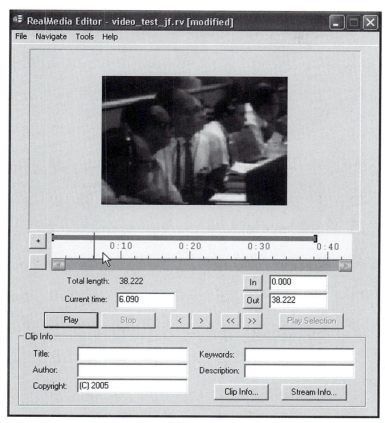

Figure 6-2
Drag the red line with your mouse to the new beginning of the file.

5. Mark the new beginning by clicking and dragging the left bracket ("[") on the timeline to the new begin point, as shown in **Figure 6-3**.

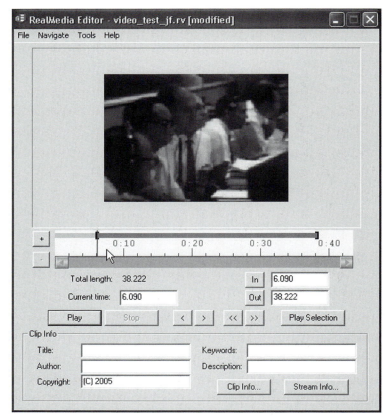

Figure 6-3
Mark the new beginning of the file with the left bracket.

Find the new end of the file by moving the red vertical line to the new end point.

Mark the new end of the file by clicking and dragging the left bracket ("]") on the timeline to the new end point, as shown in **Figure 6-4**.

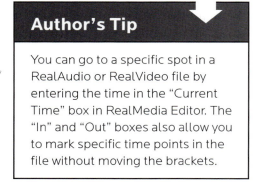

Author's Tip

You can go to a specific spot in a RealAudio or RealVideo file by entering the time in the "Current Time" box in RealMedia Editor. The "In" and "Out" boxes also allow you to mark specific time points in the file without moving the brackets.

6. Save your changes by selecting File → Save Real-Media File As... and give the modified file a new name.

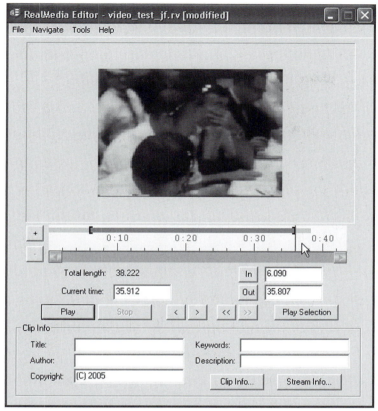

Figure 6-4
Mark the new end of the file with the right bracket.

Modify Title, Author and Copyright

1. Open RealMedia Editor and the file you wish to modify.

2. Enter new title, author, copyright, keyword and description data, as shown in **Figure 6-5**.

Author's Tip

RealMedia Editor lets you append one or more audio or video clips to each other, creating a longer file. However, all the encoded clips must have the same settings; you can't append a clip encoded for a dial-up audience to a clip meant for a high-speed LAN. See the RealProducer Help documentation for more details.

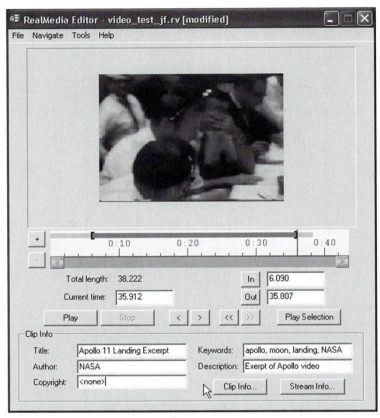

Figure 6-5
Modify title, author, and copyright information.

3. Save your changes by selecting File → Save RealMedia File As... and give the modified file a new name.

Windows Media

Microsoft's Windows Media Encoder includes a utility called "Windows Media File Editor," which functions much like RealMedia Editor, which is discussed in the previous section. The following section demonstrates simple editing tasks with the Microsoft product.

Modify the Beginning and Ending of a File

1. Open Windows Media File Editor by selecting Start → Programs → Windows Media → Utilities → Windows Media File Editor.

2. Locate and open the encoded file you wish to modify.

3. With your mouse, drag the progress indicator of the Seek bar to the new begin point.

4. Click Mark In, as shown in **Figure 6-6**.

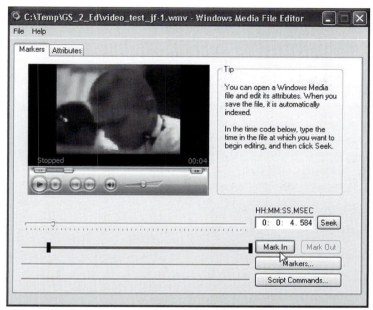

Figure 6-6
Click Mark In to mark the new begin point in the Windows Media file.

5. With your mouse, drag the progress indicator to the new end point.

6. Click Mark Out, as shown in **Figure 6-7**.

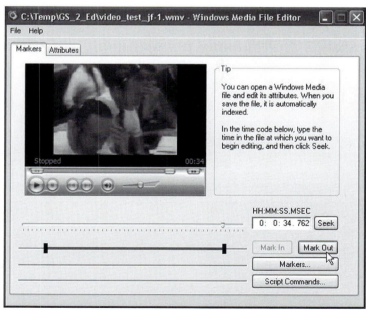

Figure 6-7
Mark the new end point of the file.

7. To save your changes, select File → Save As and Index... and give the file a new name.

ALERT Even though you may pick a precise moment to trim your Windows Media File, the actual trim may start at a different point. The new begin point starts at the key frame that is closest to the mark-in point.

Change Title, Author and Copyright

1. Open Windows Media File Editor.

2. Locate and open the encoded file you wish to modify.

3. Click the Attributes tab.

4. Modify the title, author, copyright, and description, as shown in **Figure 6-8**.

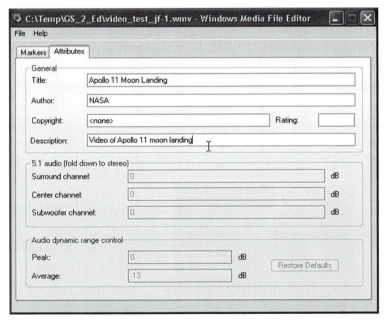

Figure 6-8
Modify the title, author, and copyright information via Windows Media File Editor.

5. To save your changes, select File → Save As and Index... and give the file a new name.

QuickTime

Editing QuickTime files is similar to editing RealAudio, RealVideo, or Windows Media files, except that you use the QuickTime Pro player, instead of a separate application. The next section shows how to perform simple edits with QuickTime Pro.

Choosing New Ending and Beginning Points

1. Open QuickTime Pro.

2. Locate and open the QuickTime file you wish to modify by selecting File → Open File... A new player will appear.

3. With your mouse, move the "out" timeline indicator to the new end point, as shown in **Figure 6-9**.

Figure 6-9
Move the "out" timeline indicator to the new end point.

4.   Move the "in" indicator to the new begin point, as shown in **Figure 6-10**.

Figure 6-10
Move the "in" indicators to the new begin point.

5.   To save your changes, select File → Save As... and give the file a new name.

Update Title, Author, and Copyright Information
1.   Open QuickTime Pro.
2.   Locate and open the file you wish to modify.
3.   Select Window → Show Movie Properties...
4.   In the Properties window, select the Annotations tab, and select the Annotation you wish to add, as shown in **Figure 6-11**.

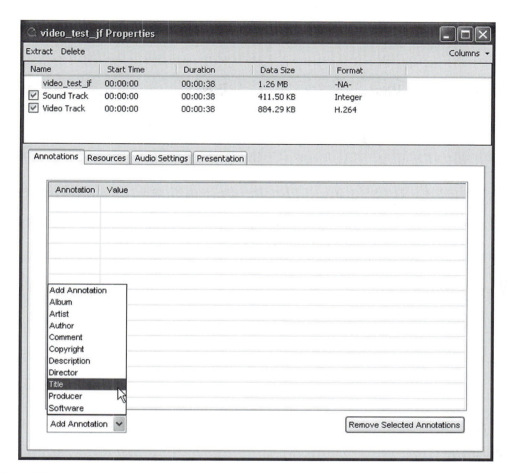

Figure 6-11
Select the annotations you wish to add to your QuickTime file.

5. Add annotation categories, such as title and author, and enter the data, as shown in **Figure 6-12**.

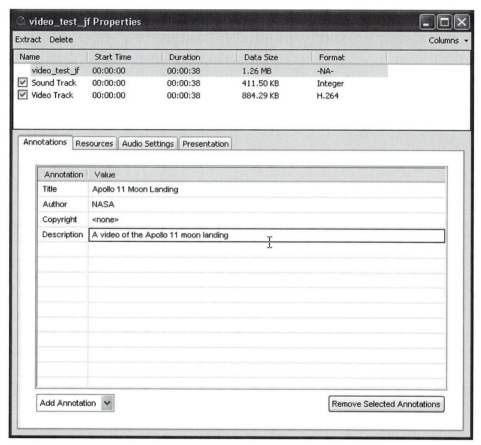

Figure 6-12
Add annotation categories and enter the data.

6. When done, close the Properties window.

7. To save your changes, select File → Save As... and give the file a new name.

Flash 8

Unfortunately, there's no easy way to edit Flash files (the ones with the **.swf** extension). Hopefully, you've saved your work as a Flash project and you have access to the **.fla** or **.flv** files. Make your modifications there, and recreate the **.swf** files.

There may be a workaround, depending on the problem you have to fix. For example, if your HTML file created via Flash 8 Pro contains title and author information, you can edit the HTML file with any text editor without using Flash 8 Pro.

Embedding Events in Your Encoded Files

Most people think of streaming media files as nothing more than computerized versions of tapes. You play back the tape, expecting to see and hear only audio and/or video. But you can tell your streaming files to do certain actions at specified points, such as open a browser window to display product information or change title information to reflect a change in the timeline. The following procedures show how to add these events to your streams.

RealAudio and RealVideo

To embed events in a RealAudio or RealVideo file, you create a text file containing the commands you need. You'll use RealMedia Editor to incorporate the file into your encoded file.

In the text file, you'll place one or more lines that direct the action, following this format:

```
flag start_time end_time data
```

Here's what each piece means.

- *Flag* – A letter value signaling the type of event
  - u – Open a Web page
  - t – Change the title
  - a – Change the author
  - c – Change the copyright information
- *Start_time* – The time the change should occur
- *End_time* – The time the change should stop
- *Data* – The required data, such as a Web address

Here's an example:

```
u 00:00:00.0 00:02:00 http://www.focalpress.com/
```

In this case, when the file starts playing, a browser window opens and sends the user to the Focal Press Web site.

To create a file with an event, use the following procedure:

1. Open a text editor, such as Notepad.
2. Write your text file with your commands, and save it with a .txt extension.
3. Open RealMedia Editor.
4. Locate and open your encoded RealAudio or RealVideo file.

5. Select Tools → Merge Events..., select your events file, and click Open.

The events file is merged with your media file. You should play the file to make sure the event occurs as you designed.

Windows Media

Adding events, or "scripts," as the Windows Media developers call them, to Windows Media files is much easier than for RealAudio and RealVideo files.

1. Open Windows Media File Editor.
2. Locate and open the **.wma** or **.wmv** file you wish to modify.
3. Click the "Script Commands" button.
4. In the new window, click the "Add..." button.
5. Enter a time for the event to occur.
6. Select "URL" or "TEXT" for the type of event. (URL refers to a Web address where you want to send your users. TEXT refers to information you want displayed in the player.)
7. Enter the appropriate data in the "Parameter" box, as shown in **Figure 6-13**. Click OK.

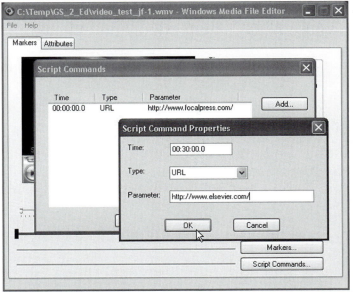

Figure 6-13
A script incorporated into a Windows Media file.

In **Figure 6-14**, you'll note three bars on the timeline to the left of the Script Commands button. These show the locations of each event. Use your mouse to modify the location of the event. You can also remove an event by double-clicking the timeline and removing the event from the list.

Figure 6-14
The embedded events are shown on the events timeline.

Be sure to save your work and play the file to check the file's new behavior.

QuickTime
Adding an event to a QuickTime file is similar to RealAudio or RealVideo: you build a text file with your commands. However, in the case of QuickTime, it's extremely elaborate and unreasonably confusing and difficult. And you can only specify Web addresses, not title, author or copyright information.

To create the text file, called an "HREF track," open Notepad and add information using this format:

```
time flag<URL> flag<option>
```

For example, the following automatically opens the Focal Press Web site at 1 minute, 30 seconds from the start of the movie file.

```
[00:01:30.0] A<http://www.focalpress.com>
```

If you leave out the letter "A" in the code above, the user must click the video image to go to the Web site.

You can also tell QuickTime to load a new movie into the same player by adding the "T<myself>" parameter. For example, the following code will automatically load the movie "new_movie.mov" into the player at one minute from the beginning of the original movie.

```
[00:01:00.0] A<http://www.my_video.com/new_movie.mov> T<myself>
```

Once you create and save the text file with a **.txt** extension, use the following procedure to load the file into your QuickTime file.

1. Open QuickTime Pro.
2. Click File → Open File..., locate and open the HREF Track file. (You may have to list all files in the folder.) A new window appears, as shown in **Figure 6-15**.

Figure 6-15
An HREF Track file opened in QuickTime Player.

3. In the new window, select File → Export...
4. In the dialog box, select "Text to Text" from the Export drop-down menu.
5. In the dialog box, select "Text with Descriptors" from the Use drop-down menu.
6. Click the Options... button.
7. In the Text Export Settings dialog, choose the Show Text, Descriptors, and Time options. Also, choose Show Time Relative to Start of Movie, and set fractions of seconds via the down arrow.
8. Click Save to create a new file with **.txt** extension.
9. Open the new file in Notepad.
10. Open the movie you want to contain embedded events in QuickTime Pro.

11. Move the timeline indicator to the point where you want the event to occur. Note that time value.

12. In the HREF Track file, change the time stamp just before your URL to the time value for your event, as shown in **Figure 6-16**.

Figure 6-16
Modifying the HREF Track file.

13. Modify the last timestamp to match the length of the movie.

14. Save the text file.

15. In QuickTime Pro, open the text file via File → Open File...

16. In the new player, click Edit → Select All...

17. Click Edit → Copy.

18. Close the new window.

19. Click the window containing your video.

20. Click Edit → Select All... and Paste the event file.

21. Select Window → Movie Properties.

22. Rename the Text Track to "HREFTrack".

23. Uncheck the check box next to the name.

24. Close the Properties window.

25. Save as a self-contained movie.

Flash

Events are a strong component of Flash design. But you will need to option your original Flash project to add or modify the events in your **.swf** file.

Batch Encoding

If you start to do a lot of encoding, you may waste a lot of time encoding files one at a time. To solve this problem, use *batch encoding*, wherein you can encode several audio and/or video files at one time, automating the process. In batch encoding, you pass a list of file names and parameters to the encoding application (or a script), and the encoder steps through each file until all are encoded.

The downside to batch encoding, at least for RealProducer and Windows Media Encoder, is that you have to get your hands dirty on the command line, which can be frustrating and confusing if you're used to graphical interfaces. However, once you get started, you'll find the tools very powerful. And if you get into industrial-strength encoding, scripting the encoders for different situations can be a challenging and satisfying experience.

As for Flash, Macromedia again demonstrates its user-friendly savvy: its Flash 8 Video Encoder utility, included with Flash 8 Pro, is GUI-based and very easy to use.

Author's Tip

To use the command line, click Start → Programs → Accessories → Command Prompt. Then navigate to a working directory or the encoder's home directory.

RealAudio and RealVideo

To batch encode WAV and AVI files into RealAudio and RealVideo files, you pass one or more file names and accompanying parameters to the main executable file, **producer.exe**.

Here's the basic syntax:

```
producer.exe -i path/file -o path/file options
```

For example, you may need to encode a multiple bit rate video file for a dial-up and a cable/DSL audience. Here's one way to do it.

```
producer.exe -i c:\videos\myfile.avi -o c:\encoded\
-ad "56k,150k"
```

In this example, producer.exe takes the following arguments:

Author's Tip

The commands in this section assume you are in the home directory of RealProducer, which is usually C:\Program Files\Real\ RealProducer Basic\. If you are in a working directory, you'll need to add the full path to the producer executable.

- *"–i"* (*input*) – tells the encoder the file to be encoded

- *"–o"* (*output*) – tells the encoder where to put the encoded file

- *"ad"* (*audience*) – tells the encoder to create the file for the two audiences, dial-up and cable/dsl

In this scenario, the output file in the "c:\encoded\" directory will have the same name as the input file, but with the .rm file extension—i.e., "myfile.rm,"—though you can give it another name if you like.

To take this one step further, batch encode a set of files in a directory.

```
producer.exe -i c:\videos\*.avi -o c:\encoded\ -ad "56k,150k"
```

In this case, the "*" character, used as a wildcard, signals the encoder to encode all the **.avi** files in the "c:\videos\" for a dial-up and cable/DSL audience and store them in the "c:\encoded\" directory.

To see all the audience command line options, type "producer.exe –pa" on the command line and producer will spit them out. You may want to print this to a file to make it easier to view. Check your Windows documentation and RealProducer documentation for more information. You can also view the options online at:

http://service.real.com/help/library/guides/uproducerplus/htmfiles/command.htm

ALERT RealProducer Basic contains only elemental command-line functionality for batch encoding. RealProducer Plus features a utility called "rmbatch," which is much more flexible.

Windows Media

The Windows Media Series 9 Encoder includes a utility that allows you to encode source files into Windows Media files on the command line. The "cscript.exe" executable takes a Visual Basic Script file and a number of command line options as arguments, similar to RealProducer. You can encode all files in a directory by typing all the commands during a single session or, if you run the same commands frequently, write a batch (**.bat**) file containing the commands to save typing.

To run the command line encoder, you need to be in the encoder directory, typically "c:\Program Files\Windows Media Components\Encoder\".

Here's a simple command line example:

```
cscript.exe wmcmd.vbs -input c:\source\video.avi -output c:\encoded\video.wmv
```

The file cscript.exe takes these arguments:

- *wmcmd.vbs* – the encoder command line utility
- *–input* – the switch telling the utility the input file name
- *c:\source\video.avi* – the input file name and location
- *–output* – switch telling the utility the output file name and location
- *c:\encoded\video.wmv* – the output file name and location

Here's a more complex example:

```
cscript.exe wmcmd.vbs -input c:\source\*.avi -output c:\
encoded\ -profile av100 -v_codec WMV8
```

This script tells the encoder to encode all the **.avi** files in "c:\source\" directory into the "c:\encoded\" directory. The audience is a 100-kbps broadband audience, and the codec is Windows Media Video 8.

The Windows Media Help files contain detailed instructions for using the command line tools. To see all the options at once, run this on the command line:

```
cscript.exe wmcmd.vbs /?
```

Author's Tip

Microsoft offers to Windows developers a sample GUI batch encoder in the Windows Media Encoder Software Development Kit (SDK). You can download the kit from the Microsoft Web site.

If you do not specify audiences or codecs, the command line tools typically default to the newest audio and video codecs and a broadband audience. In Windows Media Series 9 Encoder, the defaults are Windows Media Audio 9 and Windows Media Video 9.

QuickTime

QuickTime Pro does not include any command line utilities for batch encoding. However, there are a number of third-party command line scripts available for Mac OS X, such as QTCoffee and QuickTime QuickBatch.

Flash 8

The installation of Flash Professional 8 includes a separate encoder utility, called "Flash 8 Video Encoder." Usage is extraordinarily simple. Just start the encoder, drag and drop as many files as you want into the main window, and click "Start Queue," as shown in **Figure 6-17**.

To modify settings for each source file, highlight the file, click the "Settings" button, and select the appropriate audience.

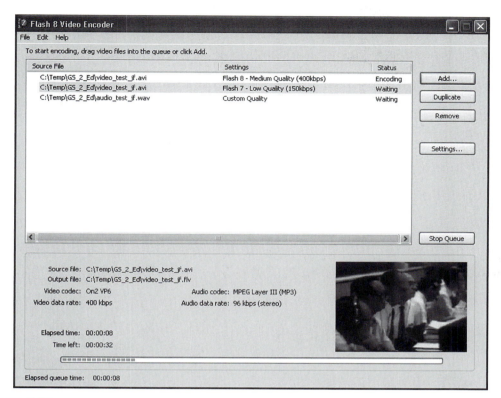

Figure 6-17
The Flash 8 Video Encoder utility batch encoding files. (The button will toggle to "Stop" once encoding begins.)

The result is a Flash Video (**.flv**) file, which can be imported into a Flash project.

Conclusion

The encoders of three of the four major streaming media vendors feature utilities or command line options that let you manipulate files in several ways. Although it's recommended that you use encoders solely as encoding tools, you can perform some editing functions and modify information such as title, author and copyright. The encoders also offer utilities or command-line options that let you script encoding, also called batch encoding, which automates large encoding jobs. In the next chapter, you'll learn the background needed to understand streaming media distribution.

CHAPTER 7

Streaming Media Distribution

Once you have encoded and edited your files, you're ready to distribute them to the world. In some ways, this is the biggest challenge facing a streaming producer. You will have to work closely with the people who manage your organization's streaming server and network resources. Frankly, these professionals aren't always the most easy-going colleagues. Streaming media is a demanding technology, especially on bandwidth, which is the amount of data that can be transmitted over a network per second. Network and system administrators have to balance all the demands made on a network, and streaming can throw their systems out of kilter. Hopefully, you've explained your plans to your IT high priests from the beginning, so they can prepare for today, when you deliver your content. It's important to have them on your side throughout the process.

To that end, this chapter is somewhat different from previous chapters. It won't show you how to install and configure a streaming server. Rather, it focuses on giving you enough information to help you have intelligent conversations with network/system administrators. You want to make good decisions about your infrastructure needs. Unless you're a server administrator/networking specialist, it's best for most streaming producers to leave the details of server and network configurations to the experts.

In this chapter, you will:

- Make preparations for serving, i.e., delivering your streams
- Learn about buying a streaming server

Streaming Server Overview

When you approach your IT department or a Web-hosting company about serving your streams, you should have a grasp of the technology fundamentals and the infrastructure needs that go into streaming delivery. You'll find it easier to trust networking professionals if you know something of what they talk about. The basics are relatively easy to grasp, even if you're not a techie. The next few sections will give you the background necessary for making good decisions in partnership with the pros. As the saying goes, forewarned is forearmed.

You may want to review *Evaluating Your Audience and Resources* in Chapter 5. Many of the issues, such as bandwidth, have counterparts on the delivery side of the equation.

Operating System and Streaming Server Considerations

Just as you evaluated the potential streaming media platforms of your audience (RealPlayer, Windows Media Player, QuickTime Player, Flash Player, or some combination thereof), you need to evaluate the platforms available to you on the server side. The server-side platform is usually thought of in terms of the operating system, followed by the streaming server supported by the operating system.

There are two basic server operating system choices: Microsoft products, such as Windows NT and Windows Server 2003, or the family of systems that trace their roots to the original Unix operating system developed by Bell Labs in the 1970s. Unix-like systems include:

- HP-UX (Hewlett Packard)
- Solaris (Sun Microsystems)
- AIX (IBM)
- BSD (open source)
- Linux (open source)
- Apple's OS X, which is based on BSD

Once you know the operating system your network servers use (as opposed to desktop computers, which run either Microsoft Windows or Apple Computer's operating system), you'll know more about your streaming server options. That's because some streaming servers run on some operating systems and not others. Here's a general rundown:

- RealNetworks Helix: Runs on Windows servers and major Unix OSs
- Microsoft Windows Media Services: Runs on Windows server only
- QuickTime Streaming Server: Runs on Macintosh server only
- Macromedia Flash 8: Streamed by Web servers, which run on virtually all operating systems

Furthermore, most streaming servers support more than one format. But format support is not equal among all streaming platforms. For example, RealNetworks Helix will stream almost any kind of audio or video file, including those of the company's archrival, Microsoft. However, Bill Gates won't allow Microsoft Media Services to stream files created with RealNetworks' tools. Moreover, because the streaming landscape is constantly shifting, there's a chance (however slight) that Bill might change his mind, muddying the waters.

Confused? No? You must be a genius, because this stuff confuses and frustrates the heck out of a lot of people. Your only solution is to carefully study the system requirements and capabilities of all the streaming servers on the market and compare your findings to the capabilities in your shop. Then you can work with your system administrator to make the wisest choice.

Here's an example. Assume your network has no streaming capability at all. You want to stream QuickTime files. You learn from your IT priestess that your network runs on Microsoft Windows 2003 Server. However, the QuickTime streaming server only runs on the Mac OS. That means she can install the RealNetworks Helix Server (which serves QuickTime files), or the *open source* version of the QuickTime streaming server, which is known as Darwin.

Inside the Industry

 Streaming Protocols

All data needs to be organized in a certain way to make sense. Books have chapters, sections, and paragraphs. The rules of grammar in a human language let two or more people communicate, because they agree on the rules. Computer data has a kind of "grammar" as well. When computers talk to each other across a network, they use a *communications protocol* or just *protocol*.

Computer programmers have come up with an alphabet soup of protocols. A few are directly related to streaming media. The protocols control the communications between the media player and the streaming server, and vice versa. Here's a list of the most important, plus a brief explanation. **Figure 7-1** shows how the protocols work together.

User Datagram Protocol – UDP is one of the most common Internet protocols used for sending data in a continuous stream. It uses less error correction than another common Internet protocol, Transmission Control Protocol (TCP), meaning fewer transmission delays.

Real-Time Streaming Protocol – The RTSP protocol is an open-standard application-level protocol endorsed by the Internet Engineering Task Force (IETF), a body of prominent Internet engineers. Internet clients—i.e., media players—use RTSP to talk to streaming servers, allowing features such as play/pause/stop. If you look inside a RealNetworks or Apple QuickTime metafile (see Chapter 8, *Linking to Your Streaming Files*, the first four letters are often "rtsp." That tells you the player will use RTSP to communicate with the streaming server. RTSP is supported by virtually all streaming media vendors.

Real-Time Transport Protocol – Streaming media servers build packets of data and send them off to the media player. RTP (it's unclear what happened to the other "T") governs how the server constructs these packets. For example, RTP

(continued on following page)

Inside the Industry (continued)

lays out rules for identifying the type of packet, how packets are numbered in sequence, and how they are stamped with the date and time. The architecture is similar to UDP and TCP, though RTP packets are meant to work specifically with the RTSP and RTCP protocols.

Real-Time Control Protocol – RTCP packets work with RTP packets to check the delivery of other packets. RTCP packets are often used to monitor quality of service.

Real-Time Messaging Protocol – RTMP was initially developed by Macromedia for remote programming calls, but is now also used to control their streaming media files.

Progressive Networks Audio – RealNetworks was dubbed "Progressive Networks" by its founders, and its early engineers developed a proprietary protocol called "PNA." It's rarely used these days.

Microsoft Media Services – Microsoft also developed a proprietary streaming protocol, MMS, which is widely used today on its Windows Media servers. Real-Networks supports MMS on later versions of its media player and server. If you open a Windows Media metafile, the first three letters of the streaming URL are usually "mms."

HyperText Transfer Protocol – Most kinds of data on the Internet, particularly Web pages, travel via HTTP. Every time you see an "http" in a Web address, you know it's using HTTP as the communications protocol. In streaming, HTTP is most often used for "progressive downloading," sometimes called "pseudo-streaming," because it doesn't have the control and data management features of "true" streaming protocols, such as RTSP. Flash 8 audio and video are usually placed on Web servers, and the files are streamed under HTTP.

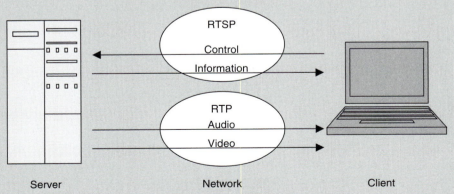

Figure 7-1
How streaming media protocols work together.

Security

Most of us have heard of computer viruses, malicious lines of code that invade desktop computers and erase files and even erase hard drives. Criminal coders also attack servers, and streaming servers are no exception. But security issues in the streaming world go far beyond self-protection. Some protection methods, such as *firewalls*, can even be a handicap to delivery of your streams to the end user.

Firewalls

A computer *firewall* takes its name from a barrier that protects something valuable from something dangerous on the other side. In an automobile, the firewall protects people from a catastrophic failure in the engine compartment. Computer firewalls typically limit the kinds of Internet data that can pass into and out of an internal network. Most network administrators think of the Internet as a dangerous wilderness full of virtual beasts that could attack at any time. For them, a firewall is like a castle wall with limited access points, allowing only certain kinds of information in or out.

Most firewalls are configured out of the box to reject streaming media. The nature of the back-and-forth communication between the media player and server and the types of proto-cols and packets exchanged are usually problematic to firewalls. People behind a firewall at government organizations and large corporations are the most frequent victims of firewall issues; System administrators are correctly trying to limit access in an effort to thwart invad-ers. However, with a little bit of persuasion and elbow grease, firewalls and sysadmins (a nickname for system administrators) can be trained to safely allow streaming media data.

Here are some methods of coping with firewalls:

- *HTTP cloaking* – Most firewalls allow data packets that use the HTTP protocol, the protocol for Web pages. If you are sending streams to others you think are behind a firewall, consider using "http cloaking," which wraps data packets in a kind of HTTP envelope. The packets may get past the firewall, though the user experience may not be as good as it would be without cloaking. But at least they're getting the audio or video.

- *Special server location* – It's just unnatural for streaming media servers to live behind firewalls. They crave the freedom of the Internet, because they need to communicate back and forth with media players. If you run a streaming server, ask your network administrator to put it in a *demilitarized zone*, or *DMZ*, as shown in **Figure 7-2**. The term comes from international politics. Two warring nations, when they get tired of shooting at each other, agree to a buffer zone a few miles wide. No soldiers or weapons are allowed in the DMZ, and people feel safer. In computer networking, the DMZ is just outside the firewall facing the stormy, unpredictable Internet "cloud." You have control of the streaming server, and it can talk freely to end users out in the wider world.

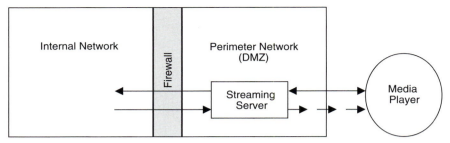

Figure 7-2
A typical network configuration with a "demilitarized zone," or DMZ.

- *Education* – You should prepare yourself to educate end users, as well as network and system administrators, about configuring media players to work behind a firewall. Some networks may dedicate *ports*, a kind of virtual window, through which streaming data travels. Or your network administrator may prefer to use a *proxy* server, which is a way to store Internet data for use by designated people. In each case, the media player's settings need to be modified, as shown in **Figure 7-3**.

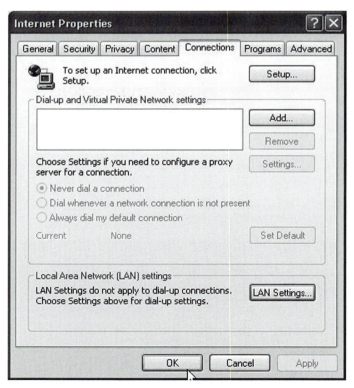

Figure 7-3
RealPlayer's proxy configuration window.

Proxy Servers and Streaming

A special server called a *proxy* is a security measure of choice for many network administrators. If you configure a media player to use a proxy server, you're asking it to ask the proxy server to get the information for you. It acts as a kind of go-between, so that you don't ever connect to the Internet directly. Governments and corporations use proxy servers to hide information about themselves from folks who aren't supposed to know, such as hackers. Proxies can also filter incoming information, hiding it from people behind the proxy.

Authentication and Authorization

The major streaming software manufacturers include "authentication" and "authorization" features in their streaming systems. *Authentication* is the process of verifying who you say you are, while *authorization* is the process of giving you the right to view content based on that identity. When implemented, the end user is asked for a username and password in order to access a stream. You usually see authentication and authorization systems when producers want to limit access to special groups of people, such as subscribers. However, most producers password-protect their content via the Web server, rather than the streaming server.

Author's Tip

Most software has imperfections. Malicious programmers know this, and they relish the challenge of finding the problems and exploiting them. Software vendors release code *patches* to plug holes hackers and others discover. Your server administrator is responsible for keeping your organization's systems up-to-date. As a streaming producer, it's wise for you to keep an eye on the streaming vendors' Web sites for news about their products. When you see security warnings or patch announcements, notify your IT department.

Digital Rights Management

Digital rights management or *DRM* was mentioned in Chapter 5 during the discussion about encoding. Streaming media server vendors also sell DRM tools for the server side. Music producers and retailers in particular want a way to ensure that their copyrights are protected. DRM is important to you if you want to prevent piracy of your media. You'll find more information on DRM in Chapter 11.

File Storage Requirements

Streaming media files take up a lot of room, even though they're highly compressed. If you plan to serve a large amount of video, you will need very large hard drives, perhaps even whole systems devoted to file *storage* and retrieval. How much do you need? That depends on several factors, such as your encoding practices. Files encoded for dial-up delivery need less space than files encoded for delivery over a corporate LAN. See **Table 7-1** for some guidance. Use the table's per-minute figures to estimate the final sizes of encoded audio and video files. Multiply the length of the file in minutes by the number of megabytes per minute. If you use multiple bit rate encoding, add the figures for each type (audio or video) and bandwidth together. The figures in the table come from RealNetworks. But they should be more or less applicable to other vendors' codecs. Be conservative in your estimates.

Table 7-1
Streaming media file sizes.

Target Bandwidth	Audio	Video
56 kbps modem	.24 MBs/minute	.25 MBs/minute
112 kbps dual-ISDN	.47 MBs/minute	.59 MBs/minute
225 kbps Corp. LAN	.70 MBs/minute	1.10 MBs/minute
256 kbps cable/DSL	.70 MBs/minute	1.65 MBs/minute
512 kbps cable/DSL	.70 MBs/minute	3.30 MBs/minute

Bandwidth

Bandwidth needs up to this point have been discussed in the context of the end user. (Are they connecting with dial-up, cable/DSL, or by a corporate LAN?) The end user needs only enough bandwidth to view one audio or video stream. When you serve streams to your internal audience or the outside world, you think about bandwidth in terms of the aggregate number of simultaneous connections to your streaming server. In other words, if ten dial-up users connect to your streaming server, you'll need at least 600 kilobits per second of out-going bandwidth (10 × 56 kbps = 560 kbps + 40 kbps [headroom] = 600 kbps). Realistically, however, you should probably have a lot more outgoing bandwidth to get the performance you want. You also have to take into account other activity on your network, such as e-mail and Web browsing.

Where's this leading? You may have to add extra bandwidth capacity to your network, which may mean increased costs. Bandwidth is the single largest ongoing technical infrastructure expense in the streaming-media delivery equation.

To understand this better, here's a quick review how the client and the server work together. You'll recall that the server sends continuous streams of data to the media player. Just like autos on an expressway need space to move smoothly and freely, data needs space in the form of bandwidth to travel. If too many autos try to reach the same destination, you get a traffic jam. If too much data tries to elbow its way through the network, data gets backed up, and you get a frustrating user experience.

 ALERT   It's worth remembering that video streams are actually *two* streams, one for the sound and one for the pictures. For example, a 56K stream may reserve eight kilobits per second for audio, 26 kbps for video, and 5 kbps for "overhead," which is data that controls the delivery of the entire stream.

How much bandwidth do you need? Go back to your audience analysis in Chapter 5. Two main questions apply:

- What's your best estimate of the peak number of connections you expect at a given moment? Ten? Hundreds? Thousands? This number is usually discussed using the term *simultaneous connections* or *simultaneous streams*.

- What streaming bit rates does your audience expect? Dial-up only? Cable/DSL? Higher?

Use these two variables to calculate a rough estimate of the amount of bandwidth you need. For example, if you expect a peak of 100 simultaneous connections at 225 kbps (a common bit rate for cable/DSL connections), you'll need at least 2.25 megabits of bandwidth.Double your estimate for safety. Let your network administrator know you need at least 4.5 megabits per second of outgoing bandwidth. Ask for as much bandwidth as you can get. You'll never have enough.

Unicasting and Multicasting

Most streaming media over the Internet follows a simple model: one stream for each client connection. This is called *unicasting*. It's the easiest model to grasp and implement, but it also uses the most bandwidth. What if you could get all your players to tap into a single stream? You'd need far less bandwidth. This is called *multicasting*, which requires a specially configured network, as shown in **Figure 7-4**.

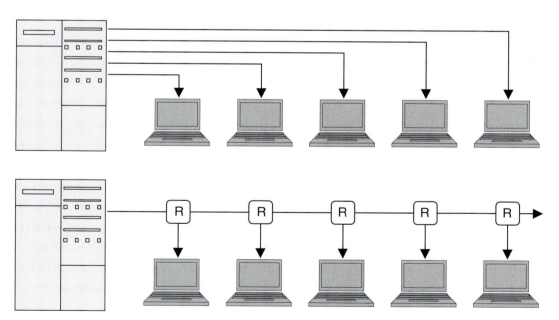

Figure 7-4
The unicasting and multicasting delivery models for streams.

In unicasting, the server delivers as many streams as requested by as many clients as it can handle. In multicasting, the server delivers a single stream to multicast-enabled routers ("R" in the diagram), which allow clients to tap into the single stream.

Ask your IT department if your network is multicast-enabled. If so, you may be able to add streaming capacity without drastically increasing your bandwidth consumption. It's unlikely, though, you'll be able to multicast to audiences outside your internal network. The public Internet isn't set up for it.

Edge-Cached Delivery

The typical piece of Internet data, whether from a Web page, an e-mail, or a video stream, gets bounced around from place to place before it reaches its destination. It's a little bit like an international letter going from your local post office to a first then a second distribution center before getting on a plane and ending up at the recipient's neighborhood post office before getting delivered to his door.

In the Internet world, the fewer "hops" in this trip, the higher the quality, because the data, like a letter, has less chance of getting directed to the wrong place. *Content delivery networks* (CDNs) mitigate this problem by placing storage servers with your on-demand streaming files closer to final recipients. This idea, called "edge-cached" delivery, can improve the experience of your users by reducing the number of data hops.

Buying a Streaming Server

You've analyzed your audience and reviewed your organization's streaming capabilities, and you've decided you should purchase a streaming server. Here are a few points to consider.

Licensing

The main drawback of specialized streaming servers is cost. You have to buy the server, or more accurately, the privilege of using the server. Remember when you installed your media players and encoders? Part of the installation process included a screen which asked you to accept or reject a bunch of legalese. If you rejected it, the software wouldn't install. When you accepted it, you in effect said that you agree to abide by the conditions of a *license* offered by the manufacturer. Even though the software is installed on your hard drive, you don't really own the software, just the right to use it in a way defined by the manufacturer.

The same goes for streaming servers. However, different manufacturers license their servers in different ways. Here's a breakdown of the different licensing approaches.

- *RealNetworks* – RealNetworks licenses its streaming server by the number of simultaneous streams you can deliver. Their free version is limited to five simultaneous streams. From there, you can upgrade to a 25-stream, 100-stream, or unlimited version. Pricing starts in the low four figures and goes up from there.

RealNetworks' serving license pricing changes fairly frequently. Check the Web site for the latest.

- *Microsoft* – Windows Media Services comes "free" with its enterprise server products. Of course, you have to buy the server products, which are sold based on the number of users. Costs for enterprise servers can run from several hundred dollars to darn near infinity, depending on your overall networking needs. However, if your network already runs on Microsoft products, you can install Windows Media Services without spending more money.

- *Apple Computer* – Apple's QuickTime Streaming Server has the simplest licensing arrangement. You buy a license for the server itself; licensing is not related to the number of streams you serve. In fact, Apple touts this as a feature, jibing its competition for what Apple calls a "server tax," that is, charging more money for streaming licenses as streaming volume increases.

- *Macromedia* – Macromedia sells a server with streaming capacity, but most Flash 8 developers deliver their work from Web servers. You should do the same with your Flash 8 until you have a stronger grasp of streaming technology.

Inside the Industry

 You may have heard of another class of software licensing called *open source*. The price for an open source license is pretty compelling: $0. Chapter 11 will look at open source streaming solutions in some detail. But it's worth noting here that Apple has released an open source version of its QuickTime Streaming Server. Called "Darwin Streaming Server," it follows the open source licensing model.

Technical Support

What do you do if the server's not working and the manual is no help? The answer is often technical support provided by the manufacturer. The purchase of a server license usually includes some level of technical support, ranging from an online archive of accumulated experience (a *knowledgebase*) to a dedicated human being 24 x 7 x 365. One factoid: If you think you're talking to a support person in Anytown, USA, you may in fact be talking to someone in Anytown, India. American software manufacturers of all types are outsourcing more and more help-related services overseas.

There are a few other options. When an error message pops up or something else breaks, there's a very good chance that someone else has experienced the same problem. You might find a local user's group that has an online bulletin board where you can post questions. Several Web sites cater to techno-geeks, and they include message board areas. The vendors themselves run message boards. Try solving your technical problem by performing a global Web search or a search of online news groups using the text of an error message. You might be amazed at what turns up.

Conclusion

Distributing your encoded streaming-media files is a major component to your streaming strategy, but it's not for the faint of heart. You have to balance several factors, such as storage capacity, security and bandwidth needs. It's important that you work with your IT and networking professionals to complete a successful streaming-media project. In the next chapter, you'll learn the first steps toward integrating your streams with your Web site.

CHAPTER 8

Streaming Media and Metafiles

When you click a link on a Web page, the browser contacts the Web server and requests the page you want to look at. A link to streaming media works differently. Instead of linking directly to your newly uploaded media file, there is an intermediate step using something called a *metafile*. The "meta" prefix, especially in computer applications, most often refers to data that describes or relates to other data. A streaming media metafile describes a streaming media audio or video file to the browser in terms of the location of the media file on the streaming server. It can be very confusing, but by the end of this chapter, you'll be master of metafiles.

In this chapter, you will:

- Learn the difference between Web servers and media servers
- Consider the relationship between metafiles and media players
- Write a metafile for three of the four vendors
- Discover how to link to a metafile via a Web page
- Pick up some advanced techniques in metafile creation
- Be introduced to dynamic metafile creation

Web Servers vs. Media Servers

Web servers are one of the core pieces of the Internet software suite. They are fairly simple networking applications. When you click a link in a browser, the browser sends a request via the *HyperText Transfer Protocol* (HTTP) to the Web server, which responds by sending the requested *HyperText Markup Language* (HTML) file to the requesting browser, along with associated graphics and text. There are some other important features, such as requesting and sending encrypted information. But that's the extent of it.

Media servers, on the other hand, are more complex and specialized. Unlike a Web server, a media server stays in constant contact with the media player while it delivers a media file.

The media server uses a variety of protocols, including HTTP, to deliver the media file to the player and manage its progress. And because of the huge amounts of data involved, most media servers are designed to manage player connections and bandwidth consumption better than Web servers.

In fact, you should determine whether your organization or Internet service provider (ISP) runs its media server on a separate computer. Most media server vendors recommend that media servers run on a separate computer because of their specialized nature. And that leads to the need for a metafile.

Metafiles and Media Players

A streaming media metafile is a small text file containing the location of the encoded audio or video file on the streaming media server. The location is stored as a URL, which points to the streaming media server. The link to an audio or video file on a Web page points to this metafile. As shown in **Figure 8-1**, when the link is clicked, the Web server delivers the metafile to the browser, which hands the file to the correct media player on the user's computer. The media player opens the metafile, loads the URL, and requests audio/video data from the streaming server—that is, it plays the file. For this process to work, you need to write a metafile and place it on your Web server.

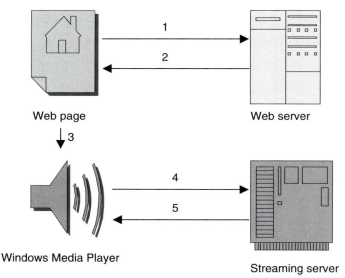

Figure 8-1
How the browser, media player, Web server, and streaming server work together.

Creating a Metafile

Metafiles range from very simple to highly complex. They can simply point to an audio or video file, and they can set all kinds of parameters. This step-by-step guide aims to keep things as simple as possible. But, as usual, different vendors implement the metafile model differently. First, the section lists common steps for all the vendors. Then, it goes through the vendors one by one.

Common Metafile Creation Steps

Here are metafile creation steps common to all major streaming media systems.

1. Make note of the URL/location of your encoded file on your media server. That URL goes in the metafile. If you're having trouble, speak to your IT support staff or network administrator.

2. Open a text editor such as Notepad or SimpleText. (Avoid word processors such as Microsoft Word. These files incorporate hidden code that can confuse media players.)

3. Type the URL into the text file, using the syntax appropriate to the streaming platform you're using.

4. Save the text file with the appropriation extension.

5. Upload the new metafile to your Web server.

The next sections go through each of the vendors' implementations.

Figure 8-2
A media file URL pasted into a new text file and saved with an extension, in this case, **.ram** for RealAudio or RealVideo.

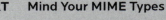
RealNetworks RealPlayer/Helix

The RealNetworks metafile syntax is very simple. Essentially, all you have to do is place the URL to your streaming media file inside your metafile.

1. Note the URL to your media file on the streaming media server.

2. Open a new text file with a text editor.

3. Write or copy/paste the URL in the text file. Your line will look something like this:

    rtsp://www.yourcompany.com:554/pathtofile/filename.rm

4. Save the text file with the extension **.ram**. This extension identifies the file as a metafile for the RealNetworks system. If you're using an embedded player, use the **.rpm** file extension.

5. Upload the text file to your Web server with your FTP client and note the file's location.

Author's Tip

Troubleshooting Your Metafiles

To test metafiles for any vendor's system, type the location of the metafile on your Web server in the location bar of your Web browser and click Go or hit Enter. For example, your location could be:

http://www.yourcompany.com/pathtometafile/mymetafile.ram.

If you get a "file not found" error from your browser, check the location of the metafile. If the media player starts, but it gives you a "file not found" error, then the URL in the metafile is wrong. If the URLs appear correct and still have problems, see your network administrator and show them the error message.

Microsoft Windows Media Series 9

1. Windows Media metafiles have a completely different structure from RealNetworks metafiles. They use *XML* (eXtensible Markup Language) syntax, which resembles HTML syntax. Here's how to create a Windows Media Metafile. Note the URL to your media file on the streaming media server.

2. Open a new text file with a text editor.

3. Write the following code *exactly* into the text file.

```
<ASX version = "3.0">
  <Entry>
    <Ref href = "[placeholder]" />
  </Entry>
</ASX>
```

4. Replace the text "[placeholder]" with the URL to your audio or video on your streaming server. (Keep the quotes.) The URL should look something like this:

```
mms://www.yourcompany.com:1755/yourpath/yourfile.wmv
```

5. Save the text file with the extension **.asx**. This extension identifies the file as a metafile for the Windows Media system.

6. Upload the text file to your Web server with your FTP client and note the file's location.

Apple QuickTime

Apple recently added the QuickTime Link metafile syntax. If you're going to use this syntax, it's important to check with your network administrator to make sure the Web server is configured for this new MIME type.

1. Ask your network administrator whether there is a MIME type associated with the **.qtl** file extension in your Web server's MIME type lookup table. If not, your network administrator will need to add an entry using the following MIME type:

```
application/x-quicktime-media-link
```

2. Open up a text editor such as Notepad or SimpleText.

3. Type the following into the file, replacing the URL in the `<embed>` tag with the URL to your file:

```
<?xml version="1.0"?>
<?quicktime type="application/x-quicktime-media-link"?>
<embed src="http://www.myserver.com/Movies/My.mov" />
```

Author's Tip

XML and XML Compliant
XML (eXtensible Markup Language) is the current darling of the programming world. It's an extremely flexible way to describe data within a document. You don't need to know XML to create streaming media, but it's worth learning about. Both the Windows Media and QuickTime metafile code are "XML compliant," meaning they use standard XML syntax.

4. Save the file with the **.qtl** file extension.

5. FTP the file to your Web server and note the location.

Macromedia Flash 8

Flash audio and video files are always played back via an embedded application in your Web page. Therefore, you don't need a metafile. Place the link to your streaming file in the **.swf** file that contains the embedded Flash player.

Linking to Your Metafile

The last step is creating a link in your Web page to your metafile. Now is a great time to meet your Web designer/developer and explain what you're doing. (Actually, you probably should've given them a heads up at the beginning.) Or you may have access to your organization's Web pages. You almost certainly have access to your personal Web pages. If you haven't worked with an HTML page for a while, you might refresh your memory with an HTML tutorial or book.

Build a Link to Your Metafile in Your Web Page

Here is some very simple code for linking to your metafile. It actually creates an entire, though small, Web page. You can adapt this code to your specific needs.

```
<html>
    <body>
    <a href="http://www.yourcompany.com/pathtometafile/mymetafile.XXX"/>My Audio/
Video</a>
    </body>
</html>
```

Important! Don't forget to replace the XXX with the correct file extension for your metafile, such as **.ram**. It doesn't have to be capitalized. Finally, upload the modified Web page to your Web server, load it into your browser, and test the link.

Advanced Metafiles

As you'll recall from earlier in the chapter, the divided functions of Web server and streaming media server require the use of a metafile. Here's a quick review of what happens:

1. User clicks a link to the metafile.

2. The browser downloads the metafile.

3. The browser hands the metafile to the media player.

4. The media player looks inside the metafile for the URL of the streaming media file.

5. The media player contacts the streaming media server and plays the file.

Metafiles can do more than just point to the streaming server. They can control several features in the player. You can override some data encoded into a file with new information, such as the copyright information. This section goes through each vendor's main metafile features to show you your options.

More on Metafiles

Every metafile has at least a URL to a streaming file. Each piece of the URL has a meaning. Here's a typical URL:

mms://streams.yourhost.com:1755/pathtofile/filename.wmv

Another way to look at a streaming URL is:

```
[protocol]://[your.domain]:[port]/[mount_point]/[path]/[file.name]
```

Here's the URL taken apart, piece by piece.

- *Protocol* – This is the streaming protocol used by the server. In the example, it's Microsoft Media Services protocol. Note the following colon and pair of forward slashes.

- *Domain* – This is the familiar string of characters ending in .com. Note the following optional colon.

- *Port* – The number in the example, 1755, identifies the requested service to the computer where the service lives, in this case Windows Media Services. The RTSP protocol uses port 554. Port numbers are usually optional.

- *Mount point* – The mount point is the beginning place in the streaming media server's file system or directory structure where streaming files are located. The mount point is set in the server's configuration files.

- *Path* – The directory or directories under the mount point where a specific file is located. A file could be located directly under the mount point.

- *File name* – The name of the file to stream. In the example, the **.wmv** extension signals it's a Windows Media file.

RealNetworks Metafile (.ram, .rpm) Options

You can put options at the end of a URL to a RealNetworks streaming file that specify start and end times, and/or modify title, author and copyright information. Here's the format:

```
rtsp://streams.helixserver.com/filename.rm?[parameter]=[value]&[parameter]=[value]
```

Note the "?" after the filename and the "&" between the first and second pairs of parameters and values.

Here's a simple URL with options that specify a start and end time of the file:

```
rtsp://streams.helixserver.com/filename.rm?start="30"&end="1:45"
```

This tells the server to begin playing back this file from the 30 second mark and stop at the 1 minute 45 second mark. See **Table 8-1** for common RealNetworks metafile parameters.

Table 8-1
Common metafile parameters for RealNetworks metafiles.

Parameter	Values	Purpose
Start	Written as dd:hh:mm:ss.xyz where: dd = days hh = hours mm = minutes ss = seconds xyz = milliseconds	Sets a start time within a file
End	Written as dd:hh:mm:ss.xyz where: dd = days hh = hours mm = minutes ss = seconds xyz = milliseconds	Sets an end time within a file
Title	Any string of characters	Overrides title info encoded in the file
Author	Any string of characters	Overrides author info encoded in the file
Copyright	Any string of characters	Overrides copyright info encoded in the file

Windows Media Metafile (.asx) Options

Here's the contents of a simple Windows Media metafile, using some advanced parameters:

```
<asx version="3.0">
    <entry>
        <starttime value="30" />
        <duration value="1:15" />
        <title>My New Title</title>
        <ref href="mms://streams.wmserver.com/filename.wmv" />
    </entry>
</asx>
```

This metafile tells a Windows Media server to play the file starting at 30 seconds from the beginning and run it for 1 minute 15 seconds. The file will stop playing at the 1 minute 45 second mark. This metafile also changes the title displayed to "My New Title." Carefully note the syntax of each line, down to the slashes, which are easy to miss.

Also note the difference between the **starttime** tag and the **title** tag. **Starttime** and **duration** take a value, in this case the time in seconds to start the file and the amount of time to play the file. **Title** is a *container* tag. It doesn't take a value, but wraps around some information with a closing tag. See **Table 8-2** for common Windows Media metafile options.

Author's Tip

There are a number of other metafile parameters available. For a full list, consult the documentation available on the RealNetworks site.

Table 8-2
Common metafile parameters for Windows Media metafiles (.asx).

Parameter	Options	Purpose
`<starttime value="x"/>`	dd = days hh = hours mm = minutes ss = seconds Written as dd:hh:mm:ss	Sets a start time within a file
`<duration value="x"/>`	dd = days hh = hours mm = minutes ss = seconds Written as dd:hh:mm:ss	Sets a duration for playback
`<title>` `</title>`	Any string of characters	Overrides title information encoded in the file
`<author>` `</author>`	Any string of characters	Overrides author information encoded in the file
`<copyright>` `</copyright>`	Any string of characters	Overrides copyright information encoded in the file

QuickTime Metafiles (.qtl) Options

QuickTime metafiles also offer a number of additional metafile options. These options can be added via the QuickTime Media Link Settings dialog (see **Figure 8-3**) or added by hand using a simple text editor.

Author's Tip

There are a number of other Windows Media metafile parameters available. For a full list, consult the documentation available on the Microsoft site.

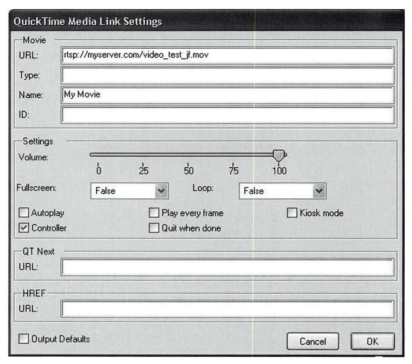

Figure 8-3
The QuickTime Media Link Settings dialog.

Here's a breakdown of the advanced options available in a QuickTime Media Link file:

- *Type* – Ordinarily left blank, the Type field lets you override the XML type.

- *Name* – Lets you specify a movie name.

- *ID* – Lets you specify a movie ID number, perhaps from a database.

- *Volume* – This slider sets the opening volume when the file begins to play.

- *Fullscreen* – This allows you to set a default playback size. In addition to full screen, you can also specify full, double, half, or current size.

- *Loop* – Sets whether the file should play through once or loop continuously. The "palindrome" option causes the movie to play forwards and backwards alternately.

- *Autoplay* – Tells the player to begin playing the file as soon as the player opens.

- *Controller* – Instructs the player to show the play/pause button.

- *Playeveryframe* – Do not skip any frames.

- *Quitwhendone* – Checking this open forces the player to close when the file stops playing.

- *Kioskmode* – Disables saving the file to disk.

- *QTNext* – Plays this video file after this current file is finished.

- *HREF* – Link the video image to this Web page.

If you want to add any of these options manually, simply add them inside the `<embed>` tag. For example, to make a file play automatically, set the autoplay option to true using the following syntax:

```
<?xml version="1.0"?>
<?quicktime type="application/x-quicktime-media-link"?>
<embed
        autoplay="true"
        src="rtsp://www.myqtserver.com/myfile.mov"
        />
```

ALERT   **No Metafiles for Flash**

Macromedia Flash MX does not use metafiles, since they are usually served from a Web server. See the next section for information on using Flash 8 files in your Web page.

Dynamically Generated Metafiles

If you produce a lot of streaming media files frequently, creating tons of metafiles by hand would take too much time and present a file management and tracking problem. The solution is to generate your metafiles dynamically, or "on the fly," as the phrase goes. For example, imagine a set of 50 training videos residing on your streaming server. Instead of writing 50 **.asx** files, you can put the URLs plus any other information into a Microsoft Access or SQL Server database. You then write code that generates the **.asx** file "on the fly" using a scripting language such as ASP.net, PHP, or perl. As you add training videos, you simply enter the data in the database, and the script automatically writes the metafile whenever the video is requested. For an example of how this can be done, check the tutorial at:

http://www.streamingmedia.com/tutorials/view.asp?tutorial_id=105

RealNetworks Server's Special Feature

RealNetworks' Helix Server offers an easy way to skip all this metafile rigmarole. The server will generate a metafile when you need it. You don't have to worry about building it and uploading it to the Web server. To generate a metafile dynamically, create a *hypertext reference* (HREF) directly to the streaming server. The HTML link will look something like:

```
<a href="http://streams.helixserver.com:80/ramgen/video_file.rm">
```

Note the path "ramgen" in the URL. This tells the Helix server to build the **.ram** file automatically and send it to the browser. The browser then sends the **.ram** file to the media player, which opens it, and locates the video file.

Later versions of RealServer, including Helix, also contain a way to generate an **.asx** metafile on the fly for Windows Media Players. Use this syntax for **.asx** files:

```
<a href="http://streams.helixserver.com:80/asxgen/video_file.wmv">
```

Check your Helix server documentation for exact use of the ramgen and asxgen features.

Conclusion

Because Web servers and streaming servers perform different functions, and because users typically find video links via Web sites, developers created the metafile to allow browsers to hand off streaming media files to streaming players. Each streaming media vendor uses metafiles, but they each have slightly different syntaxes. To improve efficiency, developers often build systems that create metafiles dynamically. In the next chapter, you'll learn how to embed media players directly in a Web page.

CHAPTER 9

Embedding Streams in Your Web Pages

Putting streaming media in a Web page is more complicated than most types of Web content, and it's potentially the most confusing. That's because streaming media requires the use of a *helper application*, a piece of software that's not part of the Web browser. In the case of streaming media, the helper application is the media player. And the media player can be used in two ways: as a standalone application, or as a browser *plug-in*. Each has advantages and disadvantages and different implementations. But using embedded players, the subject of this chapter, creates some interesting options not available through use of the standalone player. The chapter will take you through each vendor's implementation, step-by-step, and show you some code examples.

After reading this chapter, you will:

- Understand the difference between external and embedded players
- Learn HTML coding for embedded players
- Get an overview of testing
- Be encouraged to promote your hard work

For purposes of clarity and brevity, the chapter assumes you're using a video file, not an audio-only file. Of course, you can use the code discussed here for audio-only applications.

External vs. Embedded Players

As a Web developer, you can take advantage of a media player's capabilities in two ways. First, you can tell the browser to play the stream in an external player. This is usually a standalone application—that is, RealPlayer, Windows Media Player, or QuickTime Player. (The Flash Player works only within a browser.) When a user clicks a streaming link, the browser tells the media player to start up and play the file.

The developer can also tell the browser to play the media file within the browser window. In this case, you're using the player as an *embedded* application. When the player is installed, certain components are also installed to enable this functionality. These are a bit like the attachments to your vacuum cleaner. When you need to reach into a tight spot, you attach the crevice tool to the hose. The hose becomes part of the vacuum cleaner for a short time. When a developer wants to play a streaming media file in a browser window, he or she adds some HTML that tells the browser to attach the streaming media components and play the file in the browser. When the user goes to a different page, the plug-in components are unloaded from the browser.

Should I Use the External Player or an Embedded Player?

Each form of the media player, external and embedded, has advantages and disadvantages. Web page coding for the external, standalone player is easiest. All you need to do is point to a metafile using a standard HTML hypertext anchor tag. (See the section "Build a Link to Your Metafile in Your Web Page" in Chapter 8 and the review in the next section.) However, some users might be confused when the standalone player starts up on their computer. Also, media player branding may compete with your own, especially if you're targeting a consumer audience. As always, consult your audience analysis and communications goals for guidance.

If you use an embedded player, you have almost total control over the look and feel of the media player in the user's browser. You decide where to put the video image, the play/pause/stop buttons, even what the buttons look like. However, it's harder to code HTML for embedded players. You'll need some advanced HTML knowledge and some knowledge of how different browsers behave. For really advanced control, you'll need to know some JavaScript or VBScript.

HTML Coding for Embedded Players

HTML code for embedded players differs significantly from player to player, although they share several components. Most importantly, they all use the **<object>** and **<embed>** tags. Here's another confusing bit:

- **<object>** tags are used by Microsoft Internet Explorer to embed helper applications, which are called *ActiveX* controls.

- **<embed>** tags are used by Netscape Navigator to embed helper applications, which are called *plug-ins*.

Because you may not know which browser will display the page containing the code, including browsers such as Firefox and Opera, you need to create *cross-platform* HTML. To do this, you can include code for both by simply placing your **<embed>** tags within the **<object>** tags. The following code examples for each media player demonstrate this practice.

HTML for the RealPlayer Plug-In

Use this code for embedding RealPlayer components in a Web page. It's important to note the components of the RealPlayer are embedded individually. For instance, in this example the image window and controls for the RealPlayer are embedded using separate code.

Before the book explains each piece, here's all the code in one chunk.

Author's Tip

A ClassID by Itself
You'll note that the **<object>** tags for each of the following examples use a parameter called *classid* followed by a seemingly random string of letters and numbers. It's important that you use the string *exactly as shown*. That code is needed by Internet Explorer to know which ActiveX control to load. To learn more about ActiveX and classes, read the documentation on Microsoft's Web site. Several good how-to books on ActiveX are also available.

```
<OBJECT ID="video_image" CLASSID="clsid:CFCDAA03-
8BE4-11cf-B84B-0020AFBBCCFA"

WIDTH="320" HEIGHT="240">

        <PARAM NAME="AUTOSTART" VALUE="true">

        <PARAM NAME="TYPE" VALUE="audio/x-pn-realaudio">

        <PARAM NAME="SRC" VALUE="my_video.rpm">

        <PARAM NAME="CONTROLS" VALUE="ImageWindow">

        <PARAM NAME="CONSOLE" VALUE="_master">

        <EMBED NAME="video_image" SRC="my_video.rpm" WIDTH="320" HEIGHT="240"
        AUTOSTART="true" CONTROLS="ImageWindow" TYPE="audio/x-pn-realaudio-plugin"
        CONSOLE="_master">

        </EMBED>

</OBJECT>
```

```
<OBJECT ID="video_controls" CLASSID="clsid:CFCDAA03-8BE4-11cf-B84B-0020AFBBCCFA"
HEIGHT="36" WIDTH="320">

        <PARAM NAME="AUTOSTART" VALUE="true">

        <PARAM NAME="TYPE" VALUE="audio/x-pn-realaudio">

        <PARAM NAME="SRC" VALUE="my_video.rpm">

        <PARAM NAME="CONTROLS" VALUE="ControlPanel">

        <PARAM NAME="CONSOLE" VALUE="_master">

        <EMBED NAME="video_controls" SRC="my_video.rpm" WIDTH="320" HEIGHT="36"
        AUTOSTART="true" CONTROLS="ControlPanel" TYPE="audio/x-pn-realaudio-plugin"
        CONSOLE="_master">

        </EMBED>

</OBJECT>
```

N.B.: The first set of components controls the video image. The second set controls the play/pause/stop buttons.

Now for the details. The text discusses each piece after the corresponding line of code.

```
<OBJECT ID="video_image" CLASSID="clsid:CFCDAA03-8BE4-11cf-B84B-0020AFBBCCFA"
WIDTH="320" HEIGHT="240">
```

This line opens the **object** container, names the object in memory (important for JavaScript coding, if you elect to do so), sets the ActiveX control **classid**, and sets the **height** and **width** of the video image. The height and width should match the image size of the encoded file.

```
<PARAM NAME="AUTOSTART" VALUE="true">
```

The **autostart** parameter tells the player plug-in to play the video file when the Web page loads. If you don't want the behavior, set the value to "false" or omit the parameter.

```
<PARAM NAME="TYPE" VALUE="audio/x-pn-realaudio">
```

The **type** parameter identifies the MIME type of the file to the browser.

```
<PARAM NAME="SRC" VALUE="my_video.rpm">
```

The **src** (short for "source") parameter points to the metafile, which in turn contains the URL of the streaming file. Note that RealPlayer uses the **.rpm** extension to identify a metafile used in the plug-in version of its player.

```
<PARAM NAME="CONTROLS" VALUE="ImageWindow">
```

The **controls** parameter tells the browser what part of the RealPlayer is being embedded. In this case, the code refers to the video window.

```
<PARAM NAME="CONSOLE" VALUE="_master">
```

The **console** parameter is used to tie together the different parts of the RealPlayer that have been embedded. All components that share a common console name will work together. In this case, the "ImageWindow" controls described in the previous parameter will be linked to the "ControlPanel" controls parameter below via the "_master" console value.

```
<EMBED NAME="video_image" SRC="my_video.rpm" WIDTH="320" HEIGHT="240"
AUTOSTART="true" CONTROLS="ImageWindow" TYPE="audio/x-pn-realaudio-plugin"
CONSOLE="_master">
```

The opening **embed** tag for Netscape browsers. You can see the corresponding parameters. However, Netscape Navigator does not have a parameter corresponding to Internet Explorer's **classid**.

```
</EMBED>
```

The closing tag for the **embed** container.

```
</OBJECT>
```

The closing tag for the **object** container.

```
<OBJECT ID="video_controls" CLASSID="clsid:CFCDAA03-8BE4-11cf-B84B-0020AFBBCCFA"
HEIGHT="36" WIDTH="320">
```

The opening **object** tag for the player controls. Note the different value for id and the smaller height value compared to the first set of tags.

```
<PARAM NAME="AUTOSTART" VALUE="true">
<PARAM NAME="TYPE" VALUE="audio/x-pn-realaudio">
<PARAM NAME="SRC" VALUE="my_video.rpm">
<PARAM NAME="CONTROLS" VALUE="ControlPanel">
```

This value for **controls** tells the browser to load the play/pause/stop components.

```
<PARAM NAME="CONSOLE" VALUE="_master">

<EMBED NAME="video_controls" SRC="my_video.rpm" WIDTH="320" HEIGHT="36"
AUTOSTART="true" CONTROLS="ControlPanel" TYPE="audio/x-pn-realaudio-plugin"
CONSOLE="_master">

</EMBED>
</OBJECT>
```

HTML for the Windows Media Player Plug-In

Use this code for embedding the Windows Media Player in a Web page. Again, here's the code in one big listing, followed by a detailed explanation for each piece.

```
<OBJECT ID="MMPlayer1" WIDTH="320" HEIGHT="350" CLASSID="clsid:22d6f312-b0f6-11d0-
94ab-0080c74c7e95" TYPE="application/x-oleobject">
        <PARAM NAME="scr" VALUE="my_video.asx">
        <PARAM NAME="ShowControls" VALUE="1">
        <PARAM NAME="AutoStart" VALUE="1">
        <EMBED NAME="MMPlayer1" TYPE="application/x-mplayer2" SRC="my_video.asx"
        AUTOSTART="1" SHOWCONTROLS="1" WIDTH="320" HEIGHT="350">
        </EMBED>
</OBJECT>
```

Here is each line with a corresponding explanation.

```
<OBJECT ID="MMPlayer1" WIDTH="320" HEIGHT="350"
CLASSID="clsid:22d6f312-b0f6-11d0-94ab-0080c74c7e95" TYPE="application/x-oleobject">
```

The opening **object** tag includes **id**, which is a name in memory for the player object. **Width** and **height** parameters correspond to the video image size *plus* the height of the player controls. The MIME **type** is also included in the opening **object** tag.

```
<PARAM NAME="src" VALUE="my_video.asx">
```

The **src** parameter tells the plug-in where to find the metafile. You may need to add more path information to this value.

```
<PARAM NAME="ShowControls" VALUE="1">
```

The **ShowControls** parameter tells the browser to show the play/pause/stop controls.

```
<PARAM NAME="AutoStart" VALUE="1">
```

The **autostart** parameter tells the browser whether or not to start the video when the page loads. In this case, the value of "1" means "Yes." A value of "0" means "No."

```
<EMBED NAME="MMPlayer1" TYPE="application/x-mplayer2"
SRC="my_video.asx" AUTOSTART="1" SHOWCONTROLS="1" WIDTH="320" HEIGHT="350">
```

The opening **embed** tag for Netscape Navigator.

```
</EMBED>
</OBJECT>
```

HTML for the QuickTime Player Plug-In

The following HTML code will embed QuickTime Player in a Web page. First, all the code in one place:

```
<OBJECT ID="my_video" CLASSID="clsid:02BF25D5-8C17-4B23-BC80-D3488ABDDC6B"
HEIGHT="350" WIDTH="240">

        <PARAM NAME="TYPE" VALUE="video/quicktime">

        <PARAM NAME="SRC" VALUE="my_video.qtl">

        <PARAM NAME="AUTOPLAY" VALUE="true">

        <PARAM NAME="CONTROLLER" VALUE="true">

        <EMBED NAME="my_video" SRC="my_video.qtl" TYPE="video/quicktime"
        WIDTH="350" HEIGHT="240" AUTOPLAY="true" CONTROLLER="true">

        </EMBED>

</OBJECT>
```

Here's each component, followed by an explanation.

```
<OBJECT ID="my_video" CLASSID="clsid:02BF25D5-8C17-4B23-BC80-D3488ABDDC6B"
HEIGHT="350" WIDTH="240">
```

The opening **object** tag for QuickTime Players.

```
<PARAM NAME="TYPE" VALUE="video/quicktime">
```

The **type** parameter identifies the MIME type to the browser.

```
<PARAM NAME="SRC" VALUE="my_video.qtl">
```

The **src** parameter tells the plug-in where the metafile is located on the Web server.

```
<PARAM NAME="AUTOPLAY" VALUE="true">
```

An **autoplay** parameter set to "true" will start the video immediately after the Web page loads. The default value is "false."

```
<PARAM NAME="CONTROLLER" VALUE="true">
```

The **controller** parameter shows the play/pause/stop buttons.

```
<EMBED NAME="my_video" SRC="my_video.qtl" TYPE="video/quicktime" WIDTH="350"
HEIGHT="240" AUTOPLAY="true" CONTROLLER="true">
```

These are the **embed** tag parameters for Netscape Navigator compatibility.

```
</EMBED>
```

```
</OBJECT>
```

Embedding the Flash 8 Player Plug-In

Flash is unique in that there is no standalone Flash player. Instead, you have to create a custom embedded Flash player application, complete with a link to your streaming Flash file. However, the Flash authoring environment makes it very simple to author your embedded Flash player. The following steps walk you through the wizard Flash tool provides to create a simple embedded Flash player.

1. Start Macromedia Flash 8 by clicking Start → Programs → Macromedia → Macromedia Flash 8. (If you're using a trial period version, click the "I want to try…" option and the Continue button.)

2. Click on the link to create a new Flash Document from the center of the interface (see **Figure 9-1**).

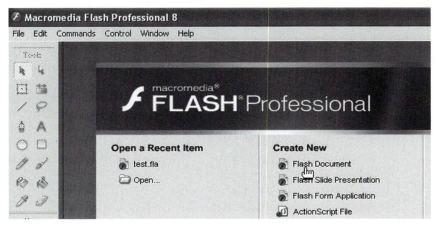

Figure 9-1
Choose "Flash Document" to start a new project.

3. From the File menu, select Import → Import Video. This opens the Import Video window (see **Figure 9-2**).

4. Click the "Already Deployed…" option, and enter the URL to your Flash file. It should look something like this:

    rtmp://flv.world.mii-streaming.net/lux/MyVideo.flv.

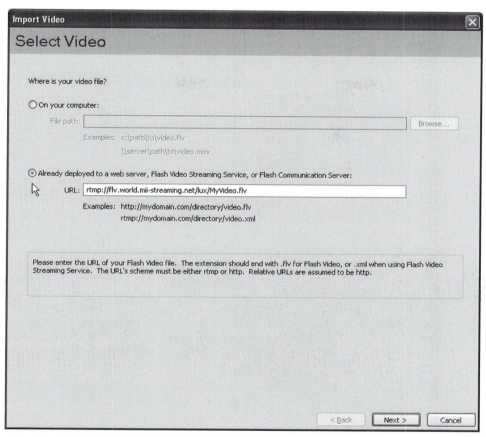

Figure 9-2
Enter the URL to your Flash video in the Import Video window.

5. Click Next. This brings up the Skinning window (see **Figure 9-3**).

6. Choose a "skin" for your video. A skin determines the appearance of your embedded Flash player. There are a number of options available.

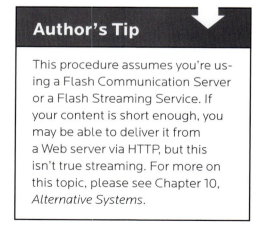

Author's Tip

This procedure assumes you're using a Flash Communication Server or a Flash Streaming Service. If your content is short enough, you may be able to deliver it from a Web server via HTTP, but this isn't true streaming. For more on this topic, please see Chapter 10, *Alternative Systems*.

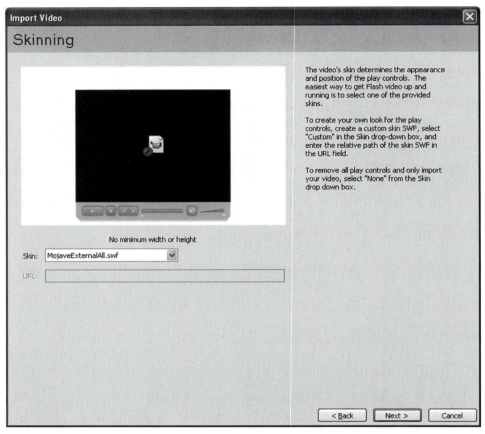

Figure 9-3
Do your users a favor and choose a skin with full playback controls.

Author's Tip

The great strength of Flash 8 is the flexibility of its environment. In the case of *skins*, you can choose one of the selections, or you can create your own skin, and load by selecting "Custom." Furthermore, you can link player controls elsewhere in the presentation to the player behavior. See your Flash 8 documentation for more information.

7. Click the Next button. This takes you to the Finish Video Import screen (see **Figure 9-4**). Be sure to read all the information on this page, as it details the steps that must be taken to finish publishing your embedded player.

8. Click the Finish Button. This brings up the "Save As" dialog box. Type in a name for your Flash project, and then click the Save button.

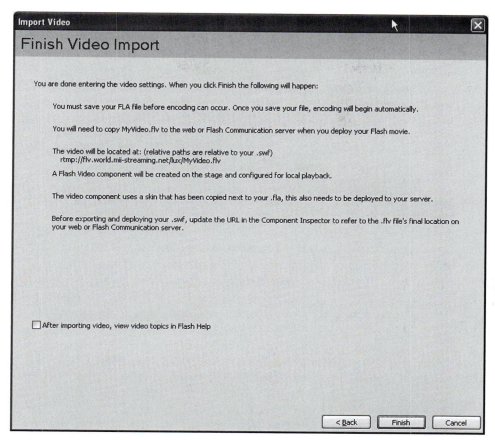

Figure 9-4
The Finish Video Import screen.

ALERT Flash will attempt to connect to your published file to find out what dimensions the Flash player needs to be. If Flash cannot connect to the video file, it will display an error, which indicates that there is something wrong with your URL.

9. If you'd like to preview your movie, choose Publish Preview from the file menu, and then choose Flash. This will bring up the embedded player in a small window.

10. If you're satisfied with your embedded player, select Publish Settings from the File menu. In the Format tab, select the Flash (**.swf**) and HTML types. Give the files unique names.

11. Click Publish and the files are created. You can test your files locally by double-clicking on the **.swf** file to view the presentation in the Flash Player or on the **.html** file to view the presentation in a browser.

Look in your working directory for files with the **.swf** and **.html** extensions. The **.swf** file is the embedded Shock-Wave Flash application, which is the embedded player. This is embedded in the **.html** file.

Remember, all Flash files are played back in an embedded player. If you look inside the HTML, you'll see code that looks something like this:

```
<OBJECT ID="my_video" CLASSID="clsid:D27CDB6E-AE6D-11cf-96B8-444553540000"
WIDTH="320" HEIGHT="240">

        <PARAM NAME="TYPE" VALUE="application/x-shockwave-flash">

        <PARAM NAME="movie" VALUE="my_player.swf">

        <EMBED NAME="my_video" SRC="my_player.swf" WIDTH="320" HEIGHT="240"
        TYPE="application/x-shockwave-flash">

        </EMBED>

</OBJECT>
```

Once again, here's each line of the code, followed by an explanation.

```
<OBJECT ID="my_video" CLASSID="clsid:D27CDB6E-AE6D-11cf-96B8-444553540000"
WIDTH="320" HEIGHT="240">
```

The opening object tag for Flash.

```
<PARAM NAME="TYPE" VALUE="application/x-shockwave-flash">
```

The MIME type for Flash 8.

```
<PARAM NAME="movie" VALUE="my_player.swf">
```

The **movie** parameter points to the **.swf** video file, rather than a metafile for other players. That's because the **.swf** file has the URL to the streaming file "baked in."

ALERT You must regenerate your **.swf** file if you want to point to another streaming file, because embedded Flash players have the URL to the streaming file inside them.

```
<EMBED NAME="my_video" SRC="my_player.swf" WIDTH="320" HEIGHT="240"
TYPE="application/x-shockwave-flash">
```

The opening **embed** container tag for cross-platform compatibility with Netscape Navigator. The **src** parameter corresponds to the movie parameter in the **object** tag.

```
</EMBED>
</OBJECT>
```

ALERT   **Sorry, No Guarantees**

It's unfortunate, but there's no guarantee the code above will automatically work for you. There are enough differences among player versions and browser versions to make universally compatible code almost impossible. This is the bane of all Web developers and it causes sleepless nights. Maybe someday all the media player and browser vendors will agree to using standard tags, parameters, values, etc. In the meantime, you'll have to experiment some and test rigorously.

Upload Your File(s)

When you have completed your HTML coding, upload the file to your Web server. If you're using Flash, you'll also need to upload the **.swf** file to your Web server. You'll probably use your FTP program to do this. Note the location of the Web page. You'll need it to test and announce your work.

Testing Your Embedded Player Code

Every software project includes a testing phase. Yours is no different. Depending on the complexity of your project, you should consider writing a test plan. Software engineers spend weeks writing test plans, which can run dozens of pages long. Yours could be as simple as a single page. The first thing to do is go back to your audience analysis. Try to test on all the variables you expect to encounter. Test variables could include:

- Operating systems
- Browsers and Web pages, including the streaming links
- Media player(s)
- Player performance
- End user bandwidth (dial-up, cable/DSL, etc.)
- Server-side bandwidth usage

A tutorial on testing is beyond the scope of this book. But if you try to emulate as many of the technical conditions of your audience as best you can, you'll be more confident that your streaming project will perform as designed. And get your systems and network administrators involved. They will help you set up tests and troubleshoot problems.

Promote Your Streams

It sometimes amazes me that people sweat blood to make a killer streaming project, but don't bother to tell anybody about it! You've worked dang hard. Tell the world! Again, keep your audience in mind. Targeted announcements work best. Some of your options include:

- An e-mail with a link directly to the metafile or to a Web page with instructions
- Notices on all relevant Web pages on your intranet
- Banner advertising on Web sites your audience visits
- Embedding stream URLs in RSS and Atom feeds
- An announcement on a printed postcard sent via snail mail
- Standing on a corner and shouting at the top of your lungs (well, maybe not)

The important thing is relevance. Where do you think the audience is most likely to see an announcement about your stream? You might ask someone with public relations or advertising/marketing experience for advice. They can help your investment pay off by finding ways to maximize your exposure in a productive way.

Conclusion

Embedding your media player and streaming video into a Web page creates a customized experience for your users. However, you need some advanced understanding of HTML to write the code needed to make embedding work. All vendors implement embedding in a slightly different way, and the code required for different browsers is slightly different. It's important to write cross-platform code, test your pages thoroughly, and promote your streams once they are ready to go. In the next chapter, you'll learn about some alternative streaming media systems and technologies.

CHAPTER 10

Alternative Systems and Methods

Everyone has daydreamed about chucking it all, packing the family, and starting over. The daydreams usually occur when something about what you're doing at the moment doesn't feel quite right, though you can't put your finger on it. Maybe you've successfully implemented a streaming strategy at work, or put your home video online. You may be thinking there's got to be a better way, or just a different way.

The wonderful thing about software is that there's always a different way of doing something. The universe of 1s and 0s is the most plastic ever conceived. In the streaming world, some people believe all codecs should work on any streaming platform. They shouldn't be limited to a single platform built by a private company. Others believe the source code behind the media players and streaming servers should be viewable by all; they distrust the inherent secrecy of proprietary software. Still others believe the dominant client/server architecture of streaming is wasteful. They prefer a model called *peer-to-peer*. All of these streaming practitioners have come up with solutions based on their own engineering principles and philosophical beliefs.

Although this book focuses on the streaming media methodologies that currently dominate the Internet, you don't have to limit yourself to them. That's the point of this chapter. You can dare to be different. In this chapter, you will:

- Receive some cautions before trying non-mainstream systems
- Get a detailed introduction to MPEG
- Learn how *open source* technology plays a role in streaming media
- Examine a way to serve streams without a streaming server
- Look at whether outsourcing your streaming might be the right choice
- Discover an alternative to the client/server streaming architecture called *peer-to-peer*

Before You Veer Off the Main Highway

The writer William Least Heat Moon unfolded a road map one day and noticed something about lonely county roads and backwoods routes. He saw that many were colored blue, unlike the major trunk roads. He called a book about his treks on these "roads less traveled" *Blue Highways*. Sometimes he had grand adventures. Other times, he found himself alone and lonely.

If you decide to try alternative streaming solutions, go with your eyes open. Some of the advantages will appeal to you. But there are also important disadvantages. On the up side, you'll find yourself almost completely independent of proprietary systems, especially if you choose a fully open source solution. (Open source is discussed in detail in following sections.) Some people chafe at the idea of dependency on a large corporation for a critical business system or personal service. They'd rather work within a community of equals dominated by an ethic of helpfulness and engineering elegance, rather than profit. Alternative streaming systems are worthy choices for individuals or small, flexible organizations willing to experiment and take risks in an unstructured environment.

On the other hand, if you prefer structure, or you work in an organization that has strong demands for accountability, a nonstandard (read: nonproprietary) solution may create too much stress. Some people don't like working with tools that don't have the imprimatur of a Microsoft or Apple Computer. Others want a phone number to call or a printed manual from a bookstore, neither of which may be available for an alternative solution. You can mitigate potential conflict over nonstandard solutions by educating your colleagues and bosses and showing the organizational and financial value of an alternative streaming solution. In some cases, particularly in the technical arena, you can take advantage of the comfort of brand by using alternative solutions that people have heard about, though they may not have tried them.

MPEG: The Most Talked-About Alternative to Proprietary Architectures

Every discussion about the relative merits of one streaming media solution over another includes an argument over *MPEG-4* (pronounced "em-peg four"), one of the handful of open standards for recording, storing and sending digitized audio and video. MPEG-4 is the standard that directly affects streaming media. The argument revolves around whether MPEG-4 is an important factor in the development of streaming as a technology and an industry. But no one argues about the importance of MPEG as a group of standards.

What Is a Standard?

A *standard* is a set of rules practitioners of a particular discipline agree to follow. In computer engineering, they often define the architecture of a particular type of solution. It's a little like agreeing on the general rules for constructing a building, but letting each architect design his or her application of the rules, as long as everyone can use the building.

Nonstreaming examples of computer standards include HTML, which is actually a set of rules for telling Web browsers how to display information in a text file, among other things.

Open Standards vs. Proprietary Models

Open standards appeal to many computer engineers in part because of the transparent process behind the standard. A group of leading lights in a field get together in a public forum and hash out the rules that will govern anyone who wants to build something that works in that arena. Participation is voluntary. But a nonstandard solution, even if it works, is often excluded by default if enough people adopt the standard.

Almost every popular piece of computer hardware is based in large part on some kind of engineering standard. The open standards allow different manufacturers to design different ways to solve a problem. If the solutions follow the standard, related pieces of hardware doing different jobs will work together. Success is not dependent on someone following a single manufacturer's way of doing things. Rather, success depends on sticking to a set of rules. Vendors compete on how they implement a standard, their pricing, and their support.

On the other hand, the history of technology in business is replete with stories of companies whose proprietary solutions became a standard without the blessing of a committee. The company and its owners/shareholders grew very rich when the marketplace made the rules—i.e., adopted the standard—which everyone else had to follow. This is a powerful incentive to create useful tools that solve real problems.

Microsoft is the best example in the software industry. Bill Gates made Windows the de facto standard for desktop and laptop computer operating systems. He used aggressive marketing, enjoyed technological prowess, and made the most of the opportunity presented by the dawn of the personal computer in the early 1980s.

The prospect of market dominance encourages all software companies to compete with each other for the best solution to a particular problem. In the ideal scenario, all potential customers eventually come to your "one-stop shop" and you reap the rewards of their long-term dependence on you. However, you cannot sit on your laurels. IBM is much less powerful than it was a generation ago because it missed the sweeping changes in computer technology that led to the dominance of the personal computer.

In the streaming world, the proprietary solution dominates. The leading companies, RealNetworks, Microsoft, and Apple Computer, ultimately want to "own" the streaming marketplace. Their software works pretty well and it's getting better all the time. They may not admit it, but they don't want to be tied to committee-created standards that can be slow to change in a dynamic environment, such as the Internet.

However, one can argue that the intense competition has held up the wider adoption of streaming. If these companies had followed open standards, some would say, people at home and at work who just want to hear some music or watch a sports highlight could simply click a button and listen or watch. They wouldn't have to worry about whether they have a particular media player or the latest codec or spend hours downloading stuff and other silliness. Shouldn't streaming be like turning on the radio or starting a car? Why not?

How Does MPEG-4 Fit?

The story of MPEG standards predates streaming media. MPEG-1, adopted in 1992 by the *Motion Pictures Experts Group* (MPEG), defined how video is stored digitally on CD-ROM. At the time, CD-ROM was the multimedia rage. Before the Internet as the world knows it appeared, software companies believed the world would get its media fix via a plastic-coated metal platter, which had already taken over the music industry. MPEG-1 included *MPEG-1 Audio Layer III*, an audio compression standard that would lead directly to the *MP3* file-sharing phenomena of the late 1990s.

More MPEG standards followed. MPEG, which works under the direction of the International Standards Organization (ISO) and the International Electro-technical Committee (IEC), developed a new compression standard in 1994 dubbed MPEG-2. Now you could store video on a CD and play it back with "VCR-like" quality. MPEG-2 would become the basis of DVD and satellite TV technologies.

MPEG-4 arrived in 1998. It was originally designed for teleconferencing applications. But engineers started applying it to streaming media as an alternative to the rapid rise of proprietary technologies introduced by RealNetworks, Microsoft, and others a few years before. MPEG also grew into a way of packaging all kinds of data, such as text and still images. Interactivity is also a part of the standard. MPEG-4 is also discussed in the context of video distributed over wireless networks to Personal Digital Assistants (PDAs) and advanced cell phones. MPEG is more likely to have an impact in these delivery arenas in part because they're so new. In these areas, MPEG-4 doesn't have to play catch up with the proprietary big boys.

MPEG is also branching out into standards that aren't directly related to delivering audio and video data. MPEG-7, for example, defines video and audio metadata. It was adopted in 2001. The goal is to make identification of audio and video material easier by search engines. See **Table 10-1** for a list of the current MPEG standards either adopted or under discussion.

Table 10-1
MPEG standards.

Standard	Adopted	Purpose
MPEG-1	1992	Store video on CD-ROM and early set-top boxes.
MPEG-1 Audio Layer III (MP3)	1992	Audio compression standard.
MPEG-2	1994	Store VHS-quality video on CD. Used by DVD and satellite TV.
MPEG-3	1995	An early HDTV standard, later folded into MPEG-2.
MPEG-4	1998	Video compression for teleconferencing, adapted for streaming media.
MPEG-7	2001	Defines metadata standards for sound and images.
MPEG-21	(in dev)	An overarching standard covering all previous MPEG standards.

Inside the Industry

MPEG and Fees

A number of private companies own patents related to the MPEG standards. Normally, people who want to develop products based on those patents pay a license fee to the patent owner. MPEG requires the fees to be fair, reasonable, and nondiscriminatory. The fees compensate the companies that participate in the MPEG process.

Why MPEG Standards Are Important

Implementing a standard such as MPEG breaks the potential of a single company to dominate a marketplace. If every streaming media vendor supported MPEG-4 from the beginning to the end of the streaming process, for example, none could control the streaming market. You could encode a file into an MPEG-4 format with one vendor's tool and play it back with another. Users and producers are no longer locked into a particular way of doing things. Vendors would have to compete on other aspects of streaming, such as the availability of the latest Hillary Duff video or major league baseball games.

More on MP3

As mentioned above, the MPEG-1 Audio Layer III standard is part of the original MPEG-1 standard for storing video on CD-ROM. Don't confuse MP3 with MPEG-3, which is a defunct High Definition Television (HDTV) standard that was folded into MPEG-2. Software manufacturers have developed tools to encode audio files into MP3 format, which has become a popular streaming media format as well as file storage format.

MP3 first gained notoriety when college students started sharing music files encoded into the format. The files were far smaller than the original files on their CDs and maintained most of the musical quality. Most CDs can store a little more than an hour's worth of music. With MP3, you can store up to 12 hours of high-fidelity audio. You could put hundreds, perhaps thousands of songs on a CD. The compression also led to the popularity of MP3 for portable digital music players and to MP3 streaming solutions, especially on peer-to-peer networks. Streaming MP3s also support standard encoding features such as multiple bit rates ranging from 8 kilobits per second to 1.5 megabits per second.

More on MPEG-4

MPEG-4 is usually discussed in the context of audio and video delivery. But it actually covers all types of media that can be delivered over a computer network. MPEG-4 is a set of tools. The MPEG-4 video tool is only one of many in the toolbox.

MPEG-4 supports encoding at very low bit rates, starting at 2 kilobits per second for audio and 5 kilobits per second for video. High bit rates are also supported: 64 kbps for CD-quality audio and up to 5 megabits per second for video. MPEG-4 is "transport-agnostic," meaning you can use practically any protocol to deliver MPEG-4 files. MPEG-4 supports intellectual property protection to combat piracy. It's also backward compatible with other major existing standards.

Inside the Industry

The Rise of H.264

An important rising star in the MPEG-4 universe is the *H.264* standard, also called *MPEG-4 AVC*, which achieves very high data compression. Though it's been around for several years, the standard went mainstream when Apple Computer added H.264 playback capability to its fifth-generation iPod in 2005. The company already supported it in QuickTime 7. The standard is also gaining traction among software developers and broadcasters. RealNetworks' Producer for mobile streaming and its mobile streaming server support the MPEG-4 standard. In fact, MPEG-4 in general and H.264 in particular is becoming a major standard for streaming to mobile phones, as shown in **Figure 10-1**. Microsoft does not support the standard in its streaming media products, preferring to push its own solution, called *VC-9*. Sorenson, which supplies Macromedia with codecs, does support the standard.

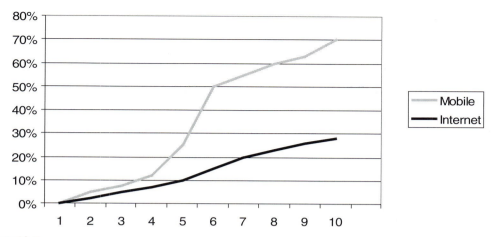

Figure 10-1
MPEG market penetration from the standard's introduction in 1992 through 2002.
(Data source: The MPEG Industry Forum.)

How the Major Streaming Media Vendors Support MPEG Standards

The Big 3+1 streaming media vendors (RealNetworks, Microsoft, Apple Computer, and new-comer Macromedia) support MPEG standards to one degree or another. Here's how their support shakes out.

1. *RealNetworks* – The pioneer streaming media company is committed to a propri-etary software model where it can gain competitive advantage through techno-logical advances. But it also supports serving, creation and playback of MPEG files. The company hopes to dominate the market by supporting virtually every streaming media format, including competitors' formats.

ALERT Producers should note that RealNetworks' free encoder does not sup-port MPEG encoding. You'll need to upgrade to RealProducer Plus if you're interested in MPEG encoding with RealNetworks products.

2. *Microsoft* – The ultimate proprietary software company is by its nature lukewarm to standards it cannot control. This leads to an inconsistent and contradictory implementation of these standards. The company supports MP3 file playback. But it has its own implementation of the MPEG-4 format, developed before the standard was finalized. Microsoft uses the term "MPEG-4" to describe this codec, but files created using this codec do not always play in competitors' media players. (One of the purposes of MPEG is cross-platform compatibility.)

However, third-party software vendors have built plug-ins to Windows Media Player that allow playback of their MPEG implementations.

3. *Apple Computer* – Apple is the most aggressive among the Big 3+1 in touting its support of MPEG standards, especially MPEG-4. The company notes that the MPEG group chose the QuickTime file format as the "foundation" for the MPEG-4 standard. The company sees MPEG support as a key differentiator for its products, compared to RealNetworks and Microsoft.

4. *Macromedia* – The Flash 8 creator is the new kid on the streaming block, and its MPEG strategy is fuzzy. It supports MP3, but not MPEG-4. It may not need to support the video format at the moment, given the extreme ubiquity of its Flash Player. However, Macromedia may change its mind if its main customers, designers and Web developers demand MPEG-4 support.

Inside the Industry
Podcasting and MPEG

Podcasting, that is, the distribution of audio and video files for storage and playback on a handheld, portable device, is technically not a part of the streaming world. For one thing, there's no such thing as a live podcast. However, it's worth noting that a large share of podcasted audio and video is encoded in MPEG formats used in streaming, such as MP3 for audio and MPEG-4 for video. It's another example of MPEG standards' penetration into audio and video distribution.

Open Source: An Alternative to Proprietary Systems

Most consumers and businesses use software created by companies eager to keep their methodologies secret or tightly protected by intellectual property law. These laws are an important part of capitalism. If companies could not benefit exclusively from their ideas, they'd have little incentive to come up with these ideas. And keeping their methods secret helps companies maintain an edge in the marketplace.

However, some people view the software world as another kind of marketplace, where ideas are debated publicly. The best ideas survive, while the rest are discarded. And they say no one should own the mechanisms behind products that have become a central, almost indispensable, part of everyone's life.

Imagine a different history of the internal combustion engine. What if the inventors never shared the ideas and methods behind their creation? What if Henry Ford kept his ideas secret, yet managed to sell hundreds of millions of vehicles? And what if his competitors held only small parts of the car market? The consumer would be completely tied to his company for maintenance and new models. You couldn't tinker with the motor in your backyard to make it run better to suit your own particular needs or taste. And the cost of switching to a different manufacturer could outweigh the benefits.

Proponents of the "open source" model of software believe that placing ideas before a community leads to better software for everyone. They believe everyone should have a chance to view and modify the *source code*, the ideas and methods executed by software developers in programming languages such as C++ or Visual Basic. Tens of thousands of developers around the world create Web sites, post on newsgroups, and write to Internet e-mail lists about their ideas. They criticize other ideas and propose new solutions. Often, ad hoc teams grow out of a common interest in solving a problem. And in some cases, these teams, even individuals, have changed the software world.

Inside the Industry

The "Free" in "Freeware"

Some people prefer to use the term *freeware*, rather than *open source*. Freeware means that the source code is "free" for anyone to view, and "free" from the normal constraints of intellectual property law, including some provisions of copyright law. The "free" in freeware does not refer to the software's cost, although it's true that freeware/open source software can be downloaded and used at no charge.

Open Source Success Stories

The most famous example of the open source model is Linux. Finnish computer science student Linus Torvalds created Linux in the early 1990s because he wanted a Unix operating system for his IBM personal computer. Building on the ideas of others, he wrote an operating system, got it working, and shared the source code with some like-minded programmers on a computer bulletin board. He incorporated the suggestions of other programmers and posted the results. The project began to snowball.

The world of computer science is peppered by egomaniacs and bullies. Torvalds did not fit the mold. He brought a unique humbleness and ability to facilitate conversations missing from many discussions about software. He was also a good engineer. Furthermore, his operating system had strong networking features, which made it ideal for the new world of the Internet. First academic institutions, then new Internet businesses started by former students started using Linux for their Internet servers. The operating system continued to improve, and it now accounts for a large chunk of servers directly connected to the Internet. Today, Torvalds still directs the development of the Linux kernel, the core part of Linux, which now includes thousands of utilities and applications, all available as open source software.

One of those applications accounts for two-thirds of the Web servers on the Internet. You'll remember that a Web server is the software that delivers a Web page to you when you request it with your Web browser. In 1995, the most popular Web server was public-domain software designed by Rob McCool at the National Center for Supercomputing Applications at the University of Illinois. But many webmasters had developed their own extensions and bug fixes to what was cryptically called the "HTTP daemon." A group got together and organized all the bug fixes, sometimes called "patches." The result was a Web server called *Apache*, as in "a patchy server." Apache is the single most successful open source application on the Internet, as shown in **Figure 10-2**.

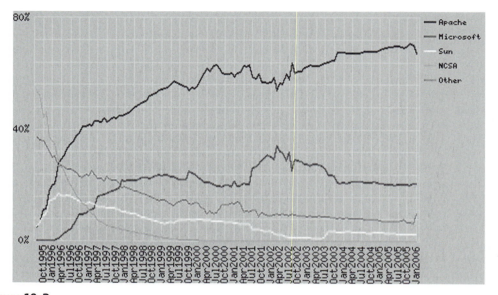

Figure 10-2
The Apache Web server (top line) accounts for nearly 70% of all Web servers deployed on the Internet. (Source: Netcraft. The latest figures are available at *http://www.netcraft.com*.)

Advantages and Disadvantages of Open Source Tools

The open source model of development has some distinct advantages and disadvantages. Some of the most important advantages include:

- An opportunity to know exactly how a mission-critical piece of software works.
- Ability to modify the software to suit your particular needs.
- Up-front costs often close to zero.
- Licensing often extremely liberal (see following box on licensing).
- Support available in two basic forms:
  - Vendors specializing in open source software support.
  - Participation in the open source community.

The disadvantages of open source software include:

- Usually requires strong knowledge of operating systems, especially Unix and its clones, including Linux.

- Rarely backed by a major organization with large resources. The exceptions are the major names, such as Linux or Apache.

- Community support can be spotty and response times irregular or infrequent.

- Good documentation can be difficult to find. Again, exceptions to this are the popular open source solutions, such as Linux.

Inside the Industry

 Open Source Licensing

The document that makes open source "open" is the license. As explained elsewhere, you don't actually own the software installed on your computer. Rather, you own a license to use it and the license sets the rules for its use, most often that you can't copy it and give it away or sell it.

There are several types of open source licenses. The most popular is called the General Public License (GPL). All open source licenses grant you the right to view the source code of your software and make changes as you see fit. Differences often occur in permissions you have to distribute changes. If you want to learn more about open source licensing, visit the Web site for the nonprofit Open Source Initiative, *http://www.opensource.org/*.

Open Source Streaming Solutions

Most of the open source work in the streaming realm has focused on the server side. The best example is Darwin, a variant of the QuickTime Streaming Server. The project is sponsored by Apple Computer. Darwin has many of the features of the QuickTime Streaming Server, and it runs on Mac OS X, Linux, and Microsoft Windows NT/Server 2000. Darwin serves MP3 audio and MPEG-4 video files to QuickTime Player. RealPlayer and Windows Media Player can play MPEG files served with Darwin if users install the EnvivioTV MPEG plug-in.

RealNetworks has also taken up the open source banner. The company has created a community of software developers around its "Helix DNA Platform," which is a facet of its effort to create a universal digital media platform that includes streaming. RealNetworks allows participating developers to view the source code of Helix clients, encoders and servers, and modify it for their own use. Developers can also suggest changes to Helix code for the wider Helix community. RealNetworks has written special open source licenses that allow the company to retain property rights while taking advantages of the "marketplace of ideas" concept at the heart of open source development.

"Streaming" with Your Web Server

This book has assumed you'll use server software specially designed to deliver audio and video over a computer network. That's usually the best option. However, you have another option which won't cost you a dime. It's very different from "true" streaming, which uses specialized streaming protocols, such as RTSP. This second type goes by various names, including *pseudo-streaming*, *progressive download*, or *HTTP streaming*. As the last name suggests, the second type of streaming uses the HTTP protocol. It's the same protocol Web browsers use to communicate with Web servers.

The principle is pretty simple: You treat your encoded file just like an HTML file or graphics file by putting it on your Web server. You create a link to the encoded file in the same way you create a link to another Web page. The user clicks the link and the encoded media file starts to download. As it downloads, it starts the media player, which plays the file as it comes through. In many cases, the user experience with HTTP streaming is virtually the same as "true" streaming. But there are limits.

First, your system administrator will have to configure your Web server to understand the MIME type associated with your type of encoded file. That's actually pretty easy. (See **Table 10-2** for a list of common streaming MIME types.) Second, you'll probably run into performance problems with the stream after a certain amount of time. The longer a stream is, the more problems you'll experience, such as sudden stops.

Third, if large numbers of people request the stream all at once, your network could be easily swamped. Web servers, unlike streaming servers, typically don't know how to manage the bandwidth allocated to them. You also miss out on such features as multiple bit rate encoding, because Web servers can't detect player connection speed. Therefore, they don't know when to serve a high-bandwidth or low-bandwidth version of your stream.

Since HTTP isn't a streaming protocol, the amount of control a user has over the experience is extremely limited. For example, you can't fast-forward through a stream when you're using HTTP. Playback will not begin until a substantial portion of the file has been downloaded. If your file is large, this could take quite awhile.

And finally, since files served via HTTP are downloaded, a copy is saved to the user's hard drive. Some browsers try to obscure the location of this file, but with a little effort it's not too hard to find these files. So Web servers don't offer any security for your files, as opposed to streaming servers.

However, if for whatever reason you don't have access to a streaming server, HTTP streaming can be a viable option under these circumstances:

- Your audio/video files are less than 60 seconds in length.
- You expect a minimal number of simultaneous requests.
- You encode with only one bit rate.
- You need on-demand access only. (Web servers can't serve live streams.)
- You don't mind people having a copy of the file.

Table 10-2
Common Streaming MIME types.

Vendor	File Extension	MIME Type
RealNetworks	.ra, .rv, .rm	audio/x-pn-realaudio
Microsoft	.asf, .wma, .wmv	video/x-ms-asf
Apple Computer	.mov .qtl	video/quicktime application/x-quicktime-media-link
Macromedia	.swf .flv	application/x-shockwave-flash video/x-flv

The Advantages of "True" Streaming

As mentioned previously, "true" streaming relies on specialized network transport protocols, such as RTSP, which are supported by streaming servers, not Web servers. The protocols allow the client and server to speak to each other and adjust to net weather, the dynamic network conditions that pervade the Internet and even some internal networks. The final result is better network performance, more efficient use of resources, and a higher-quality user experience. Use a streaming server under these circumstances:

- Your encoded files are more than 60 seconds long.
- You expect more than a minimal amount of simultaneous connections.
- You plan multiple bit rate encoding.
- You may stream live events sometime in the future.
- You want consistent performance for long files.
- You need intelligent management of your outgoing bandwidth.
- You want to give your audience the maximum amount of control over their streaming experience.

Do You Need a Streaming Server?

Streaming media is a demanding technology. Network and system administrators in organizations large and small have to balance all the demands made on a network, and streaming can throw their systems out of kilter. You may decide that your network can't handle streaming. Maybe the network expertise you need isn't available in-house. Perhaps you don't have enough bandwidth for the traffic you expect. You have another option: *outsourcing*.

ALERT The up-front discussion of outsourcing isn't meant to discourage you from distributing your streaming media from your own system. But reliable distribution is the key to success in any media project, and you should be ready to make a major commitment in time and resources to make an in-house distribution strategy work.

Outsourcing to a Streaming Media Hosting Service

Most small to medium-sized businesses contract with a hosting company or their Internet Service Provider (ISP) to host their Web sites. The ISP handles all the files and processes that make a site work, such as HTML files, databases, and programs that make the site dynamic.

Many *hosting companies* and ISPs offer streaming media services. Web hosting has evolved a standard set of options, such as Web serving, e-mail accounts, and credit card order processing. However, streaming services vary wildly from one hosting company to another. Some offer none. Others offer everything. Furthermore, a few companies have sprung up devoted exclusively to streaming media hosting and delivery. The industry of streaming media hosting is something of a wilderness at the moment. But it has definite staying power, given the background trends.

Is outsourcing streaming media hosting a good option for you? Review your audience analysis and your assessment of internal resources. If the two seem out of balance, and it seems impractical in terms of time and/or money to bring them into balance by adding internal capacity, outsourcing streaming media hosting and delivery is a viable option.

What Hosting Companies Can Do For You

The most important benefit of a hosting contract is peace of mind. You'll rest easy because the hosting company is taking care of important variables that could make or break the success of your streaming project. This is especially true if you plan to stream audio or video to a consumer audience. All you have to do is supply the content.

Hosting companies offer another important advantage: cost control. If you contract out hosting, you don't have to spend the money to upgrade your network and systems infrastructure. Your upgrade could be as simple as adding streaming services to your current Web-hosting arrangement. Your monthly or quarterly charge goes up by a few percentage points, and you get all the streaming capacity you need. Because you pay a set amount per month or quarter, your streaming costs are more predictable, and budgeting is easier.

If you prefer to go with a streaming media hosting specialist, expect to purchase an account based on key streaming variables, notably storage space for files and the amount of data transferred per month, which is another way of talking about bandwidth. The more you need, the higher the cost, though economies of scale play a role in lowering unit costs. In addition, streaming specialists may offer encoding services, priced on a per-minute basis. The longer an audio or video program, the more you pay. (Common pricing by streaming specialists is shown in **Table 10-3**.) But the process becomes much easier and simpler for the customer. You drop off a Beta SP or DV tape; they encode it, host it, and deliver it.

Other advantages of outsourcing include:

- *Security* – Hosting companies make security a top priority or they're out of business.

- *Dedicated infrastructure* – Streaming specialists and some Web-hosting companies optimize their networks for the unique demands of streaming. They design fault-tolerant systems—that is, if one piece fails, another piece automatically jumps in to take over, meaning little if any interruption in service.

- *Advanced technology* – Hosting companies have to keep up with the latest technological developments or they risk falling behind competitors. This means you don't have to worry about buying the latest and greatest versions of everything every year or so.

Table 10-3 shows a pricing sample for selected streaming media encoding and hosting components offered by streaming media specialists. Caveat emptor: Use this table for your own rough guesswork only. Actual pricing formulas vary wildly among providers. You should also expect to pay setup charges for some or all of these services.

Table 10-3
Monthly Pricing for Streaming Media Services (2006).

Encoding per format per bit rate	
Media length	**Rate per minute**
0 to 30 minutes	$5.00 – $10.00
30 to 60 minutes	$2.50 – $7.50
More than 60 minutes	$1.00 – $3.50
Media storage	
Total amount	**Rate per megabyte**
Up to 1 gigabyte	$.05 – $.10
Up to 500 gigabytes	$.03 – $.07
Up to 1,000 gigabytes	$.01 – $.07
Data transfer	
Total amount	**Rate per gigabyte**
Up to 1 gigabyte	$10.00 – $15.00
Up to 500 gigabytes	$4.50 – $7.50
Up to 1,000 gigabytes	$3.00 – $7.00

Inside the Industry

 There are a number of resources available on the StreamingMedia.com Web site that can give you up-to-date information about current industry pricing schemes.

Reasons to Avoid Outsourcing

The main thing you give up when you outsource is control. You are handing over an important part of your communications strategy, as well as tangible assets in the form of media files, to others. Granted, a hosting company has a compelling interest in providing good service and helping you succeed. But ultimately you have the responsibility to ensure they can deliver your streams to your audience in a way that meets your goals. This can be as simple as clicking your stream links once a day to make sure they work. Keep your hosting provider up-to-date on your needs and expectations, and monitor performance.

How to Shop for Streaming Media Hosting

You should shop for streaming media hosting just like anything else. Review your audience analysis and develop some criteria for deciding whether a hosting provider can meet your needs. Then call around. These questions will get you started.

1. What streaming formats do you support?

2. What is the range of your services? End-to-end? Encoding only? Hosting only?

3. What is your streaming media infrastructure? Do you have redundant backup systems? Load balancing? What is your stream capacity?

4. Do you offer Digital Rights Management (DRM) services?

5. What security features do you offer?

6. How often do you upgrade your streaming servers?

7. Do you offer any uptime (service availability) guarantees or Service Level Agreements (SLA)?

8. What production facilities do you have? Do you offer live encoding at remote locations?

9. How much streaming experience do you have?

10. Can you show me a client list and references?

11. Can you report streaming media traffic?

12. Can you create customized Web pages or embedded players?

13. Can you support advertising features, such as streaming ad insertion or banner ads?

14. What kind of customer support do you offer?

Peer-to-Peer (P2P) Streaming

The most common network architecture for streaming media is client/server. Numerous software clients on computer desktops contact a central server, which delivers the data to the client. It looks a lot like the familiar one-transmitter-to-many-receivers model in over-the-air broadcasting.

But streaming producers have a second network architecture choice: peer-to-peer or *P2P*, as shown in **Figure 10-3**. All the computers, or *workstations*, in a peer-to-peer network have more or less equal status and share resources, such as files and printers. There's no hierarchy implied with a centralized server. The difference can be subtle. If you have a computer hooked up to a printer, and all the other workstations use the same printer, the first computer can be called a "server." If the server also performs workstation tasks, such as word processing, then it's technically not a server, because it's not dedicated to server-related tasks. Many small businesses and most home networks use a peer-to-peer model.

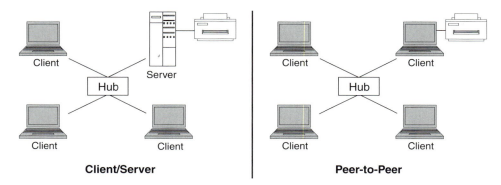

Figure 10-3
The two main network architectures, client/server and peer-to-peer.

The difference becomes clearer when you talk about peer-to-peer streaming. And the difference shows the peer-to-peer architecture's ability to overcome the most important streaming resource problem, bandwidth. In the client/server model, dozens, hundreds, or thousands of clients may contact a single server all at once. If dozens, hundreds, or thousands of clients contact your server all at once, your bandwidth could be overwhelmed and your whole system may fail.

In the peer-to-peer model, there's no division of labor; computers consume and serve/relay streams at the same time. Bandwidth needs are distributed equally among all the client machines. And adding new clients doesn't necessarily lead to capacity problems. In other words, the bandwidth bottleneck is removed. Peer-to-peer, or *distributed content*, advocates say many computers over many small connections can do the same work as a single computer with one fat connection at lower costs and higher return for the content provider.

The main problem with peer-to-peer is not technical, but political. Much of the illegal sharing of music files since the dawn of the Internet has happened over peer-to-peer networks, which are much harder to control than client/server networks. In the client/server model, all the content files are stored in one place, the server. In the peer-to-peer model, the content files can be shared on any, or perhaps all the participating computers. Music companies and other purveyors of copyrighted material (including software companies) lose tight control over their intellectual property on peer-to-peer networks. And most intellectual property business models depend on ownership and control of the product by a single individual or corporate entity.

Another problem has to do with *free riders*. The success of peer-to-peer architecture, including streaming, depends on users who are willing to relay streams. However, a large portion of peer-to-peer users consume files and streams without passing them to the next user. Free riders take advantage of the benefits of peer-to-peer streaming without contributing to the community effort.

Two Popular Peer-to-Peer Streaming Implementations

Several software companies have developed peer-to-peer streaming solutions. Here are two of the most popular, SHOUTcast and ICEcast.

1. *SHOUTcast* – Prospective online broadcasters interested in SHOUTcast start by installing an MP3 media player such as Winamp for Windows or Audion for the Mac. To broadcast a stream, you install a SHOUTcast Distributed Network Audio Server, which allows you to receive and relay streams to other peers. As with any streaming, it's important that you have a robust connection to the Internet, such as cable/DSL. To find out more, visit *http://www.shoutcast.com.*

2. *ICEcast* – ICEcast is one of the leading open source peer-to-peer streaming solutions. It's completely community based, and it supports an open source streaming format called *Ogg Vorbis* that can be played by the Winamp player. The ICEcast architecture is similar to SHOUTcast, but ICEcast runs only on Linux. To learn more, visit *http://www.icecast.org.*

Conclusion

Though proprietary systems dominate the streaming world, enterprising streaming media producers have other options, notably MPEG-4 and open source servers, encoders, players, outsourcing options, and alternative architectures such as peer-to-peer. Alternative systems will become more important as streaming moves into other areas, such as mobile networks. However, one should make use of these tools with eyes open, because they require a higher level of technical expertise and a commitment to open standards and the open source community. In the next chapter, you'll study more advanced topics related to streaming technology and the industry.

CHAPTER 11

Advanced Topics

Streaming audio and video is great, you may say to yourself, but can't I make this stuff more interesting, more interactive? Yes, you can. In this chapter, you'll learn a little about live streaming. You'll also study a couple of methods that improve interactivity. You may remember the heyday of the 1990's Internet bubble, when almost no one seemed to care about business models to back up the fancy new technologies, streaming included. Make a profit? Who cares! Well, believe it or not, solid business models are emerging in the streaming space, although it's still too early to tell whether any of them have long-term viability. Also, technologies have emerged that protect the copyrights of the content holders. Finally, when your boss asks you for some numbers to measure how your new investment in streaming is paying off, you'll have a method ready to go.

In this chapter, you will:

- Understand the differences between live and on-demand streaming
- Experiment with a markup language for streaming media
- Learn about the potential of streaming high-definition video
- Examine streaming media on portable devices, such as cell phones
- Learn about digital rights management (DRM)
- Consider potential business models for streaming
- Study ways to measure streaming media success, including calculating a return on investment

Live Webcasting vs. On-Demand Streaming

The Hands-On Guide to Streaming Media Basics is designed with the intelligent beginner in mind. To keep things simple and straightforward, the book focuses almost exclusively on the "on-demand" streaming option—that is, archiving streams for access whenever the audience chooses. That's why you've shot and encoded an on-demand file, the one that's in your hands right now.

However, you may find yourself in the position of choosing whether to produce a live broadcast, usually called a *webcast*, as opposed to an on-demand broadcast. Or you may have to do both for the same content. Here's some advice: If you decide to produce live and you have little or no experience in producing live events, look seriously into outsourcing the project. (For more on outsourcing, see Chapter 10.) Live events of all kinds, not just live streaming-media broadcasts, have their own unique demands that go beyond the scope of this book and the abilities of most beginners, even smart ones. Nevertheless, this section will help you decide whether your project is appropriate for a live broadcast or archiving for on-demand access.

When Should I Produce Live?

Live events are among the most exciting and compelling experiences people enjoy. It's fun to watch actors on a stage, because the action unfolds before your eyes. You know anything can happen, including the unexpected. Live broadcasting is similar. Ever wondered why television news departments go "live to the scene" whenever possible? Because a "live" storyteller (the reporter) adds an extra emotional edge, even drama, to a story when he or she tells it as it happens. That feeling is very hard to capture in a recording.

You should consider producing a live broadcast when you can capture and deliver action as it happens. And you need to judge whether the action, or the information delivered as part of the action, would have the most impact if delivered immediately, rather than at some later point. Here are some good candidates for a live streaming-media broadcast:

- An annual address by a CEO or prominent political leader
- A new product rollout at an important industry conference
- An event where the outcome is uncertain, such as a game or debate

If you decide to produce an event live, you should probably double or triple your time and financial budgets, depending on the nature of the content. (A simple speech is easier to produce than a football game, for example.) Again, unless you have experience with live event or broadcast production, consider outsourcing at least part of your live webcast, at least until you understand the resources required.

When Should I Produce for On-Demand Delivery?

One of the great advantages of the Internet is instant access at any time to untold amounts of stored information, including audio and video information. But step back for a minute and consider the reasons for on-demand delivery of streams over live broadcasts.

You should consider producing for on-demand delivery when the content stays relatively fresh over time. Some people called this kind of content *evergreen*, because it reminds them of the pine and fir trees that retain their green color over the darkest winter, unlike their deciduous cousins. Another factor that argues for on-demand is audience interest. Will the potential audience want to watch this content long after it was first produced? If the answer is yes, you should produce and store an on-demand streaming media file.

Some streams may fall into both live and on-demand categories. A live broadcast of a presidential speech is usually archived, because the president's words carry interest both at the time they were delivered and for many days, perhaps years afterward. Some good candidates for on-demand production and/or archiving include:

- A training presentation on sexual harassment (this could be delivered live and archived for later access)
- An early audio recording of the community's first radio station
- Almost any kind of music production

One major advantage of on-demand delivery over live delivery is your ability to enhance the stream with interactive elements. For example, you can apply some advanced techniques to add a navigation menu to a stream, allowing users to go to specific sections of a recording. This isn't possible in a live broadcast.

A decision matrix, such as the one shown in **Table 11-1**, might help you to choose live or on-demand production for your material. To use the matrix, follow these instructions:

1. Give each criterion a weighting from 1 (not important) to 10 (very important).
2. Rate how well each criterion meets the criterion.
3. Multiply the weighting by the rating for a score.
4. Add the score for each platform. The highest score suggests the right decision.

> **Author's Tip**
>
> If you're just dying to know more about live streaming-media production, the *Hands-On* series offers another book in the series, *The Hands-On Guide to Webcasting*, by Steve Mack and Dan Rayburn.

Table 11-1
A live vs. on-demand decision matrix.

| | | Broadcast Choices | | | | | |
| | | Live | | On-Demand | | Both | |
Criteria	Weight	Rating	Score	Rating	Score	Rating	Score
Uncertain outcome							
Dramatic tension							
Info stays same over time							
Potential for interactivity							
Budget							
Potential to promote stream							
Prep time							
	Totals						

Synchronized Multimedia Integration Language

The realm of streaming media tends to be limited to sending audio and video over the Internet in real time. However, you can stream other kinds of data, such as static images and text side by side with audio and video. This allows you to create different kinds of time-based media experiences that take advantage of the efficiency of streaming technology. The most flexible tool for managing a variety of streaming data types in the same application is *Synchronized Multimedia Integration Language*, or SMIL.

Think of SMIL (pronounced "smile") as a markup language for multimedia. It looks a lot like HTML with the addition of tags that let you add timing information. With the timing tags, you decide when certain things happen, such as the start and end times of an audio clip within a larger timeline. Producers can also incorporate links within a SMIL presentation for interactivity, similar to links in a Web page. SMIL is XML-compliant, meaning it follows XML's rules for tag construction. SMIL applications play in RealPlayer and QuickTime Player. Windows Media Player does not support SMIL.

A Simple SMIL Example

One of the most common SMIL implementations is the slideshow. It's also the easiest to understand. Say you want to create a narrated streaming slideshow of your family camping trip to the Grand Canyon. You've created JPEG graphics files out of your photos with a graphics programs such as Adobe Photoshop. You've arranged the photos in the correct order and recorded a simple narration. Open a text editor, such as Notepad, and type the following code.

```
<smil>
    <head>
    <layout>
        <root-layout id="root" width="320" height="240"
            background-color="black" />
        <region id="slides" width="320" height="240" />
    </layout>
    </head>

    <body>
    <par>
    <seq>
        <img src="photo1.jpg" region="slides" dur="5s" />
        <img src="photo2.jpg" region="slides" dur="15s" />
        <img src="photo3.jpg" region="slides" dur="10s" />
    </seq>

    <audio src="narration.rm" />
    </par>
    </body>
</smil>
```

Here's an explanation for each of the tags:

- **<smil></smil>** – These are the opening and closing container tags to all SMIL files, similar to the **<html></html>** tags in a Web page.

- **<head></head>** – These define the header for the file, which is primarily for setting basic layout parameters.

- **<layout></layout>** – The layout tag holds information about the layout.

- **<root-layout/>** – The **root-layout** parameter tag lays the foundation for the rest of the presentation. In this case, it tells the media player that the presentation is 320 pixels wide and 240 pixels tall. It also sets the main background color to black. Note the lack of a closing container for this tag.

- **<region/>** – The region tag, in this case, tells the media player where the slides should play within the **root-layout**. For your camping trip slideshow, the slides take up the whole **root-layout** area. You could make the region smaller, but not larger. Don't forget to give the **region** a name, signaled by the **id** parameter.

- **<body></body>** – The **body** tags, similar to the body tags in HTML, hold the data types to be displayed and the timing information that controls playback.

- **<par></par>** – The **par** tags tell the media player about a group of items that play in "parallel," or simultaneously. In this case, you have only one group of items, so you need only one set of **par** tags.

- **<seq></seq>** – The **seq** tags define the items that play in "sequence," or one after the other.

- **<img/>** – The three **img** tags in this example tell the media player which of your camping trip photos to play and in what order. The **src** parameter identifies the image. The **region** parameter places the photo in a region defined in the **<layout></layout>** container, in this case "slides," which is your only region. The **dur** tag (short for "duration") tells the player how long to show each photo. The first photo is displayed for 5 seconds, the second for 15 seconds, and the third for 10 seconds.

- **<audio/>** – The sample code puts the audio narration after the closing **seq** tag, and before the closing **par** tag. This tells the media player to play the audio file while the photos cycle through their order. The sample uses a file encoded in RealNetworks format for this example. But you could use a QuickTime streaming audio file as well.

Playing the SMIL Slideshow

Save the SMIL file with the extension **.smi**, as in **slideshow.smi**. (Some people like to use the extension **.smil**. Both **.smi** and **.smil** will work.) Upload the SMIL file to your RealNetworks Helix or QuickTime Streaming server, and place it in the same directory as your JPEG photos and audio narration file. Then load the URL to the SMIL file in your RealPlayer or QuickTime Player. The URL will look something like this:

rtsp://streaming.server.com/myslideshow/slideshow.smi

You can also put this URL into a metafile and put the metafile on your Web server. It will work just like a metafile to an audio or video file. An example SMIL presentation is shown in **Figure 11-1**.

Author's Tip

Metafiles are covered in detail in Chapter 8.

Figure 11-1
A simple SMIL slideshow. Clicking the names in the lower half of the presentation takes the user to specific points in the slideshow.

RealNetworks and Apple QuickTime Extensions

The SMIL language is governed by a standard similar to other standards, such as MPEG. However, RealNetworks and Apple Computer have added nonstandard *extensions* to SMIL. RealNetworks, in particular, has created a whole range of extra functionality for SMIL presentations. They also developed RealPix and RealText to extend the range of possibilities of streaming media presentations:

- *RealPix* – allows producers to add video-like effects to static images, such as wipes, fades, and crossfades.

- *RealText* – lets you add features including text crawls and closed captioning to presentations.

Author's Tip

Slideshows: A Powerful, Underused Tool

Slideshows are one of the most powerful and underused multimedia applications on the Internet. Say you have a video, but you're worried about the bandwidth capabilities of your audience. Consider taking some screenshots from the video and creating a SMIL slideshow, using the audio track from the video as the timeline. A number of JPEG graphics files paired with a low bit rate audio file take up much less bandwidth than a full-fledged video file. Now you can offer a slideshow that performs well on low-bandwidth connections, as well as a standard video for folks with more bandwidth. And you've found two uses for the same content.

Note that RealText, RealPix, and RealNetworks SMIL extensions work only in RealPlayer, not other media players.

QuickTime's SMIL extensions are not as elaborate as RealNetworks, although they allow some fine-tuning of QuickTime Player behavior. Both sets of extensions require some advanced knowledge of XML syntax.

Inside the Industry

Learning How to SMIL

The SMIL section in this chapter is meant as a brief introduction to the language. If you're interested in learning how to write SMIL applications, you should visit the RealNetworks or QuickTime Web sites and study the documentation in detail. And there are a few third-party software packages that can get you started. But in the case of SMIL, there's no substitute to getting your hands dirty with the code.

SMIL's Main Drawback

As said previously, the only media players that support SMIL are RealPlayer and QuickTime Player. Of course, that leaves out one of the heavyweights, Windows Media Player. If you're interested in producing a SMIL application, go back to your audience analysis in Chapter 3. Will a large share of your audience be using Windows Media Player? If so, you may need to rethink your SMIL plans.

Streaming High-Definition Video

The greatest advance in television technology for almost half a century occurred with the advent of *high-definition television* (HDTV) in the 1980s. Though adoption by broadcasters and producers has been relatively slow, more and more consumers are enjoying video with larger images and sharper pictures produced and broadcast in HDTV format.

Inevitably, streaming media developers jumped on the HDTV bandwagon, creating tools and technologies for taking advantage of high-definition video on computer displays. For example, the Windows Media Series 9 Encoder features codecs specifically designed for encoding high-definition video into Windows Media files.

High Definition and Streaming

Typical high-definition video differs from standard video in three main ways, insofar as streaming is concerned.

1. 16:9 aspect ratio (standard video has a 4:3 aspect ratio).

2. Much higher resolution, meaning a lot more information in each frame of video.

3. Multichannel or surround-sound audio (standard audio for video is mono or stereo).

The result is an extremely sharp image that's been compared to 35-millimeter film, the standard film size for movies and professional photography. The audio has more depth and detail as well.

Inside the Industry

High-def video comes in two resolutions, 720p and 1,080i, which refer to the number of lines of resolution in the image. High-def resolution is at least two-thirds greater than standard video, which means a sharper, more realistic image.

The "p" in "720p" refers to *progressive scan*, the method for displaying an image on a computer screen. Traditional television monitors use another method called *interlacing*.

For the streaming media specialist, working with high-def video poses a number of problems:

- *File size* – Because high-def video contains much more information than standard video, the sizes of source files and encoded files are much larger. A full-length movie can take up hundreds of gigabytes of storage.

- *Processing power* – Both encoding and playback of high-def files requires much more processing power than standard video. In fact, high-def pushes even the most advanced personal computer hardware, including processors, hard drives, and other peripherals, to its limits.

- *Bandwidth* – The bit rates for streaming high-def start at the 1-megabit range, which is near the limit of the fattest DSL lines. In fact, most material encoded into high-def today is either downloaded for playback from a hard drive or burned onto a DVD.

As you can see, the problems are similar to the ones you face working with standard video, just magnified.

ALERT

The book has used the term "streaming" in conjunction with HD video. But the reality is that most HD video is downloaded for playback, rather than streamed, because current bandwidths available to just about everyone other than major research institutions can't support HD streaming. Maybe in ten years or so...

Put Punch into Your Playback Computer
Playback computers for high-def require nearly the same power as encoding computers. Microsoft recommends the following configurations for playing Windows Media High Definition files without too many hiccups.

Minimum Configuration for 720p high-def video
- Windows XP
- 2.4-GHz processor or equivalent
- 384 MB of RAM
- 64 MB AGP4s video card
- DVD drive
- 1024 × 768 screen resolution
- 16-bit sound card
- Speakers

Optimum Configuration for 1080p with Dolby 5.1 surround sound
- Windows XP
- DirectX 9.0
- 3.0-GHz processor or equivalent
- 512 MB of RAM
- 128 MB AGP4x video card
- DVD drive
- 1920 × 1440 screen resolution
- 24-bit 96-kHz multichannel sound card
- 5.1 surround sound speaker system

The monitor is key to a good high-def experience. You can get good results with the latest flat-panel displays, provided you get a big one. You can also hook up your playback computer to flat-panel TVs that hang on the wall. Visit the Microsoft Web site for more information. Lastly, make sure your computer supports DXVA (DirectX Video Acceleration). This helps the decompression of your video for playback.

Building a High-Def Encoding Machine

An encoding computer for high-def needs much more power and storage than a standard encoding computer. The sheer amount of information in a high-definition AVI file would overwhelm most off-the-shelf boxes. Here are a few requirements:

- *Multiple, high-speed processors*: Windows Media Encoder, for example, can take advantage of dual-processor machines, encoding audio with two processors and video with four. Pick a machine with a pair of high-speed Pentium 4 or Athlon 3000 processors.

- *Multiple, high-speed SCSI hard drives and other high-performance hardware*: SCSI drives running at 15,000 rpm in a redundant array of independent disks (RAID) level 0 are about the only drives that can handle the work needed to store and access high-def files. You'll need a minimum of 300 gigabytes of storage for one full-length movie. It's also a good idea to get a dual PCI bus motherboard. This allows you to separate the capture card from the SCSI card, reducing the chances for dropped frames. Finally, install a multichannel audio card.

- *Microsoft Windows XP Professional x64*: The newest Microsoft operating system for professionals has multi-threading technology that maximizes the use of dual processor boxes. While you're at it, upgrade to the latest service pack and the most recent version of DirectX, Microsoft's system for managing graphics of all types.

Capturing for WMHD

Although a discussion of high-definition video production is outside the scope of this book, the basic steps for capturing and encoding are similar to standard video.

You can capture video from a high-def tape or a high-def camera using specialized capture cards that create AVI files. If you already have high-def computer files, you need to convert them to AVIs using the features of a high-def nonlinear editing system. High-def MPEG2 files can also be encoded using a special plug-in for Windows Media Player installed on the encoding computer.

When capturing high-def video, Microsoft recommends keeping these practices in mind:

- Capture content at the original frame rate, especially if it's from a motion picture shot on film. Movies are shot at 24 frames per second.
- Capture to a *YUY2* format to maintain good color information.
- Capture at the video's original pixel size.
- If you capture audio separately, synchronize the audio with the video in a high-def video editing suite.

Once you've captured your video, use a high-quality high-def editing suite to add effects, titles and other enhancements, and render the files to an AVI file.

Encoding for WMHD

Encoding for high-def video is similar to standard video. The main difference is distribution. Although high-def can be streamed, most encoded high-def files are either downloaded for playback on a hard drive or burned onto a DVD. Streaming HD is about ten years behind standard video streaming, mostly due to limited bandwidth.

Because encoded high-def files are rarely streamed, you'll find yourself using *variable bit rate* (VBR) encoding. VBR codecs maintain quality of the video image no matter the type of shot or scene, whether it's high action or talking heads. VBR can be used to encode files meant for playback from a hard drive or other storage device because these devices don't have the bandwidth constraints of streaming media.

If you have enough bandwidth to stream high-def video, use constant bit rate codecs, which you'll access when you select streaming as your distribution method in the encoder.

If you choose to customize an encoding session for high-def video, keep these principles in mind:

- Preserve the aspect ratio of the source video, usually 16:9.
- Higher bit rates mean better image and sound quality.

- Match the encoded frame rate to the frame rate of the source video.

- Keep your target playback device in mind. Some high-def displays are interlaced, while others are progressive. Be sure to encode your file with the proper parameters for your target display.

- Maintain the pixel aspect ratio if your source has non-square pixels.

- Choose a key frame rate that suits the content. If your content is talking heads, fewer key frames mean a smaller file size without sacrificing quality. An action movie needs more key frames, because the image is constantly changing.

ALERT

!

Before encoding the entire video file, encode a minute's worth and play it back to check quality. Encoding high-def video is in its infancy, so don't be surprised if you have to make further adjustments and do some troubleshooting before encoding the whole file.

Streaming on Portable Devices

Two related communications technologies promise a revolution comparable to the emergence of the Internet in the early 1990s. Multifunctional cellular telephones and the growing capabilities of wireless communications are combining to form a mobile communications network that puts a planet-full of information at your fingertips, whether you're at a mall, on the freeway, or on top of Mount Everest.

Streaming video on wireless networks is taking the first baby steps toward reality, at least in the United States, where wireless technology and deployment is several years behind the rest of the world. Even so, a revolution is happening all around. Just look at picture phones. It's fun to send a picture of your daughter playing softball on a muddy field to grandma's cell phone 500 miles away.

Wireless streaming isn't limited to the cellular network. People are using 802.11b networks at their local coffee shop with laptops and *personal digital assistants*, or *PDAs*, such as Pocket PCs. But the real buzz is about streaming to cell phones.

The key to the success of streaming media over the cell-phone network is the deployment of *3G wireless networks*, which feature as much as 2 megabytes per second of bandwidth when the viewer is standing still. (The amount of available bandwidth falls as the viewer moves, such as walking or driving.) Japan and other Asian countries, as well as Europe, have enjoyed 3G for years. American companies are just now deploying 3G networks.

Differences between Mobile Streaming and Wired Streaming

The basic client/server model of streaming media as described in this book applies to mobile streaming. Source files are encoded, placed on a server, and made available through the wireless telephone network. But mobile streaming faces some important challenges.

- *Inconsistent hardware* – Streaming media professionals can safely assume that the hardware player streaming media over a wired connection or even certain kinds of wireless connections, such as 802.11b, are using an IBM-compatible personal computer or an Apple Computer product.

Wireless phones, however, are built with proprietary technologies often incompatible with one another. Mobile devices vary widely in terms of processor power, memory, operating system, protocol support, client software, screen size, and color depth. Furthermore, new devices are introduced every day, it seems, and the new features in new phones are sometimes incompatible with similar features in older cousins.

- *Video formats* – The only common video format supported by all 3G phones is MPEG-4. Support for MPEG-4 is mandated by the *3rd Generation Partnership Project* (3GPP), the leading industry standards body for 3G devices and networks. In addition to designating MPEG-4 as the standard video format, the 3G industry has set media format standards regarding audio, graphics, and MIDI support.
- *Mobility* – The cell phone's greatest strength, its mobility, is the major technological drawback from a streaming perspective. Whereas the bandwidth for a wired connection can remain fairly consistent over time, the amount of bandwidth on a mobile network can change dramatically from one city block to the next.

Two other factors affect bandwidth:

1. The number of devices operating simultaneously within a cell.
2. The speed at which the device is traveling through the cell. (You have less bandwidth when talking while driving than talking while walking.)

Lastly, high-bandwidth coverage remains spotty within the emerging 3G networks, and seamless roaming between 3G networks is problematic.

Solutions for Mobile Streaming

Several mobile streaming media companies are working on the problems. Packet Video has focused on porting their software client to a wide selection of handsets and operating systems. Vidiator Technology is enabling its server to *transcode* and *transform* streams to match the capabilities of the target device. Transcoding involves a format change, such as delivering a RealVideo file as a 3GPP-compliant MPEG-4 file. Transforming involves changing display characteristics of a file such as dimensions, aspect ratio, pixel density and color depth.

The big streaming media vendors are in the thick of mobile streaming. RealNetworks has developed media player, encoding and serving tools specifically designed for mobile streaming. Microsoft has built Windows Media Player 10 Mobile, specially designed for cell phones that run Microsoft Windows Mobile 2003 SE operating system.

Digital Rights Management

One of the most heated debates of the last years of the dot-com boom concerned file sharing. Music lovers, particularly college students, found they could convert music files on CDs to MP3 format and send them to friends over networks or burn custom CDs. Thus began the controversy over copyright protections for digital media. Although file-sharing continues, copyright protection and media distribution technologies have advanced significantly, allowing companies and individuals to enjoy income from their work while distributing their creations to fans over the Internet and recently over cellular telephone networks.

The most sophisticated protection technologies come under the heading of *digital rights management* or *DRM*. In simplest terms, the 1s and 0s of a digital media file, whether audio or video, are scrambled or *encrypted* in the encoding process. The file (live or on-demand) is said to be *protected*. To hear or see the file, the user must purchase a license, often via a Web site with a credit card. Media players apply the license key to the encoded file and unscramble the data.

DRM can be applied to a variety of business scenarios:

- Individual songs
- Sets of songs or whole albums
- Pay-per-view movies or TV programs
- Movie rentals (license limited by time or number of playbacks)
- Subscriptions (license applied to range of services for limited periods of time)

A prerequisite for a successful application of DRM is a business model. How do you want to limit access? For example, do you want to allow a limited number of playbacks for promotional purposes before requiring a fee for unlimited use? What value do you want to place on the exclusivity of your encrypted content? In other words, can a user get the same content for free or a lower price somewhere else? (See the following section for more on business models.)

How DRM Works

DRM starts with one or more *rights* sold to a media user allowing him or her to play an encrypted file. The rights are available only to that user on that device. If an encoded file is copied to another device, it can't be played unless another license is acquired.

From a technological point of view, it's relatively easy to apply a set of rules to a file and match a right to the file allowing playback. The hard part is managing those rights to thousands, perhaps millions of individual files or sets of files. The rights themselves can be very complex. Variables include time, number of plays, fee or no fee, artist, publisher, country, anything that a company or individual (or lawyer) can come up with. Different rights could be applied to the same content at different times. And you may even need to revoke all licenses if the copyright comes into dispute or you detect tampering. In short, DRM rules can be designed to meet just about every need.

Here's one scenario from the user's perspective:

1. User visits a Web site and registers.
2. User downloads a protected music file.
3. The license allows the user to play the file three times.
4. At the fourth playback attempt, the user is prompted to revisit the Web site and purchase a license to play the file again.
5. The user purchases the license with a credit card.
6. At the next playback attempt, the file plays normally.

Most of the background stuff is invisible to the user. At each playback attempt, the media player checks whether the user has the correct rights, first by looking on the hard drive, then by checking a database at a remote computer with license information. The database may be run by a third-party license provider. Throughout the process, the player reacts accordingly to the rules you have written.

Figure 11-2 shows a simplified DRM process.

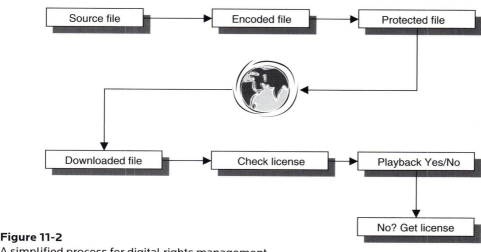

Figure 11-2
A simplified process for digital rights management.

Streaming Business Opportunities and Models

The end of the 1990s Internet bubble left a single question still unanswered: Can anyone make money with these new networking technologies? No one in the streaming arena has come up with a slam-dunk formula for a sustainable business model. But that doesn't mean the potential for profit went away with the last bull market of the twentieth century. In fact, marketers have identified an entirely new market segment called *streamies*, which is growing as fast as cable and DSL connectivity providers can hook them up. Marketers have invented a term for the person who uses online audio or video.

The streamie has important demographic characteristics that make them attractive marketing targets. In 2005, according to Arbitron, 61% of people who watched video online were men, 39% were women. 45% of streaming users are between the ages of 18 and 44, a prime age for spending. Businesses large and small are now positioning themselves to benefit from the demands of streamies.

The Streaming Media Consumer

Arbitron publishes studies that try to nail down the streamie, the individual who listens to or watches some form of streaming media. In 2003, the company came up with these characteristics:

- More likely male than female
- Generally 25–45 years old
- Has a full-time job
- Has a household income of around $50,000
- Largely Caucasian
- Better than 50/50 chance of having broadband at home
- Spent $861 online in the past 12 months

The average weekly streamie spends almost two and a half hours a day online. In contrast, only 7% of streamies thumbed through a newspaper in the previous week.

Programming Preferred by Streamies

Another study by the Cable and Telecommunications Association for Marketing found that streamies are interested in particular forms of programming. More than a third of streamies are touring travel destinations or listening to Internet radio, while 26% watch online news clips. See **Figure 11-3** for more of their results.

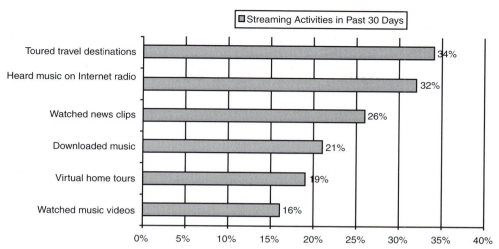

Figure 11-3
Results of a 2002 streaming media programming study by the Cable and Telecommunications Association for Marketing. (Source: CTAM.)

Four Potential Business Models

You now have a picture of the average streaming-media consumer and their viewing habits. What are some ways of serving that market and making a profit? Here are four basic business models to spark your thinking.

Content Creation

Streamies won't go online if there's nothing to watch or hear. They're looking for compelling programming. Most streaming media content these days is repurposed from over-the-air or cable broadcasts. In the case of music, they are repurposed music tracks that would have been heard exclusively on CDs or radio stations a few years ago.

However, Arbitron advises streaming-media producers to develop new programs to spur growth and create "buzz" that will encourage more visitors to play streams. Think of cable television in the late 1970s and early 1980s, when all-movie channels such as Showtime and HBO attracted more viewers to cable TV. In 1980, cable TV entrepreneur Ted Turner created CNN, the world's first 24-hour television news channel, something completely new in television news broadcasting. CNN sparked a consumer rush to cable TV and turned it into the media force known today. It's impossible to say whether a new streaming program will build a new "CNN effect." But no such program has appeared on the horizon so far.

Content Delivery

If someone did create a wildly popular streaming media program, someone would have to host and deliver those streams. As of today, most Web-hosting companies offer some streaming-media hosting as part of a larger package. The streaming services add incremental revenue. But a few businesses make streaming-media delivery a core service. Real Broadcast Network, for example, is a division of RealNetworks. RBN's sole purpose is streaming-media delivery. Other businesses focus exclusively on streaming-media delivery, whether it's simple hosting of files or soup-to-nuts production of a live streaming-media event. They serve both Internet and intranet audiences as streaming contractors. As stream volume increases and technical demands grow, more streaming specialists are likely to emerge.

Advertising

Contrary to popular belief, the advertising model on the Internet is not dead. The question has become: What kind of online advertising works? The banner ad, the first widespread form of Web site advertising, is in decline (though it has shown some recent life again). According to Arbitron, the proportion of online users who have clicked on a banner ad has fallen steadily since the summer of 2000. The days of other ad forms may also be limited. Arbitron says 65% of Internet users find pop-up ads annoying. One quarter of Web users have installed a program to block pop-ups.

In contrast, Arbitron says only 3% of people online object to commercials during an audio or video stream. Only 2% dislike streaming ads played before an on-demand stream. Why the difference? Perhaps the audience is accustomed to these kinds of interruptions, since it sees/hears them all the time on cable and over-the-air broadcasts. Whatever the reason, these figures suggest that ads on streams won't alienate streamies the way other ad forms do. Arbitron recommends streaming producers should consider advertising as a viable revenue model. And it says advertisers, especially those who want to reach techno-savvy, upscale audiences take streaming seriously as a communications channel.

Potential Value of the Internet Audio Audience
If sold as a single radio network today
($ Million/Year)

	Units per hour									
CPM	**1**	**2**	**3**	**4**	**5**	**6**	**7**	**8**	**9**	**10**
$1.00	$4	$9	$13	$17	$22	$26	$30	$34	$39	$43
$1.50	$6	$13	$19	$26	$32	$39	$45	$52	$58	$65
$2.00	$9	$17	$26	$34	$43	$52	$60	$69	$77	$86
$2.50	$11	$22	$32	$43	$54	$65	$75	$86	$97	$108
$3.00	$13	$26	$39	$52	$65	$77	$90	$103	$116	$126
$3.50	$15	$30	$45	$60	$75	$90	$105	$120	$136	$151
$4.00	$17	$34	$52	$69	$86	$103	$120	$138	$155	$172
$4.50	$19	$39	$58	$77	$97	$116	$136	$155	$174	$194
$5.00	$22	$43	$65	$86	$108	$129	$151	$172	$194	$215

How to read: "CPM" indicates the cost of buying 1000 impressions. "Units per hour" means the number of commercials aired per hour. Select a CPM and the number of commercials per hour to determine the annual value of the Internet audio broadcast market. Example: With current Internet audio broadcast audience levels, a $5.00 CPM with five commercials per hour would yield a $108 million annual Internet audio broadcast ad market.

Figure 11-4
Potential cost per thousand (CPM) value of the Internet audience sold as a single audience. (Source: Arbitron/Edison Media Research, 2003.)

Subscription

The subscription model for Internet content is one of the most controversial. It's no surprise that Internet audiences prefer free access to content. Arbitron says audiences prefer ad-supported content over content they have to pay for directly. That signals an opportunity to advertisers, if they can find the right delivery model. But another study has found that pay-for-play may have a future. The Cable and Telecommunications Association for Marketing found in 2002:

- 27% of streamies somewhat or very likely to pay for full-length movies
- 23% somewhat or very likely to pay for streamed music
- 20% somewhat or very likely to pay for live sports events

Here's an important clue to understanding the potential. CTAM found that around a quarter to a third of people open to buying a streaming subscription buy premium cable services. They're used to paying extra for special content. Put another way, the general outline of the basic/premium cable channel model may work on the Internet.

Exclusivity is the key. Again, cable provides the model. For a subscriber to sign on, he or she must see the programming as unique, compelling, and unavailable anywhere else. If the programming is available on another "channel" for free or at lower cost, the viewer will abandon the subscription.

Success Measurement

Every serious business model requires a method for measuring return on investment. Media owners typically measure success of properties, such as radio shows and TV sitcoms, with ratings. Streaming media also requires measurement of stream quality and the user experience. Online technology provides the most detailed types of data for gauging by storing information from each click in a log that can be analyzed in near real-time.

Log Analysis

Every streaming media server has a logging feature. The logs are text files that store information about the stream, such as the IP address of the computer that viewed the stream, the codec for the stream, and the version of the media player. The text files can often be enormous, especially on a busy site. Here's a single entry from a Windows Media Server 4.1 stream log:

```
192.168.0.2 2001-03-05 00:29:09 carl.elltel.net mms://134.121.239.122/stream.wma 0
4292073 1 200 {2801dd60-63ce-11d3-86b7-ce1b99aa2d9d} 6.4.7.1112 en-US - -
MPLAYER2.EXE 6.4.7.1112 Windows_98 4.10.0.1998 Pentium 0 494 4 http TCP
Windows_Media_Audio_V2 - - 0 0 0 0 0 0 0 0 0 0 0 0 0 100 134.121.239.122
videoserver2.urel.wsu.edu 15 0
```

Here's what some of the fields mean:

- *192.168.0.2* – The IP address of the requesting media player.
- *2001-03-05 00:29:09* – The date and time of the request.
- *mms://192.168.0.1/stream.wma* – The URL of the requested stream.
- *6.4.7.1112* – The version of the media player.
- *Windows_Media_Audio_V2* – The version of the audio codec.

Streaming producers can parse these logs looking for patterns or trends in streaming media usage. For example, does the traffic vary or peak during certain times of the day? Is the use of older media players falling over time? Which streams are more popular than others? Some of the fields record data that network administrators can use to diagnose problems or optimize the network for better streaming performance.

If you've done analysis of Web server logs, you'll notice some similarities. Streaming-server log formats are based on the standard Web-server log format. But there's no standard streaming-log format. In fact, at least with RealNetworks' server logs, you can set the types of data you want to record on top of a basic set of data fields. And streaming logs store data that Web-server logs do not, such as the amount of time a media player played a streaming file.

You have two choices if you want to analyze your streaming-server logs. You can build your own tools, parsing logs with scripts written in the Perl language, for example. Your homegrown tool could store the data in a database for more flexible types of analysis. And you could build a Web page interface to allow other folks to monitor traffic.

Your other choice is a third-party tool, such as WebTrends or the XStream Logger plug-in from SyncCast.

Audience Measurement

Log files provide detailed information about the stream. But logs can't tell you anything about the person playing the stream. You could infer preferences. For example, if you see the same IP address requesting the same set of football video highlights week after week, you could say the person likes to watch a lot of football. But this kind of inference is prone to all kinds of errors. How do you know it's the same person every week?

Streaming producers should pair log analysis with standard types of market analysis, such as telephone surveys and focus groups. Compare the results of your marketing studies against your log files. Do the types of files stored in your server logs match the preferences expressed by individuals in your surveys? Do focus groups say they watch movie trailers all the way through, but your logs show people stop the stream after a few seconds? An integrated approach using a variety of tools is likely to provide the most accurate answers.

Stream Quality Measurement

Streaming server logs can also give you some insight into the quality of the user experience and the ability of your network to deliver the streams in a reliable way. Networking gurus and programmers can design software tools that make use of the error reporting in the Real-Time Protocol (RTP), assuming the client is using RTSP to request the stream. These tools are very complex to build and maintain.

Many streaming producers who want to monitor quality over the long term make use of content monitoring services, such as Keynote. These companies use automated tools that contact your streaming server on a regular basis from several locations and report reliability statistics. You can use these to find bottlenecks in your network, for example.

Author's Tip

Use Your Own Products
All this gobbledegook about log analysis and focus groups and automated monitoring isn't going to make a whit of difference if you don't click your own streams once in a while. It's stunning how streaming producers forget to click links on their own Web pages. And when they do, and something is broken, they act surprised. First rule of quality assurance: Use your own products! At least pretend to be an average user to get a feel for what their streaming life is like.

Calculating a Return on Investment

Your return on your streaming media investment depends on how you use it and its purpose. It's extremely important to see streaming media as one facet of a complete communications strategy. It's a new tool, but it shouldn't be the only tool in the toolbox. At this stage of the game, streaming media provides incremental benefits to people trying to deliver a message to certain audiences. But streaming media won't save a flawed strategy—it certainly won't save a broken business model.

Having said that, streaming media can provide a tangible return almost immediately. Take the example of employee training, one of the fastest growing applications of streaming. In a study conducted in 2001, *Streaming Media* magazine found several cases where streaming saved a significant amount of money in training costs.

- A network equipment maker reduced training costs by a factor of seven. The company spends $10 million on streaming to send an average of 8.5 hours of content annually to its 40,000 employees, saving money it would have spent flying those employees to training venues, conferences, and so on.

- A semiconductor manufacturer went from spending $500,000 per year for on-site training of its 500 new employees and distributors to $100,000 for streamed training.

- A major oil company keeps up with its corporate compliance requirements through streaming. The company reaches 31,000 employees at 8,300 gas stations with one stream. Previously, it had to ship some 350,000 videotapes around the country.

According to the report, the same principles that apply to training apply to corporate communications. The content in this area is for employees, business partners and customers, and includes such events as "the boss talking to the troops," human resources policy announcements, and financial disclosures.

A detailed method for figuring out ROI is beyond the scope of this book. But check out **Figure 11-5** for some ideas on figuring out whether you're getting something for your streaming-media money.

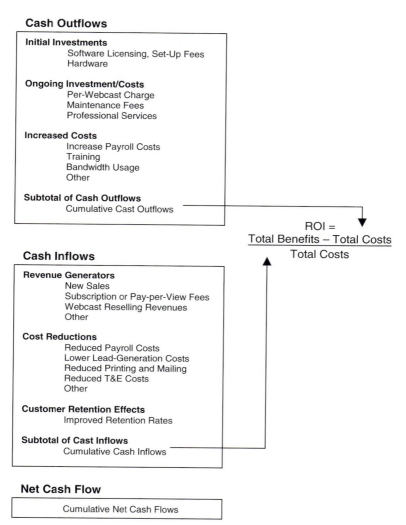

Cash Outflows

Initial Investments
      Software Licensing, Set-Up Fees
      Hardware

Ongoing Investment/Costs
      Per-Webcast Charge
      Maintenance Fees
      Professional Services

Increased Costs
      Increase Payroll Costs
      Training
      Bandwidth Usage
      Other

Subtotal of Cash Outflows
      Cumulative Cast Outflows

$$ROI = \frac{Total\ Benefits - Total\ Costs}{Total\ Costs}$$

Cash Inflows

Revenue Generators
      New Sales
      Subscription or Pay-per-View Fees
      Webcast Reselling Revenues
      Other

Cost Reductions
      Reduced Payroll Costs
      Lower Lead-Generation Costs
      Reduced Printing and Mailing
      Reduced T&E Costs
      Other

Customer Retention Effects
      Improved Retention Rates

Subtotal of Cast Inflows
      Cumulative Cash Inflows

Net Cash Flow

Cumulative Net Cash Flows

Figure 11-5
Elements for determining ROI for streaming media investments. (Source: Yankee Group, 2002.)

Conclusion

Streaming media offers highly flexible tools for creating interactive presentations around dynamic audio and video. The technology is steadily moving into the still-murky territory of high-definition television and wireless communications. But the potential, especially in wireless, for new types of streaming content and applications is enormous. The new channels of distribution call for more vigilance in the fields of copyright protections, which digital rights management attempts to provide. In the long run, streaming as a business has great potential as new business models evolve to meet the challenges of the future.

APPENDIX A

Case Studies

The following case studies illustrate how streaming media was used to solve communications problems in governments, not-for-profit organizations, and enterprises. The case studies were supplied by the organizations cited.

Case studies are provided in the following sectors:

- Government
- Enterprise
- Media and Entertainment
- Broadcasting
- Education

Government

U.S. Nuclear Regulatory Commission

The U.S. Nuclear Regulatory Commission set a goal of improving public access to its public meetings. NRC planned two to three video webcasts per month to more than 500 viewers. The main challenges were security and engineering redundancy to ensure availability. The commissioners also wanted the webcasts archived for on-demand viewing at a later time.

The NRC contracted with Online Video Service, a private streaming-media hosting service, to webcast the meetings in both the Windows Media and RealNetworks formats. Specific tasks included:

- Setup and installation of two proprietary encoding stations
- Making sure security and redundancy met federal compliance standards
- Quality assurance tests the day before each scheduled event

- Webcast management during events to ensure continuous, uninterrupted service
- Host archived video for 24 × 7 access nationwide

Since May 2004, the NRC has webcast more than 50 NRC public meetings and has renewed its contract with Online Video Service.

For more information, visit Online Video Service, http://www.onlinevideoservice.com.

Federal Deposit Insurance Corporation

The Federal Deposit Insurance Corporation's Outreach Program group wanted to educate the banking industry and the public on the benefits of deposit insurance. Because of the large and dispersed audience, the FDIC could not easily reach all interested parties. FDIC developed an integrated marketing approach using print materials and webcasting to disseminate information on deposit insurance. Under a 4-year contract with FDIC, Vodium, a streaming-media service company, delivered two Web-based on-demand training modules with streaming video. In addition, DVDs were made and are available in English with closed captioning and Spanish-language subtitles.

Financial institutions and consumers may view FDIC's Video on Deposit Insurance Coverage on the FDIC's Web page. Incorporating webcasting as part of its outreach initiatives has enabled FDIC to reach a widely dispersed audience and effectively communicate the benefits of deposit insurance. The online seminar serves as a knowledge repository, allowing users to search specific areas of the presentation, bookmark areas of interest and e-mail the presentation link to others.

For more information, visit http://www.vodium.com/.

Enterprise

Eastman Chemical Company

Eastman Chemical Company, the world's largest producer of plastics for packaging, began using streaming media in 1999. With a workforce of 12,000 employees, Eastman needed to migrate from an internally developed solution to one capable of supporting large-scale webcasts—including webcasts accessed by over half of its employees simultaneously—while meeting tight timelines and budgets.

Eastman selected products created by Accordent, a Los Angeles-based streaming-media presentation software company, to multicast high-bandwidth, medium-bandwidth, and audio-only rich media presentations to its employees across the world. Using Accordent's PresenterPRO Enterprise Edition, all presentation authoring, including the synchronization of PowerPoint slides, occurred during the live presentations, significantly reducing the workload on the streaming-media group staff and turnaround time from "live" to "on-demand" accessibility. On average, up to 6,000 employees across the world watch the live weekly webcasts with even more views once the presentations are archived for later viewing. George Baker, manager of the streaming-media group at Eastman, is happy with the product. "The Accordent Solution just worked from day one," he said.

For more information, visit http://www.accordent.com/.

General Motors

General Motors recognized the potential of streaming video early on, and the company wanted a way to take advantage of consumers' increasing use of the Internet to shop for automobiles and trucks. The company's global communications group sought out an online video solution that would be cost-effective on a large scale, and viable as a public relations and marketing tool. In 2003, GM chose The FeedRoom as its streaming-media vendor.

With The FeedRoom providing the live and on-demand streaming-media infrastructure, General Motors directs specialized video content to its 7,600 North American dealers. The FeedRoom helps the company manage and leverage an archive of more than 300 video clips, encoding them for online delivery. In 2005, The FeedRoom managed GM's webcast of its first live online product release of two new models. The FeedRoom also delivered excerpts from a private concert by the popular group, the Black Eyed Peas.

For more information, visit http://www.thefeedroom.com/.

Media and Entertainment

American Museum of the Moving Image

In July 2004, the American Museum of the Moving Image, based in Astoria, New York, launched *The Living Room Candidate*, an innovative online exhibition presenting more than 250 television commercials from every presidential campaign year since 1952. Anticipating its groundbreaking exhibition would attract a large audience to its Web site, the museum needed a solution to handle the traffic boost and reliably deliver all the streaming video clips within a limited budget.

The museum chose Mirror Image's Video On-Demand solution. Since its launch, Mirror Image has delivered more than 750,000 streams to over 100,000 unique visitors. By leveraging a global network of video delivery and storage, Mirror Image guaranteed the museum the capacity and high availability required to present its exhibit. In addition, the solution has saved the museum more than $40,000 in annual capital expenditures, and increased the length of time visitors stay on the site. An estimated 20% stay longer than 15 minutes.

For more information, visit http://www.mirror-image.com/.

IFILM

IFILM, a popular video entertainment Web site with 20 million visitors monthly, wanted to offer streaming-media versions of popular Super Bowl television commercials. A streaming-media hosting company would need the capability to deliver at least 8.5 million streams within 72 hours after the game. It approached LimeLight Networks, a content delivery network, to provide a highly scaleable delivery network to handle the rapid surge in viewers.

Limelight was able to serve a large volume of heavy, rich content quickly, securely and without compromising quality. Limelight provided end-to-end IP delivery solutions to IFILM, including content delivery and Tier-1 bandwidth services. The company helped its client move all its video quickly and reliably across the Internet, reducing the cost and complexity of its content delivery, while ensuring unmatched performance for its end users.

For more information, visit http://www.limelightnetworks.com/.

Broadcasting

NBC

With exclusive U.S. rights to broadcast television coverage of the 2004 Olympics, NBC decided to leverage broadband adoption to deliver real-time, interactive, and media-rich coverage of the Olympics. The goal was to make the site an interactive and definitive resource of the Athens Games for an anticipated audience of 20 million site visitors. NBC's Olympics site had the potential to become the most visited site for a one-time event. If they realized the traffic numbers they anticipated, the site would also generate significant revenues from advertisers.

NBC worked with a content distribution network, Akamai, which supported all content delivery for NBC's Olympics coverage—including streaming and dynamic applications such as polling, live event scoring, and Web e-mail that site visitors sent to friends or commentators. The CDN also streamed all pre-Games highlights, which included exclusive footage of the U.S. Olympic Team Trials, great moments from the 1996 Atlanta and 2000 Sydney Games, and interviews with more than 40 top U.S. Olympians. As predicted, the www.nbcolympic. com site beat all previous records, registering an unprecedented number of visitors and a traffic peak of 1.6 gigabits per second. NBC also sold twice as many ads as it had sold for the 2002 Olympics.

For more information, visit http://www.akamai.com/.

Education

University of Northern Iowa

The University of Northern Iowa in Cedar Falls has placed streaming-media technologies at the center of its mission since 1997. Faculty members recognized growing concerns that teacher education programs were not preparing the teachers of the 21st century to use the latest networking technologies, including online audio and video. The U.S. Department of Education awarded UNI a $2.4 million grant to address the issue, and the university invested the money into an Internet-based library of streaming-media case studies. The library disseminates best practices in technology education to a global audience.

To accomplish its goal of building the library, the school added streaming media solutions from RealNetworks to its already existing infrastructure, which included a one-gigabit backbone, one gigabit to each building on campus, and 100-Mbps bandwidth to each desktop. The technology can deliver streams in several formats, including RealAudio, RealVideo, QuickTime, MP3, MPEG-1, MPEG-2, and Flash. Developers used Synchronized Multimedia Integration Language (SMIL) to create dynamic presentations, and SMIL allows IT managers to manage bandwidth. The university believes streaming technology has allowed it to communicate better with students in teacher education programs as well as practicing teachers and alumni.

For more information, visit RealNetworks' case studies page: http://www.realnetworks.com/ industries/resources/casestudies/index.html.

Dearborn Public Schools

Dearborn Public Schools in Dearborn, Michigan, the home of Ford Motor Company, believes in streaming media as a way to communicate to the community as well as prepare children for the new economy. The district, which is the seventh largest in Michigan, serves 17,500 students who attend 19 elementary schools, six middle and intermediate schools, and three high schools. In 2002, voters approved a $150 million bond issue, with $32 million going towards district-wide upgrades to technology.

Some of that investment appears on the district's home page, *http://www.dearbornschools. org/,* in the form of streaming videos delivered in Macromedia Flash. The videos change frequently, which encourages visitors to return for the latest news and information about school activities. Videos include a monthly district report and an explanation of the impact of the federal "No Child Left Behind" law. Students in a television production class at Dearborn High School produce feature length movies, and trailers for those movies stream on the district Web site. A future project will feature videos of teachers discussing how these technology improvements are improving instruction.

For more information, visit Macromedia's showcase, http://www.macromedia.com/cfusion/ showcase/.

Conclusion

Every day, streaming media solves a wide variety of audio and video distribution and communications problems. Governments, media and entertainment companies, broadcasters, and educational institutions reach hundreds of thousands of Internet users with original and repurposed audio and video content that draws and keeps more people to their Web properties. On-demand archives and live webcasts increase the value of their audio and video properties and ensure a continuing return on these investments in the future.

APPENDIX B

Resources

The following Web sites contain information and software related to streaming media.

Leading Streaming Media Manufacturers

- RealNetworks – *http://www.realnetworks.com/*
- Microsoft – *http://www.microsoft.com/windows/windowsmedia/*
- Apple Computer – *http://www.apple.com/quicktime/*
- Macromedia – *http://www.macromedia.com/*

Media Player Download Pages

- RealNetworks – *http://www.realnetworks.com/info/freeplayer/*
- Microsoft – *http://www.microsoft.com/windows/windowsmedia/player/download*
- Apple Computer – *http://www.apple.com/quicktime/download/*
- Macromedia – *http://www.macromedia.com/downloads/*

Free Encoder ("Producer") Download Pages

- RealNetworks – *http://www.realnetworks.com/products/producer/basic.html*
- Microsoft – *http://www.microsoft.com/windows/windowsmedia/9series/encoder/default.mspx*
- Apple Computer – No free encoder here. Upgrade the player to a player/encoder.
- Macromedia – No free version. But a 30-day trial version is available. *http://www.macromedia.com/software/flash/*

Open Source Software and Information

- Apache: *http://www.apache.org/*
- Darwin Streaming Server – *http://developer.apple.com/darwin/projects/streaming/*
- ICEcast – *http://www.icecast.org/*
- Linux – *http://www.linux.org/*
- Open Source Initiative – *http://www.opensource.org/*
- SHOUTcast – *http://www.shoutcast.com/*

MPEG Resources

- MPEG.org – *http://www.mpeg.org/*
- MP3 – *http://www.mpeg.org/MPEG/mp3.html*
- MPEG-4 Industry Forum (M4IF) – *http://www.m4if.org/*

Places to Buy Audio and Video Recording Equipment

- Broadcast Supply Worldwide (audio) – *http://www.bswusa.com/*
- The Broadcast Store (video) – *http://www.bcs.tv/*
- Online auction sites, such as eBay or Yahoo! Auctions
- A local electronics store, such as Radio Shack or BestBuy, for small items you need immediately

Publications

- *Streaming Media Magazine*: *http://www.streamingmedia.com/magazine*
- *Streaming Media Bible*: *http://www.streamingmediabible.com/*
- *Hands-On Guide to Webcasting*: *http://books.elsevier.com/us/focalbooks/us/sub-index.asp?isbn=0240807545*
- *Hands-On Guide to Windows Media*: *http://books.elsevier.com/us/focalbooks/us/subindex.asp?isbn=0240807596*

Other Web Sites

- American Federation of Television and Radio Artists (AFTRA) – *http://www.aftra.com/*
- Arbitron/Edison Media Research – *http://www.arbitron.com/*
- Synchronized Multimedia Integration Language (SMIL) – *http://www.w3.org/AudioVideo/*
- Sorensen Media – *http://www.sorenson.com/*

Glossary

2-pass encoding: A process by which the encoder analyzes the entire audio or video source file before encoding a streaming file.

3G wireless network: Third-generation wireless network with high-bandwidth data transmission capabilities.

3rd Generation Partnership Project (3GPP): A standards body for 3G wireless technology.

3-point lighting: The standard method of lighting a video subject, using a key light, a fill light, and a back light.

ActiveX: A Microsoft technology for developing Web browser plug-ins.

Advanced Audio Coding (AAC): The default audio codec for QuickTime 7.

Analog: Describes data flowing in a continuously variable manner, as opposed to digital data, which is a series of discrete measurements.

Artifacts: Lines, distortion, snow or other unwanted data in an audio or video file usually introduced by poor-quality equipment or technique.

Aspect ratio: The ratio of width to height of a video frame. Common ratios are 4:3 and 16:9.

ASP: Active Server Page.

ASX: The Microsoft Windows Media Services metafile file type.

Authentication: The process by which a computer verifies who you say you are.

Authorization: The process by which you are given the right to view content based on your identity.

AVI (Audio Video Interleaved): A standard file format for personal computers that can contain uncompressed or compressed video.

Back light: A light placed behind a subject to separate it from the background.

Baffle: A piece of foam rubber placed on a flat surface to muffle sound.

Bandwidth: The maximum amount of concurrent data that can be transmitted reliably over a network.

Batch encoding: Encoding numerous source audio or video files in one session using a script.

Bit: A single unit of data.

Bit rate: A measure of the flow rate of data over a computer network, measured in bits per second (bps).

Bounce board: A large flat panel, painted white, that reflects light to fill in shadows.

Brightness: The luminosity of a video signal.

Broadband: Usually refers to DSL and/or cable residential and small-business Internet connections, though it may sometimes refer to higher data rates available on faster connections.

Browser: A software application that displays text, graphics, and some multimedia files downloaded from World Wide Web servers.

Buffer: A portion of RAM reserved for storing streaming data before rendering by a media player.

Byte: A unit of data comprised of eight bits.

Cable: 1. An insulated length of wiring connecting two hardware devices. 2. An Internet connection through a cable television operator.

Capturing: The process of recording or transferring audio and/or video information from a recording device, such as a camera, to a computer hard drive.

Capture card: A specialized computer component for capturing audio or video signals for storage on a hard disc.

CD: Compact disc.

CD-ROM: Compact disc, read-only memory.

ClassID: A string of letters and numbers that uniquely identifies an ActiveX object.

Client: Hardware or software primarily used for receiving and rendering information sent by a server.

Client/Server: A network architecture in which one computer performs a number of dedicated tasks that serve the needs of several other computers or "workstations."

Codec: Short for COde/DECode or COmpress/DECcompress. Usually refers to a mathematical formula that removes data from a source audio or video file, leaving a smaller file suitable for streaming over a network. A codec is also used by media players to decompress streaming files.

Communications protocol: See Protocol.

Compression: 1. A signal-processing technique whereby the peak volume levels are lowered (attenuated) to reduce the dynamic range of an audio signal. 2. A technique that reduces the size of a file.

Compressor: A hardware device or software application that compresses audio signals.

Content delivery network (CDN): A service specializing in hosting and delivery of Internet content.

Connectivity: A connection to the Internet.

Connector: A hardware device that connects a cable to another cable or other hardware device. They are usually divided into male/female pairs. Common connectors in audio and video production include mini-plug, quarter-inch, RCA, XLR, and BNC.

Constant Bit Rate (CBR): A constant or steady data rate traversing the Internet between a server and a client.

Container tag: An HTML or SMIL tag enclosing other data, often to define its display or action.

Copyright: The right to give someone permission to copy a work.

Covering shot: A brief amount of cutaway video that masks a jump cut.

CPU: Central Processing Unit. The main processor of a computer.

Crop: Removing unwanted portions of a frame, similar to cropping in photography.

Cross-platform: Software that is said to work across two or more platforms.

Cutaway: A video shot used to cover a jump cut.

DC (Direct Current) offset: A method for removing inaudible noise introduced into audio when recording equipment isn't grounded properly.

Decompression: The process a media player uses to read a compressed file.

Deinterlacing: The process of removing video artifacts introduced when two fields of interlaced video are combined to form one frame of progressive scan video.

Dial-up: A method for connecting to the Internet with a modem, usually at 56 kilobits per second.

Difference frame: Frames in a compressed video file between key frames, which contain the difference between the previous and next frames.

Digital: Describes data divided into discrete binary units, often referred to as 1s and 0s.

Digital rights management: Technologies and processes that protect copyright from unauthorized distribution.

Distortion: Poor quality sound caused by high volume levels.

Distributed content: A model of distribution where files are available from multiple locations. Clients are often steered to the closest point of distribution.

DMZ: Demilitarized Zone. A peripheral sub-network outside a firewall. Streaming servers are sometimes placed in a DMZ.

Domain: A group of networked computers with a common address.

DRM: Digital Rights Management.

DSL: Digital Subscriber Line. A broadband connection often carrying Internet and voice traffic over the same copper telephone line.

DVD: Digital Versatile Disc.

Dynamic range: The range of a sound from the noise floor to its loudest point.

Editing: The process of removing unwanted portions of an audio or video file. May include rearrangement of the remaining information.

Edge caching: Storing frequently used streams as close to the end user as possible to reduce network hops from the server to the client.

Effect: Usually a transition from one shot to the next, such as fade up from black.

Embedded: An application is said to be embedded if it performs its task within another application, most commonly a browser window.

Encoder: A software application that converts source files into streaming media files. Sometimes called a "producer."

Encoding: The process of converting a source audio or video file into a smaller file designed for streaming media delivery.

Encryption: A method of scrambling data used in digital rights management (DRM).

EQ: Equalization.

Equalization: A signal-processing technique that raises (boosts) or lowers (attenuates) the volume of audio within a certain frequency range.

Ethernet: The dominant method of networking computers.

Evergreen: Content that is relevant and useful for a long period of time.

Extension: Additions to the implementation of an open standard that differentiates the implementation from competitors while maintaining compatibility with the standard.

File: A file stores information. A streaming file stores compressed audio and video information.

Fill light: A light used in 3-point lighting to fill in shadows caused by the key light.

Filter: A hardware device or software application that removes unwanted image artifacts or sound from a file.

Firewall: Any of a number of software applications or hardware devices that limit the types of data that pass into or out of a computer network.

FireWire: A high-speed method of data transfer between digital devices.

FTP: File Transfer Protocol. A network communications protocol to transfer files from one computer to another.

Flash: An animation and streaming platform common on the World Wide Web developed by Macromedia.

Format: A way to organize data on a storage medium, such as a CD.

Frame: A single image in a video file, analogous to a single image in motion-picture film.

Frame rate: The number of frames shown per second.

Frame size: The pixel dimensions of a frame, sometimes referred to as resolution.

Free riders: Nodes in a peer-to-peer network that benefit from the network without contributing to content distribution.

Freeware: Open source software.

GB: Gigabyte.

Graphic equalizer: An audio tool for equalization that has a number of controls set at fixed frequencies.

GPL: General Public License. The most widely used open source license.

H.264: A high-compression video codec.

Hassle factor: The difficulty for users to configure their computer to view your streams, usually in terms of player updates.

High-Definition Television (HDTV): A television broadcast standard with higher quality audio and video, sometimes called "HD."

Headroom: 1. The amount of volume available before the sound distorts. 2. A portion of a stream reserved for nonaudio or video network packets needed for proper stream performance.

Helper application: A piece of software that assists the browser when it cannot render a file. Most streaming media players include helper applications so they can be embedded into Web pages.

Hertz (Hz): A unit of measure for audio frequency.

Hint track: Data in a QuickTime file that tells the server how to handle it as a stream.

Hosting company: A business that specializes in hosting and distributing Internet content, including streaming media.

HREF: Hypertext REFerence. The "link" in a Web page.

HTML (HyperText Markup Language): The standard language for creating pages rendered in a Web browser.

HTTP (HyperText Transfer Protocol): The standard communications protocol for delivering most kinds of traffic on the World Wide Web.

HTTP cloaking: A method for sending streams through firewalls.

HTTP streaming: Progressive downloading.

Hue: The quality of a color as determined by its wavelength.

IDE: Integrated Drive Electronics. A type of hard drive interface.

IEC: International Electro-technical Committee.

IEEE: Institute of Electrical and Electronics Engineers.

IEEE 1394: Also referred to as FireWire or iLink. An engineering standard related to high-speed data transfer between electronic devices.

IETF: Internet Engineering Task Force.

iLink: See IEEE 1394 and FireWire.

Interlacing: The method used to display an image onto a television screen.

Input: Data that flows into a hardware device or software application.

Intranet: A private computer network.

Inverse telecine: The process of removing duplicate frames from a video introduced when film content is transferred to video format.

IP: Internet Protocol. The standard networking protocol for computers connected to the Internet.

IP Address: The numeric Internet address of a computer.

ISO: International Standards Organization.

ISP: Internet Service Provider. An organization that provides connections to the Internet and other services, such as Web site hosting.

JavaScript: A common scripting tool primarily used in Web browsers. It is not related to the Java programming language.

JPEG: Joint Picture Experts Group. 1. A graphics standards group. 2. A still image compression standard.

Jump cut: A video edit manifested as a sudden change in an image that is not a scene or shot change.

Kbps: Kilobits per second. An expression of bit rate.

Key frame: A frame in a compressed video that contains information about the entire frame. Its counterpart, the difference frame, contains only information different from the preceding frame.

Key light: A light used in 3-point lighting to illuminate the front of a subject.

kHz: Kilohertz.

Knowledgebase: An online archive of experience related to a piece of software.

LAN: Local Area Network.

Lavalier: A type of microphone used in video production.

LED: Light Emitting Diode. In audio and video production, LED meters are often used to display audio volume.

Letterbox: Describes a video with a 16:9 aspect ratio superimposed on frame with a 4:3 aspect ratio.

License: A document granting a software user the right to use the software for its intended purpose and prohibiting the user from selling or copying the software.

Live: Encoding an audio or video signal as it is created, usually for immediate distribution to an audience.

Log: A text file that records the activity of software, usually a server.

Lossless: Refers to codecs that can recreate an exact copy of the original file when decompressed.

Lossy: Refers to codecs that cannot recreate exact copies of the original file after decompression. Lossy codecs try to retain as much fidelity as possible, while achieving the desired amount of data-rate reduction.

MB: Megabyte.

MBONE: Multimedia Back Bone. An early attempt at high-speed Internet transfer of audio and video information.

MBR: Multiple Bit Rate. The combination of several streams with different bit rates into a single encoded file.

Metadata: Data that describes other data.

Metafile: A file that contains metadata.

Mic: Microphone.

Microsoft Media Services (MMS): A proprietary streaming protocol developed by Microsoft.

MIME type: MIME (Multipurpose Internet Mail Extensions) types are used by a software client, typically a Web browser, to decide how to render an incoming file. When a browser encounters a streaming MIME type, it usually hands off rendering to a streaming media player.

Mixing desk: A device that allows multiple audio signals to be combined into fewer or a single signal.

Modem: The part of a computer or computer network that allows it to connect to the Internet. Modems come in several types, including dial-up, DSL and cable.

Monitor: A hardware device for hearing audio output (speaker) or viewing video output.

Mount point: The place in the server's directory structure where streaming files are located. Several subdirectories or folders may lie under the mount point. Sometimes called the "publishing point" in Microsoft products.

MOV: A standard format for storing audio and video information, often associated with Apple Computer.

MP3: MPEG-1 Audio Layer III. An open standard audio codec approved by the Motion Picture Experts Group.

MPEG: Motion Picture Experts Group.

MPEG-4: An MPEG open standard usually associated with video compression, though it actually comprises a wide framework used to create interoperable multimedia presentations.

MPG: A file extension for the MPEG format.

Multicast: A means of streaming to a large audience. Clients receive a copy of a stream via a specially configured router, rather than the server sending each audience member an individual stream. The counterpart to multicast is unicast.

Net weather: Describes the often unpredictable nature of Internet service quality and reliability.

Network: Two or more computers connected together for the purpose of communication and resource sharing.

Noise: Unwanted video artifacts or sound in a file.

Noise reduction: A complex algorithm for removing unwanted sound or video artifacts.

Nonlinear editing: Describes the ability to move sections of audio or video around in a software application.

Normalization: A signal-processing technique whereby an audio signal is turned up as much as possible before distortion occurs.

Ogg Vorbis: An open source audio codec.

On-demand: Making a stored streaming media file available to a user whenever the user requests it.

On-the-fly: Refers to the creation of a file at the moment the user requests it.

Open codec: A codec based on open standards.

Open source: A software philosophy and licensing arrangement that makes the underlying code of software available to users for viewing and modification.

Open standard: An engineering standard that manufacturers agree to follow to ensure compatibility with each other's devices.

Operating system (OS): The software that manages the communication between a software application and computer hardware. Microsoft Windows, Linux, and Apple's OS X are operating systems.

Optimize: The process of improving the quality of data in a captured audio or video file.

Output: Data that flows out of a hardware device or software application.

Outsourcing: The process of contracting a third party to perform some or all services related to streaming media.

Overhead: Data in the stream not part of the audio and/or video.

Overscan: The area of a video image usually covered by the plastic casing of a TV monitor. Overscan is usually removed before encoding.

P2P: Peer-to-peer.

Packet: A discrete chunk of data with control and addressing information sent over the Internet.

Patch: Computer code that fixes a problem.

Path: The list of directories, usually separated by the forward slash character ("/"), leading from the streaming server mount point to the streaming file.

Peer-to-peer: A network architecture where all the computers share equal status.

Persistence of vision: The principle by which we see a series of photos, such as frames in movie film, as a continuous moving image.

Personal digital assistant (PDA): A handheld device containing information such as calendar and contacts.

Pixel (Picture Element): The basic unit of composition of the video image on a monitor.

Platform: A software environment. In streaming, it usually refers to the software suite offered by the major proprietary vendors.

Platform for Internet Content Selection (PICS): A rating system for Internet content.

Player: Also media player. A software application that renders streaming media files.

Plug-in: A software application that renders audio and video data within a Netscape-based browser window.

Podcasting: The distribution of audio and video files for storage and playback on a hand-held portable device. Podcasting is not a streaming technology.

Port: A number in a URL that determines which application on a server handles the data request.

Pre-roll: The process of filling a buffer of memory before playback begins.

Proc amp: Short for processing amplifier. A software application or hardware device that adjusts the quality of a video signal.

Progressive download: A media delivery method using the HTTP protocol.

Progressive Networks Audio (PNA): An early proprietary streaming protocol developed by RealNetworks.

Progressive scan: The method for displaying an image on a computer screen.

Protected file: An encrypted file, usually for DRM purposes.

Proprietary: Refers to the practice of keeping certain methods private to create or protect a competitive advantage.

Protocol: A set of rules that govern the exchange of data over a computer network.

Proxy: A special type of server that acts as a middleman between a user and the Internet.

Pseudo-streaming: Progressive downloading.

QTL: The Apple Computer streaming metafile file type.

RAID (Redundant Array of Independent Disks): A type of computer storage using multiple hard drives.

RAM: 1. Random Access Memory. The part of a computer that stores data temporarily. 2. The RealNetworks Helix System metafile file type.

README: A file included in an installation package that has the latest information related to software, such as bugs or changes to documentation.

Real-Time Control Protocol (RTCP): An open standard protocol that works with RTP packets to check the delivery of other packets.

Real-Time Messaging Protocol (RTMP): A proprietary protocol developed by Macromedia (now Adobe) used to deliver streaming Flash video presentations, as well as elementary remote function calls.

Real-Time Streaming Protocol (RTSP): An open standard application level protocol used by Internet clients-i.e., media players-to talk to streaming servers.

Real-Time Transport Protocol (RTP): An open standard protocol defining rules for identifying the type of streaming packet, how packets are numbered in sequence, and how they are stamped with the date and time.

Rebuffering: Action by a media player to gather more data in its buffer before continuing playback.

Render: The process of saving certain changes, usually effects, to an audio or video file.

Rights: In digital rights management, the rights of a user to play back and copy a protected file.

ROI: Return on Investment.

Sample: A measurement of an analog input signal taken when converted to digital format. These samples are stored and played back sequentially to recreate the original analog signal.

Sample rate: The rate at which samples are taken.

Saturation: The intensity of a color.

Script: 1. A set of instructions, often containing dialog, for actors and directors to follow. 2. In Microsoft Windows Media, an event embedded in the timeline of a streaming media file. 3. A series of commands stored in a single file, often used in batch encoding.

SCSI: Small Computer System Interface, pronounced "scuzzy." A method of connecting peripheral devices to a computer, usually a hard drive.

Server: Computer hardware and/or software that services requests from clients on a network. In streaming, two types of servers, Web servers and media servers, typically work together.

Simultaneous streams: The number of streams sent at one time by a server. Some streaming server licenses are priced according to the number of simultaneous streams allowed.

Skin: A custom user-interface for a media player.

Slide: A frame containing title or other information about a video.

Slideshow: A multimedia presentation in which a set of images is displayed in sequence, often with an audio track.

SMPTE: Society of Motion Picture and Television Engineers.

SMIL: Synchronized Multimedia Integration Language. An open standard markup language designed specifically for combining content types that change over time. Pronounced "smile."

Sound card: Also called audio card. The part of a computer that handles the input and output of audio data.

Source code: The original ideas and methods in software code that makes up a software application.

Source file: A file before it is compressed into streaming media format. Sometimes called a "raw" file.

Standard: A set of engineering principles often based on patented ideas.

Standards-based: Refers to products that are built using industry-accepted standards.

Storage: The permanent or semi-permanent repository of a file on a hard drive, CD, or DVD.

Storyboard: A series of preproduction drawings that describe the shots in a video sequence.

Streamie: A frequent user of streaming media.

Streaming media: The process of sending a time-based computer file, such as audio or video, across a network to be rendered in real time by a streaming media client.

Tag: Code in HTML or SMIL that defines data or assigns parameters to data.

TCP: Transmission Control Protocol. One of the basic Internet communication protocols.

Transcode: The process of converting one file format to another.

Transform: Changing the display characteristics of a media file.

Uncompressed: Refers to a file where the input data has not been optimized for storage.

Unicast: A streaming media method whereby each client is sent a copy of a file. The counterpart is multicast.

Uniform Resource Locater (URL): The standard method of addressing a file on a computer connected to the Internet; often called a "Web address."

User Datagram Protocol (UDP): A common Internet protocol used for sending a continuous stream of data. UDP has very low overhead, which makes it ideal for low-bit-rate, time-sensitive applications.

Utility: A small software program that performs a limited, practical function.

Variable Bit Rate (VBR): A method of encoding a file where the bit rate is not fixed. Often used for files that are played back on hardware devices, it is unsuitable for streaming media applications.

VBScript: Visual Basic Script, a Microsoft scripting tool.

VC-1: Microsoft's alternative to the H.264 open standard.

Video card: Hardware in a computer that handles video data displayed on a computer monitor.

Video capture card: Hardware in a computer that digitizes video data from an outside source and stores it on a hard drive.

VTR: Video tape recorder.

Volume level: A measure of the audio power.

VU: Volume unit. A expression of audio volume or loudness.

WAV: A standard method for storing audio information. Pronounced "wave."

Waveform: A visual representation of audio in audio editing software.

Webcast: A live broadcast on the Web.

Workstation: A computer usually dedicated to a specific task, such as video editing.

XML: eXtensible Markup Language.

XML-compliant: Conforms to XML syntax.

YUY2: A file format used to store video information.

Index

G

general public license (GPL), 219, 266
gigabyte, 224
graphic equalizer, 83, 266

H

H.264, 144, 214, 266, 275
hassle factor, 97, 136, 266
HD, 237, 239, 266
HDTV, 213, 236, 266
headphones, 60, 85
headroom, 98, 178, 266
Helix, 20, 99–100, 172–173, 186, 193–194, 219, 234, 273
    Helix DNA platform, 219
    Helix server, 173, 193
helper application, 195, 197, 267
hertz (Hz), 77–78, 83, 110, 267
Hi-8, 54
high-compression video codec, 266
high-definition (HD), 237, 239, 266
high-definition television, 213, 236, 251, 266
    streaming high-definition video, 236
hint track, 132, 267
hosting company, 171, 222–224, 245, 256, 267
hue, 81, 267
HyperText Markup Language (HTML), 160, 183, 187–188, 193, 195–197, 199–201, 203, 205–208, 211, 220, 222, 232–233, 263, 267, 275
    HTML code, 197, 201
    HTML tag, 160, 183, 187–188, 193, 195–197, 199–201, 203, 205–208, 211, 220, 222, 232–233, 263, 267, 275
HyperText Transfer Protocol (HTTP), 132, 174–175, 183–184, 203, 218, 220–221, 267, 272
    HTTP cloaking, 175, 267
    HTTP streaming, 220–221, 267
Hypertext REFerence (HREF), 163–165, 193, 267

I

ICEcast, 227, 260
IEEE 1394, 66, 267
iLink, 62, 66, 267

Institute of Electrical and Electronics Engineers (IEEE), 66, 267
integrated drive electronics (IDE), 65, 267
Interlacing, 267
interlacing, 237, 267
International Electro-technical Committee (IEC), 212, 267
International Standards Organization (ISO), 212, 268
Internet Engineering Task Force (IETF), 173, 267
Internet protocol (IP), 248–249, 256, 268
    IP address, 248–249, 268
Internet service provider (ISP), 184, 222, 268
intranet, 95, 101, 267
inverse telecine, 89–90, 138, 268
iTunes, 42–44

J

JavaScript, 196, 198, 268
Joint Picture Experts Group (JPEG), 76, 232, 234–235, 268
jump cut, 87, 264, 268

K

key frame, 111, 141, 156, 240, 268
key light, 73, 261, 265, 268
kilohertz, 268
knowledgebase, 181, 268

L

lavalier, 58, 73, 268
letterbox, 268
letterboxing, 88–89
license, 4, 35, 43, 219, 269
light emitting diode (LED), 71, 268
lighting kit, 59
Linux, 96, 172, 217, 219, 227, 260, 271
live broadcast, 53, 230–231, 276
live streaming-media broadcast, 230
live webcasting, 230–231
local area network (LAN), 75, 99–100, 153, 177–178, 268
log, 18, 248–249, 269
lossless, 111
lossy, 111, 269

M

Macromedia, 20, 22, 24, 26, 46–47, 93,
101–102, 106–109, 115–116, 132–133,
145–146, 166, 172, 174, 181, 188, 193,
202, 214–216, 221, 257, 259, 266, 273
Macromedia Flash 8 Video Encoder, 108, 133,
145
Macromedia Flash Player, 24, 26, 46–47
MBONE, 269
MBR, 269
media player, 16, 22–27, 29–31, 33–39, 41, 43,
45, 47, 49, 51, 93–94, 96–98, 100–101,
105, 112, 114, 116, 136, 141, 172–178,
183–186, 188, 194–197, 200, 207–208,
212, 216, 219–220, 227, 232–234, 236,
239, 242–243, 248, 259, 262, 264, 269,
272–274
  installing a new media player, 25
   hardware and software requirements, 25
media server, 16, 18, 114, 149, 177, 183–189, 248
megabyte, 269
metadata, 118, 212, 213, 269
metafile, 173–174, 183–191, 193–194, 196, 198,
200–201, 206, 208, 234, 261, 269,
272–273
microphone, 52, 55, 57–60, 70–71, 73, 77,
268–269
Microsoft, 2–4, 7, 20–23, 25–26, 33–34, 65,
67, 76, 80–81, 93–94, 96–97, 99–101,
115–116, 154, 168, 172–174, 181, 185, 187,
189, 191, 193, 197, 210–212, 214–216,
219, 221, 238–239, 242, 247, 259, 261,
269–271, 273, 275
Microsoft Media Services (MMS), 172, 174, 189,
269
Microsoft Windows Media Services, 100, 172,
261
MIME type, 186–187, 198, 200–201, 206, 220,
269
mini-plug, 56, 263
MiniDV, 54
mixing desk, 61, 269
mobile streaming, 241
modem, 25, 75, 178, 264, 269
monitor, 16, 22, 60, 78, 80, 81, 125, 174, 224,
238, 249, 269, 271, 275
Motion Picture Experts Group (MPEG), 21, 93,
112, 209–216, 219, 227, 235, 257, 260,
270

mount point, 189, 270, 271
MOV, 7, 270
MP3, 131, 133, 212–216, 219, 227, 242, 257,
260, 270
MPEG-1, 212–213, 257, 270
MPEG-1 Audio Layer III, 213, 270
MPEG-2, 212–213, 257
MPEG-21, 213
MPEG-3, 213
MPEG-4, 21, 112, 210, 212–216, 219, 227, 241,
260, 270
  definition, 210
MPEG-7, 212–213
MSDN Library, 196
multicast, 180, 254, 270, 275
multicasting, 179–180
multimedia back bone, 269
multiple bit rate, 93, 114–115, 166, 177, 220–
221, 269
  multiple bit rate encoding, 93, 114–115, 177,
220–221
multipurpose Internet mail extensions (MIME),
186, 269

N

Netshow, 20
Net weather, 95, 115, 221, 270
network, 16, 18–19, 22, 52–53, 80, 95–96,
98–99, 101, 114–115, 171–173, 175–181,
185–187, 208, 214, 220–223, 225–227,
240–241, 246, 248–250, 255–256,
261–275
noise, 54, 58, 60, 67, 71, 82, 84–85, 89, 91,
264–265, 270
  noise reduction, 84, 89, 91, 270
nonlinear editing, 64–65, 239, 270
normalization, 82, 85, 270
normalizing, 85

O

Ogg Vorbis, 227, 270
on-demand, 17, 180, 221, 229–232, 242, 246,
253–255, 258, 270
on-the-fly, 270
On2 VP6, 146
open codec, 271
open source, 19, 172–173, 181, 209–210,
217–219, 227, 266, 270–271